CHASING BLACK GOLD

D1464591

There's a race of men that don't fit in,
A race that can't stay still;
So they break the hearts of kith and kin,
And they roam the world at will.

Robert Service, *The Men That Don't Fit In*

THE INCREDIBLE TRUE STORY OF A
FUEL SMUGGLER IN AFRICA

CHASING
BLACK
GOLD

ROBERT STONE

The
History
Press

For my two beautiful children and in loving memory of
my wife. In my search for riches I lost sight of the fact
that the love of your family is the most precious treasure
we can find in this world. Thank God I realised this
before it was too late.

Names have been changed in this book, not to protect the guilty but to spare their
families from the past.

Cover illustration: ©iStock.com/arinahabich

First published 2015

The History Press
The Mill, Brimscombe Port
Stroud, Gloucestershire, GL5 2QG
www.thehistorypress.co.uk

British Library Cataloguing in Publication Data.
A catalogue record for this book is available from the British Library.

ISBN 978 0 7509 6033 5

Typesetting and origination by Thomas Bohm, User design
Printed and bound in Great Britain by TJ International Ltd

Contents

Acknowledgements

Greg C. and Matthew H., the lawyers who master-minded my case and whom I now consider to be extremely close friends. They quite literally saved my life.

I could not have written this book without Alan Wilkinson. He worked tirelessly over the years helping me weave together the complicated threads of the past.

Reverend Lesley, who helped me survive through the grief-filled years after my bereavement.

Beth P., thank you so very much for patching me through on those three-way calls to my family from the various prisons in the USA that I was incarcerated in. Without you, my time away from them would've been so much harder.

Jimmy M., who first helped me to gather together and organise my notes for this book.

Thank you to Joan D. for your cheerful and positive guidance during the editing stage.

Roberto C.P., whose friendship and advice helped me immensely during the very difficult times while I was fighting extradition from Switzerland.

The late Hans Hass – your book *Diving to Adventure* inspired me and gave me the belief that there was a better world out there. I wished I could have met you to thank you in person.

The late Charlie McWhorter – always there when I needed him. Thanks for rounding up the Good Spooks to look after my family and me.

1

Warri, Niger Delta, September 1992

Up ahead, there was a row of stationary cars, half on the road and half off it. Men were standing beside them in small groups smoking and talking. Others were squatting on the ground. One or two were cooking over little fires. In the distance, maybe half a mile away, I could see the coloured flags of the gas station. Jesus, some of these people would still be here next month – guys who were being paid by the day to line up for fuel, which might be available and might not. I felt a momentary pang for my part in the shortages. But then I told myself, same as I always did, if it wasn't me operating the black market – hey, it would be somebody else. That's Nigeria for you.

Just as I thought we were clear of the hold-up, Solomon put his foot on the brake, bringing the Landcruiser to a halt. A car had rammed a minibus and a couple of injured people were lying on the road. Passers-by glanced at the scene and hurried on. The policeman in his bright-orange kiosk waved us past.

We were out of Warri now, onto the main road, leaving behind the piles of trash where kids fought over anything worth having: a screw-top plastic jug, a discarded T-shirt or a deflated football. We were speeding between rows of low trees, swinging out to pass the occasional motorbike that puttered along, piled high with sacks of produce.

Solomon leaned forward and switched the radio on to catch the hourly news bulletin. I was half listening, in case there was a story I hadn't heard already, but it was the same old thing. Some asshole decides to help himself. Maybe he has one of those DIY refineries back in the swamps. Drills through a supply line straight into a pressurised flow of light oil. Up she goes and fries half a dozen innocent kids. Next thing, a politician waddles out onto the steps of his mansion flanked by bodyguards and tells the reporters, no, he never took any bribe. Then, news from the coast – another fishing area has been wiped out after an oil spillage.

After a mile or two, I got Solomon to turn the damned thing off. It made me uncomfortable. Besides, any day that ends up with a drive to Lagos along that potholed piece of shit they call a road is not a good day to listen to bad news. There's enough on your mind with the gun, loaded and cocked, sitting in your lap, ready for the ambush you just know will happen, sooner rather than later.

And then there's the past, always there in the background, tainting everything you do. Right now, it was threatening to screw up my new life, the life that had started when my kids came along. That changed everything. Suddenly I was thinking it might be time to get the hell out of Nigeria – take the money and go. All my life, since I ran out on my parents, I'd been like a gambler on a hot streak. Right now, I had to be worth 30, 40 maybe 50 million – although, as someone once said to me, a man who can add up exactly what he's worth usually isn't worth much. Maybe this was the moment to scoop up my chips, cash them in and spread the money out on the table. For the family.

But even as all this raced through my head and the green of the jungle flashed past, I found myself thinking about the new tankers. They were going to bring a whole new dimension to the black market oil side of the business. No more shitty little barge loads picked up in the night in mosquito-infested swamps. No more dealing with punk bandits brandishing gold watches and guns.

Every time I did the sums, I found myself breathing hard. We were already taking just about every gallon they produced in Warri. No wonder there was nothing left to sell to the locals; no wonder there were lines a mile long at every gas station. I was making a million and a half bucks profit a month with a 6,000-tonne vessel, and now my man 'The Admiral' had fixed it for me bring a 90,000-tonner right slap bang into the refineries in Lagos and Port Harcourt. Ninety frigging thousand. Welcome to the big league, Rob.

I shifted forward in my seat as I caught sight of the oil drums lined up across the road and the uniformed figures lounging around them. Normally I would have a navy guard in the vehicle with me, rifle poking out the side window, and we'd sail through – but today the whole crew had gone missing and nobody could tell me why. Even as Solomon slowed the car I was fumbling around in my briefcase, feeling for the bundles of 20 and 50 naira notes.

It was the mobile police, the guys with face shields and black uniforms, leather helmets hanging low at the back to protect their necks – the 'Kill-and-Go', who could gun down an innocent civilian any time they wanted and walk away unpunished. Evil bastards – which is why I got a unit of them stationed across the road from my base in Warri, a unit whose commanding officer, Lieutenant Ogabie, now drew a nice monthly stipend from 'yours truly'. But these guys we were approaching, they wouldn't have a clue who I was.

As we pulled up, three or four of them sauntered towards the car. One tapped on my side window with the barrel of an Uzi. I wound it down. 'Open the back,' he said. I nodded to Solomon, who clicked the tailgate release.

'Where are you going to?' the guy with the Uzi asked.

'Lagos,' I said.

'Where have you come from?'

'Warri.' Where else did he think? The frigging road only went from A to B through 200 miles of jungle and swamp. In any case, this was all preamble. He soon got to the point.

'What have you got for me?'

'What do you need?'

'I need a drink of cold water.' Translation: 'gimme'.

I passed him a handful of notes. Solomon watched him pocket them. As we drove on, he said, 'Is it any wonder the entire country is in trouble?' I didn't answer. I was counting the miles as we headed towards the capital. Night had fallen and the sky was illuminated with an orange glow generated by a dozen scattered oil flares. What I now saw speeding by in the light of the headlamps reminded me of those photographs of the Somme battlefield. Bare mounds of earth surrounded by oily puddles, the stark outline of blasted trees, here and there a lazy wisp of smoke curling up from a burned-out vehicle. On the roadside were shapeless bundles, some of which might have been bodies. I wound up the window and put the AC on high. 'What the fuck happened here?' I said.

Solomon murmured something about a pipeline blowing up, but it was clear he didn't want to pursue it. I must have dozed off for a while. Next thing I saw was a blueish colour in the sky ahead – the lights of Lagos and Victoria Island. There was always heavy traffic, even at this time of night, but pretty soon we'd crossed the bridge and turned off the highway and I could make out my home. It was surrounded by a 12ft-high perimeter wall, topped with concertina wire. Tall trees grew around it, all lit up by security lights.

The guards on the outer gate stood to attention and let us pass. They were of the Yoruba tribe, from Lagos State. As soon as we were through the heavy steel gates, they closed behind us. Now the inside guards took over – Hausa, a much tougher tribe from up north. Once they'd checked that it was me in the car they opened the inner gate and we drove up to the front door.

Home was a big, two-storey place. It comprised offices, rooms for some of my expat staff and the home I shared with my wife and kids. It had white walls, red-tiled roofs and arched windows – barred, of course. Kind of Spanish. Linda had hired a bunch of gardeners and planted all kinds of fragrant flowers and vines around the home. Even on a night such as this, the scents were heavy, almost overpowering. She knew about these things and I knew I was one lucky sonofabitch to have married her.

I got out of the car and told Solomon to be ready at seven in the morning. I'd be calling on the admiral first thing. I needed to straighten out all the shit that had happened at the yard that afternoon. A riot, for Chrissake? I couldn't have that. I also needed to put some pressure on Chevron. I could do without that new health and safety guy, fresh out of San Ramon, California, telling me how to run my business. I needed to talk to him about how things worked in Nigeria.

The big wooden arched doors opened and I entered the headquarters of Coastal Shipping. Linda came down from our apartment on the upper floor. 'Why didn't you tell me you were coming home?' she said. 'I could've had a meal ready.'

I kissed her and asked, 'Kids in bed?'

'Yes,' she said. 'They crashed out early.' Then she repeated her first question. 'So why didn't you tell me to expect you?'

'Yeah, sorry,' I said, 'but the phones at the yard went out again. Damned power cuts. And a whole bunch of other problems.' She didn't pursue it, which was unusual for her. I didn't know whether it was, 'I don't want to hear it' or 'You'll only lie to me anyway', but she was well aware that I was paddling in murky waters. As for the riot, I certainly wasn't going to talk about that. That would've panicked her. Besides, it was history.

I unbelted my bum bag and dropped it on the table. 'Back in five,' I said, and went up to the bedroom. There, I laid myself out a set of clean clothes and got in the shower. I always stank of diesel after a day at the yard, couldn't wait to wash the damned stuff off. Then I'd go kiss the kids goodnight.

I was still thinking about my call to the admiral as I towelled off and started to get dressed. Why wouldn't he talk all of a sudden? Why had my guards gone missing? Jesus, I could've been killed. I had my shirt on and was just climbing into my slacks when I heard Linda call out to me. She sounded alarmed. I was already heading for the bedroom door when I heard voices. Men. I turned back, grabbed my gun from the bedside table and stuffed it down inside my waistband, zipping up as I hurried along the hall, my shirt tails flapping.

There were four of them. Two were sitting at the dining table drinking iced water; the others were standing up.

They were all in plain clothes. It was one of the guys at the table who spoke. He wore a cream-coloured suit and dark glasses. 'Mr Stone,' he said, 'I am Captain Frederick of the Federal Investigation and Intelligence Bureau. We need you to come with us to the station. Now.' He reached into his jacket pocket and pulled out his ID. Then he turned to his left and introduced the other guy. 'And this is Captain Nboyo of Force CID, head of X-squad. You will need to bring your passport.'

'You gonna tell me what this is all about?' I asked. I could already feel the sweat trickling down my ribs.

Frederick spoke as if he were making a formal charge against me. 'You have stolen our resources and corrupted the moral fabric of our country. Your history of international crimes has caught up with you and now you will be brought to justice.'

Even as Linda gasped, I relaxed. In fact, I almost laughed out loud. So that was it. I'd heard all that shit a dozen times and more. This was the standard crap they spouted when they were shaking you down. I glanced at Linda and nodded reassuringly. Then I turned to the captain, 'Who the hell do you think you are to come into my home and tell me what to do? I'm not some street trader.'

He didn't answer. The two who were on their feet moved a step closer, staring at me with cold, expressionless eyes. That's when it occurred to me that these might not be police after all, but a hit squad. Maybe they were planning to take me down the road to some quiet spot. 'Linda,' I said, 'tell Solomon to get the truck. This shouldn't take long.' She left the room and I went across to the table, picked up the bum bag and belted it around me. It contained the three things I never travelled without: my passport, my Nigerian ID and $10,000 in cash. The captain wasn't taking his eyes off me.

By the time Linda returned we were at the door, ready to go. I kissed her goodbye and told her not to worry. 'And tell Blessing to call Judge Williams for me ASAP,' I whispered. Blessing was my PA. The judge had been handling my legal affairs in Nigeria for years. He knew everyone. He was a personal friend of the president. If these guys were the real thing he would soon sort it out. If they weren't – well, there wasn't a goddam soul who could help me once we were on that highway.

Outside the house was a convoy of several dark-blue vehicles. They looked official enough. My Landcruiser was in the middle, engine running, Solomon in the driver's seat. I climbed in the back and invited Captain Nboyo to get in with me. He took the front passenger seat instead and Captain Frederick sat beside me. He told Solomon to follow the other cars. We set off, heading towards Lagos city centre, blue lights flashing.

It wasn't until we drew up at the FIIB police headquarters that I started to relax. This wasn't some death squad after all. I should have dumped the damned gun in the car, but Frederick was watching me – and Nboyo was standing there holding the door. As I left the car I realised I had no choice but to hang on to it.

The first person I saw when we walked into the building was the head of the Nigerian Drug Enforcement Agency. I'd seen his ugly face plenty of times on the television news. He was walking down the corridor with my partner Douglas Kane. How the hell had he wound up here, I wondered. The thought was soon blown from my mind as we walked past an open door. There inside was … fuck! Barry Sangster. I hadn't set eyes on the guy since he accused me of screwing him over a failed run. He had no business here. He was supposed to be in New Orleans. This didn't look good.

They took me into an office and sat me down. I wanted to put my hand down my pants and shift the gun. Instead I parted my legs and wriggled it into a more comfortable position. I expected some sort of interrogation, but instead of firing questions at me, Captain Frederick explained that my boats were being seized, every last one of them. Not only that, but everybody who worked for me was going to be arrested. They were closing my business down. The reason? Drug smuggling.

'Now listen,' I said, 'you guys have got this all wrong. I'm no smuggler. I'm a ship owner, a fuel trader. I grease the wheels for your country's oil business. I —' Captain Frederick cut me off with a wave of his hand.

'This is not our doing,' he said. 'It is your own government. The DEA and the FBI and such bodies. They have provided evidence. Now, please hand me your passport.' Ah, the passport. That was more like it. I reached into my bumbag and took it out. I didn't bother to point out that I was, in fact, a Canadian citizen. There was no need. Five minutes from now I'd be heading home for my supper. I tucked the $10,000 between the pages and handed it to him, with a nod of my head.

Usually, these people slip the money in their pocket and give you back your passport. Then it's handshakes all round and, 'here, let me show you to the door, my friend'. Not this guy. Not this time. He hurled the clip of money against the wall. 'What is the meaning of this?' He spat the words out, then stood up, towering over me. I was half expecting him to hit me. 'If you think you can use your dirty money to get out of this, I must tell you that you are mistaken, Mr Stone. Grievously mistaken.' He snapped his fingers, bringing one of the guards hurrying to the desk. 'Take this man away. Now.'

All the time I'd been in Nigeria I'd managed to buy my way out of trouble. Money talked, every time; that was how it worked. Now I had the full might of the United States Government lined up against me. The FBI, the Drug Enforcement Agency, customs and Interpol. It was going to take more than a bundle of notes to get me out of this hole. As they hustled me down the stairs, along a dimly lit corridor, and shoved me into the cell, I was shaking all over. The God's honest truth was, I was more than frightened. I was terrified. Once these people had you locked up they could do what the hell they wanted with you. At least I had the presence of mind to grab hold of the gun before it clattered onto the stone floor – although, right now, I could only think of one use for it.

2

The Indian Ocean, February 1988

My wife was lying face down on the deck above the wheelhouse in her bikini, soaking up the sun. Beside her were her sunglasses, a bottle of sun cream and the book that had first got me interested in the sea some twenty years previously, Hans Hass's *Diving to Adventure*. She'd spotted it in the cabin on day one and asked me about it. I told her this was the guy who inspired me to take up diving when I was a kid in Ontario, the guy who'd shown me there was a life beyond the dismal neighbourhood where I grew up. I said she ought to read it, get an idea of where I came from – the kind of dream I'd been chasing when I ran away from home at 15. I'd been meaning to re-read it for years – and what better place than the middle of the Indian Ocean, partway between the Maldives and the Horn of Africa?

I untied the ribbon that held her top in place and rubbed sun cream into her back. 'So tell me,' she asked, 'why does everything you do involve piles of cash?'

The question jolted me – but then I realised I'd kind of been waiting for it, ever since she walked into the cabin that morning when I was counting out the pay for my crew. She came in just as I snapped open the suitcase. I must've had – I don't know, not a huge amount, maybe a couple of hundred grand in US dollars. She'd never seen so much cash in her life. I remember slipping past her and closing the door of my strongbox. I wasn't having her looking in there.

Linda half turned to look at me. 'I mean, why not just write a cheque?' I shrugged, splashed a few drops of oil between her shoulder blades and rubbed it in. 'It's kinda complicated, you know …'

'Well, explain it to me. Some of these people you deal with, Rob, to me they seem very … shady.'

Linda was a dish. Make no mistake about that. A dazzler, long-legged, slim, athletic, sexy. But the way she spoke, with that precise Hebridean accent and that disconcerting habit of pausing before she delivered the key word, gave her an air of calm authority, something of the schoolmistress. Her questions always sounded innocent enough when she started out. She was like a boxer – cagey, but as soon as she sensed any uneasiness it was … wham! Right to the heart of the matter.

While I chewed her question over, I turned and looked at the sea, rippled by the faintest breeze, and the sky, clear blue and marked by nothing more than a couple of faded contrails. Everything seemed right with the world. As it should be on your honeymoon. With the back of my hand, I swept a long blonde strand to one side. She didn't like getting oil in her hair. 'Shady?' I said. 'Nah, don't say that. These are my friends you're talking about. We go back a long way.'

'But they're always in and out of jail.'

I laughed. 'No they're not. Well, not always. And anyway, it was just for smuggling a bit of marijuana.' That was the understatement of the year. Between them, my buddies brought 500 tonnes into the US in 1977 alone. 'Hell, Linda, everyone was at it. It was the glamorous thing to do, like Prohibition, only with dope. Douglas, Jack, sure they served time – and they learned their lesson.'

'What about that Muscles character? And why do they call him that, anyway? He's not one of those ... enforcers, is he?'

'Brett?' I said. 'Brett Eastwood used to be a wrestler. He still works out, that's all. Nothing sinister about the guy. He's a pussycat.'

'But didn't you say he was on the run or something?'

'Yeah, he has an indictment or two hanging over him.' I couldn't help grinning. Brett was a stone-cold gangster. At the last count there were 119, including racketeering and continuing criminal enterprise – enough to send him down for three lifetimes. 'But he's okay, so long as he stays away from the US.'

I continued the massage, working my way down her spine and out to her ribs, left and right, the way she liked it. 'So yeah, a couple of guys stepped over the line, but that was years ago. They've paid their dues, and me – I'm giving them a chance to re-enter society and earn an honest living.' I laughed. 'C'mon, turn over and I'll do your front, eh?'

She didn't move. She wasn't ready to change the subject just yet. 'But that doesn't answer my question. Why do everything in cash?'

'Listen,' I said, 'guys in Africa and Brazil, they bring you a boatload of fish, they expect something in return – something they can eat or sell. You want fuel? It's cash up front. They don't deal with banks. Hell, in the old days it would've been gold coins. Now it's dollar bills, that's the only difference.' She didn't speak. 'A medium of exchange,' I added.

'Hm. All right then.' She rolled over on her towel. She was letting it go, but she'd come back to it. What she wanted was the whole story – but I'd never told that to anyone, not even myself. Never really found time to sit down and piece it all together. Things happened so fast. It was one crazy adventure after another. Besides, when you're operating on the fringes of legitimacy, you learn to be wary who you talk to.

It's like Muscles said, back in the days when we were running pot across the Caribbean, the only way three people can keep a secret is if two of them are dead. So anybody who said they knew my story was lying, because nobody – I mean nobody – had more than a part of it. Not Doug, not Jack, not even Brett. Certainly not Linda, although God knows she asked me, over and over. And every time she tried to pump me I fenced. I fed her little bits, but I ducked the big issues. Of course I did. There are things I have done that still shame me to my bones.

The fact is, there were still a lot of unknowns between us. In the three years since the wedding we hadn't really spent much time together. Hardly any, if you want the truth. I was always busy, hopping flights here, there and everywhere, striking deals in Singapore, Dubai, New York, Rio, Miami or New Orleans. You get into shipping and you're always on the move. So, sure, there were gaps in her knowledge. There were things I hadn't gotten around to telling her and then there were things I never would, at any price. Who doesn't have secrets? Tell me that. So, no, she never did get to know all about me. Nobody has.

But now we had some time. We were on the *Rig Mover*, on our way to Natal in north-eastern Brazil. I had a fish processing facility there, along with a bunch of fishing boats. The business had been doing very well. The *Rig Mover* had finished a job in Asia and I wanted her in Brazil to act as a mother ship for the fleet. So I put it to Linda: why didn't I take a few months off and captain the vessel?

Give me a chance to practise my navigational skills. We'd make it a cruise, stop off at a few places en route. See the world's oceans. After all, we never did have a honeymoon, did we? So she took a leave of absence from her job as a crew member on the helicopters serving the North Sea oil rigs, and joined me out in the Far East.

I screwed the cap back on the plastic bottle and stood up. It was time to take over at the wheel and for Linda to do a few miles on her exercise bike. She was a fitness fanatic, a marathon runner. Didn't really get the concept of lazing around in the sunshine. She must've clocked up 5,000 miles on that voyage, pedalling furiously with her music playing. At least it kept her from getting seasick.

On the bridge I relieved Felipe, my first mate. Popeye, the African grey parrot we'd bought in Singapore, shouted 'Helloooooo,' his head bobbing up and down. I went over and tickled him behind his head while I listened to Felipe's report – the engines were running fine, the weather forecast was fair, next stop Djibouti.

I stood for a while, watching as the nose of the boat ploughed on through the slightest of swells. The *Rig Mover* was an ungainly old thing, an AHTS – or anchor handling tug supply vessel if you want the full industry name. At 50m long, 15m wide and with a draught of 3m, she was painted black and white. Like me, she had the kind of past you might have called 'shady'. I guess we were suited to each other.

I stepped out of the bridge, shielding my eyes against the sun, which was now almost directly overhead. I wiped the sweat off the palm of my hand and reached inside for the sextant, then my *Nautical Almanac*. We had an up-to-date navigational system, including GPS, but I'd always been interested in learning to plot my course by the sun and the stars. That's why I had hired Felipe. I needed someone with

his experience. Sure, the paperwork had me down as captain – and I had an unlimited tonnage oceangoing master's
licence – but I didn't have the experience to take the vessel
three-quarters of the way around the world. No way. The
fact about the captain's ticket was, I'd met a crooked attaché
from the Panamanian consulate in Singapore and bought it
off him for cash. So, as well as the protocols of entering and
departing ports and territorial waters, Felipe was teaching
me the old-school navigational techniques. By the end of
this voyage I would be able to locate our position the tradi-
tional way to within half a mile. And stars? I would be able
to read the night sky like a map.

I stood on the walkway outside the bridge, hands on the
hot metal rail, my face turned to the sun. I could never get
enough of that, and few days passed without me thinking
about what a lucky sonofabitch I was, the way things had
panned out. It was just two years since I'd started up in the
longline fishing business with one beat-up oilfield vessel in
the Gulf of Mexico. Now I was operating on two conti-
nents with a fleet of twenty-seven and some 450 employees.
My old smuggling buddies, those 'shady' guys Linda talked
about, were taking charge while she and I cruised the
oceans and the money rolled in.

Sometimes I wondered what Linda would've made of
me if she'd met me in Toronto, back in 1971, the angry
little punk from the broken home who laid out his high
school vice principal with a single punch, then hitchhiked
to the airport and hopped on a flight to Miami. I'd had
with me a snorkel, 50 bucks in cash and good old Hans
Hass – stolen from the school library. The book had started
me diving, given me the courage to leave Canada and
shown me there was a better life – somewhere. I couldn't
make it to the Dutch Antilles, like my hero, but headed

instead for the Bahamas, where I dived for lobsters and sold them to fancy restaurants.

It was on the docks there that I first saw those dudes in the fast boats, guys who strutted around wearing gold chains and Rolex watches, and who always seemed to have a suntanned beauty on their arm. Yeah, I thought, I wouldn't mind a slice of that. It didn't take me long to get involved. Someone asked me to be a diver on a 'salvage boat', which took me across the Caribbean to the San Andres Islands off Colombia. That first trip, I didn't realise what we were going to carry 'til they asked me en route if I was up for it. I was, but looking back I wonder what would have happened if I'd said no. We loaded and headed back north to Florida, transhipping the bulky loads off Bimini and racing into the Keys on go-fast boats. After that, I couldn't get enough. I made my first million that way and banked it in the Caymans. I was only 17 years old.

It was during this period that I met the guys who were still my buddies all these years later. We were a bunch of good-looking boys with big wads of cash, sports cars, fast boats and even faster women.

After a couple of years I decided this would never last, so I took my money and quit. I headed to New Orleans to begin a career as a commercial diver in the oilfields. Jack never did give it up. He said it was in his blood. Muscles told me it was in mine, too, although I never realised how true that was 'til it was too late. But even so, the friends I'd made – well, in my version of things, I like to say they stuck with me. Others might say they came back to haunt me.

So, when Jack told me about his failed pot runs in Thailand and asked me to reclaim the boat I'd bought for him for the specific purpose of smuggling dope, it seemed the natural thing to do to fly out to Singapore and take her back to Brazil. Along the way we could gather up another victim of a failed drug run, the *Adnil*, which I'd named after Linda and loaned out to another old friend. So that's the kind of people I was mixed up with, and that's how come we were on the high seas, on a journey taking us three parts of the way around the world.

We sailed the *Rig Mover* into Djibouti and tied up right alongside the *Adnil*. It had been laid up there almost a year now. My crew were happy to see me. They'd been killing time down there. Scooby, my pet cheetah, ran towards me. It was amazing that she remembered me so well.

How did I end up with a cheetah? Pure compassion. I'd been in the marketplace in Djibouti earlier in the year and I saw some guy with a cute little cub tethered on a piece of string. He'd killed its mother and he had her pelt stretched out in the sun for sale. It wasn't looking good for the youngster. My idea was to rescue the cub and get it to a place of safety. The man didn't want to sell, but I offered him $100 and gave him a look that said 'take this or I'll cut your fucking throat'. When we reached Mombasa I would hand her over to a cheetah orphanage that Linda had heard about.

While I was in port I was offered a job, taking a Somali fishing boat back to Berbera. $20,000 for a voyage of barely 100 miles, payable in advance? And on our planned route? Why not? Sounded like fun. It was only after I'd accepted the job and been paid that my agent in Djibouti told me I was crazy; I'd get arrested in Somalia, or pirates would seize the vessel en route. I thanked him for his concern and told Linda that maybe she'd better go home. She could fly out and meet me in Kenya in a few weeks' time. I didn't want her on board for this.

It didn't take long to tow the boat to its destination. I'd made my mind up what I was going to do when we arrived. No way was I going to enter the port officially.

Right now it seemed to me that every time I hit land some-body was putting the squeeze on me, and this was hard-core cowboy country. We'd drop it and get the hell out.

Just in case there was any trouble, I'd rigged up a couple of makeshift flamethrowers on the deck. I had two guys sta-tioned on the fishing boat – one to steer and one to release the tow-rope and drop anchor when I gave the word. Soon as we'd done that I turned the *Rig Mover* around and ran back alongside. My two guys jumped aboard and we left the harbour mouth at full throttle – all of 10 knots. I don't think we were in that place longer than it would take you to boil an egg.

Outside, I hooked up with the *Adnil* and we set off down the coast with her in tow. Destination: Mombasa. Looking back to the harbour mouth, I saw a little launch heading for the abandoned boat and a couple of guys waving their arms and shouting. My crew were laughing like idiots on the bridge. I divided all the money up with them, shared out according to their seniority. Scooby was standing up on my captain's chair, front paws on the compass looking out of the windows to see what was up. Popeye was squawking up a storm. I'd always wanted to be a pirate. Right then, it felt like I'd made it.

3

Mombasa to the Niger Delta, March–April 1988

In Mombasa, Linda came back out and joined up with me. She'd been pissed off about being sent home, but she was over that now. We delivered Scooby to the orphanage – a sad moment for me, I'd really gotten close to the wee girl. I'd miss the sound of her purring as she slept on the floor of my quarters at night.

Linda and I then settled down to enjoy a few weeks' vacation while I had the ships sandblasted and painted. We took a little time out, like regular honeymooners. We visited the Maasai Mara game reserve, took a hot air balloon ride and camped out under serene African skies. It was like an interlude of sanity.

As soon as we returned to port, it was back to reality with a bang. With no Scooby to put the fear of God into them, the locals had stolen aboard the *Rig Mover* and made off with pumps and various tools. But nobody got hurt, so we refitted and headed on down the coast of East Africa and across the equator.

It was off Durban that we hit our first serious weather. Mountainous seas crashed over us, the crew were all seasick, half of them lying on the galley floor and throwing up, and Linda was so ill she was in tears – and clean out of Kwells, or whatever it was she took. Me, I was walking around the place with a grin on my face, singing cheery numbers like 'A Life on the Ocean Wave' and shouting at the guys to get back to work or I'd have them on the next plane to Manila. I've never been troubled with nausea at sea, so I'm not the most sympathetic.

I was giving the cook a hard time, too. 'I'm hungry,' I told him. 'Get back in the galley.' He threw up on my foot. Next thing I know, Linda's stopped crying. She's standing there, just a few feet from me, pointing back at the *Adnil*. It's still bobbing along behind us in a 'now you see me, now you don't' kind of way. Mostly, though, it was 'now you don't', as she disappeared behind one giant wave after another and re-emerged in a blur of spray. Linda was reaching out to me. I tried to approach her, but had a struggle to stay upright as the boat pitched, teetering on the crest of a wave before plunging into the trough. With each rise and fall the two boats drifted apart. Then there was a crack as the towline stretched tight, the sudden lurch throwing Linda into my arms. 'What's up, honey?' I asked. 'You seasick? Homesick? Mad at me? Tell me.'

She looked right into my eyes and yelled, 'We're all going to die, Rob, and you don't even care!' And there was I, thinking it would help if I put a brave face on it. I needed to say something to make her feel better, but what? The fact was we were caught up in a dangerous storm, probably the worst I'd ever encountered – and that includes those years I was diving off North Sea oil rigs. Before I could find any words to comfort her, the gods delivered. An albatross, majestic with its 10ft wingspan, came gliding alongside, riding the wind with grace and power. 'Look, honey!' The wind ripped the words from my lips. Linda turned to look at me, wild-eyed, her face streaked with salt spray, tears and bits of her breakfast. 'Look,' I shouted, 'that's a good luck sign. You have an albatross with you, you're always gonna be okay.'

As she turned to see the bird it leaned to one side, caught an up-draught and wheeled away from the boat, disappearing from view as another wave crashed over us. 'It'll be back!' I shouted, then turned to see my chief engineer and his second-in-command approaching the top of the stairs that led to the engine room. They were drenched, from head to foot, and they were pointing below. 'Capitan, Capitan! Water! Water!'

I left Linda, who was leaning over the side, retching, and followed the pair of them down the stairs to the engine room. Water was gushing in through a hole in the bottom of the hull, a great jet of it 6in wide. There was no way the pumps could deal with this. The engine room would flood, we'd lose power and sink. I had enough energy to gasp, 'Fucking albatross!' before getting down to work. I knew exactly what was required. I'd seen it done in the Caribbean one time, and told the engineers what to do while I got ready. I went to the locker and took out my scuba-diving gear.

Linda came stumbling down. 'What are you doing? For God's sake, Rob, what are you doing?'

'Relax,' I said. 'It's just a little repair job. Shouldn't take long.'

'You're not going in that water,' she said. 'Surely not?'

'How the hell else we gonna fix it, honey? Now leave me alone, okay?'

The engineers cut a round circle from a steel plate and welded a threaded steel rod to it, 3ft long. Then they cut a circle from a rubber mat and put it over the rod. They fixed a broom down through the hole so the handle stuck out the hull. The deck hands threw a loop of 2in-diameter rope over the bow and worked it down the port and starboard sides 'til they felt it snag on the broom handle. Felipe had slowed us to a dead crawl nudging into the heavy seas, making sure we didn't drift back and catch the tow wire in our props. We hung a ladder over the side and I shackled myself to the rope and jumped over the side with the makeshift patch. I worked myself down to the broom handle, taking care not to get too close to the suction. I rammed the threaded pipe up through the hole and the rubberised plate slammed up against the hull, held there by the weight of water pressing on it. By the time I'd worked myself back up to the ladder and climbed aboard, the engineers had secured the plate from the inside.

That was the last of the dramas. The skies cleared that night and from then on it was pretty plain sailing, apart from the fact that Linda was now seasick twenty-four-seven. She wanted to be dropped off in Cape Town, but I couldn't do it. With the apartheid situation, once a ship had docked in the republic it was basically barred from entering any black African country's port.

Just to spice things up, we now entered the southern winter, and it was no surprise, in retrospect, that the sea off the Cape of Good Hope was dotted with penguins. We were so damned cold we all ended up cutting holes in the blankets and wearing them over our heads. It was *A Fistful of Dollars* all over again. It didn't help that our engineers had the air conditioning on full, thinking it was the heating system.

Chasing Black Gold

But there were compensations, like the night we went on deck to find the ship's wake glowing a bright phosphorescent green, porpoises dancing in the bow wave, dripping light from their glowing bodies, and the waves all leaving a luminous trail like you might see in some Japanese painting. It was the most heavenly event I'd ever witnessed. As I said to Linda, there's an upside and a downside to everything.

We made our way into the Atlantic and turned north towards warmer weather, stopping off at Hollingsbird Island, just off Namibia, on what is known as the Skeleton Coast. I'd read that the ocean floors around these islands were covered in lobsters and the beaches were renowned for their alluvial diamonds. Maybe we'd find us a bucketful. Or maybe not. The De Beers Mining Company owned vast tracts of the area and had surrounded it with a razor wire fence. They patrolled the shoreline with company aircraft backed up by the Namibian Air Force.

We spent three or four days anchored there, hoping the sea would calm down so that I could launch a light craft and sneak ashore, but the weather persisted and the planes finally spotted us. Over the radio we got a stern South African voice: 'Vissel, idintify yoursilf.' I had to say something. I told them we had mechanical problems. The reply was brief and unequivocal: 'Then fix them quick and fuck off away from here, mate.'

We headed north and across the equator. Soon we would be approaching the Nigerian coast, although our view was now obliterated by what we first took to be fog. It was actually the *harmattan* – dust, whipped up in the Sahara and transported south by the wind.

I met our pilot, as arranged by my Nigerian agent, a little further north of the delta at the mouth of the Forçados River, off a place called Escravos. We made contact by radio and rendezvoused easily enough, and he led us upstream around mangrove swamps and scattered islands. It occurred to me that there was no way the early Europeans could have made their way up here to capture slaves. They must have been guided by natives, just as I was now. We had jungle to either side of us, and the nights were pitch black, the only visible sign of life being the cooking fires in scattered settlements along the banks.

We moored at Bennett Island and waited for Customs & Immigration to show up. There were a few fishing vessels awaiting clearance, and several oilfield supply vessels anchored there between jobs. As soon as word got out that we had a white woman on board, people started pestering us to bring her ashore. There was a bar down by the river's edge and a bunch of captains asked us to meet them there. I was dead against going into such a place, I'd seen enough of them around the world, but Linda, after forty-five days at sea, persuaded me to take her.

We launched a small inflatable boat, a Zodiac with an outboard motor, and made for the riverbank. It was so shallow that we had to get out and paddle the last few feet. Before we were out of the water the working girls were all round Linda, stroking her hair, feeling her skin and firing questions at her. Was she my whore, my wife, or what? Did I treat her well? How many children did she have? How many wives did I have? Did I beat her?

We shoved our way through the packed bar to a table occupied by expat engineers and captains. There was a waitress in attendance and somebody asked Linda what she would like to drink. She said, 'A cappuccino would be nice,' and looked bemused when everybody cracked up.

'Honey,' I said, 'this is Nigeria. And it's a bar we're in.'

'Ah, all right then, a glass of Chardonnay?' The waitress looked baffled.

'Linda,' I said, 'either you order a beer or you don't. That's the full range of options.'

'Okay, a beer it is.' She looked around. 'Any idea where the toilet is?'

'You just walked through it,' one of the captains said, pointing towards the river.

We got talking to some of the guys. Told them our story and our adventures. I said I was looking for work for the vessels. They looked out the window and frowned. 'With those old tubs?' somebody said. 'I don't think so, mate. Our ships are virtually brand new and we're hardly keeping busy. As soon as our contracts run out we'll be off. Gulf of Mexico, Persian Gulf – somewhere like that.'

Before I could say anything, there was a commotion at the bar. A fight had broken out between two girls. A guy elbowed past them and made his way to our table with a tray of beers. 'What was all that about?' I asked.

He shrugged. 'She sold her friend a condom but her friend's refused to pay.'

'Oh,' I said, 'why's that?'

'It was a used one.' He paused, clearly not sure how to explain in front of Linda. 'The girls find them floating down the river. They wash them out, hang them up to dry and roll them back up.'

It was three days before the officials showed up. They inspected our papers, went aboard for a look around and gave us clearance to head on up to Warri, but only by speedboat. Leaving the two ships at anchor we took off upriver the next day. As we passed all the boats at anchor, the hookers we'd met at the bar, who'd spent the night aboard with clients, waved and shouted, 'Leen-da! Hello Leen-da!' Some of them weren't even dressed. I smiled at Linda and said, 'Nice company you keep.'

4

Warri, Nigeria, May 1988

The sky was clear – clear of clouds, that is – but you could hardly see the sun, despite it being directly overhead. It was obscured by a grimy veil of smoke. As the speedboat raced along the river we saw the remnants of what had been the local fishing fleet protruding from banks that glistened with oil. One or two people were paddling dug-out canoes through the gobs of tar and other rubbish. There were few trees, just their remains: splintered stumps and withered, blackened foliage. Here and there a dead fish lay on the surface of the water.

The desolation went on for many miles before the first houses started to appear, shacks with rotting tin roofs and collapsed wooden docks. There were rusted steel barges with homes built on top, children playing in filthy water, and everywhere the smoke of cooking fires. We slowed as we went past the navy yard and the depots of the oil service companies – familiar names like Halliburton, Baroid, SBM, Tidewater, Zapata and Noble Bawden.

We had entered the oil capital of the Delta State. There were no glassy, multi-storey offices here, no gleaming trucks, no superhighways criss-crossing the skyline. Houston it was not. Aberdeen it was not. It was Warri, a lousy stinking dump of a place which left you in no doubt as to the main industry, and the source of all the ugliness.

We pulled into a dock where we were met by the agent I'd appointed to clear my vessels for entry into Nigeria. He was all smiles. 'Welcome to my country, welcome to Warri,' he said. I looked around. Here and there a chicken pecked at a patch of grit where an occasional weed had sprouted. Christ knows what they were finding to eat. There was a smell in the air, the kind of smell you might get around a junkyard on a hot day — and boy, was it hot.

Linda and I got into his car, a wheezing heap of shit on which only one thing worked properly: the horn, which he leaned on most of the way through town, carving a path through the traffic. People yelled and leapt out of our way. Every time we slowed down, a bunch of kids had their hands through the open windows, palms outstretched, asking for naira.

We pulled up outside his office. Linda pointed to the sign: 'Ships Agent, Furniture Sales, High Powdered Business Deals.' She laughed at the misspelling, then she nudged me and murmured, 'Think he's in the cocaine business?'

Inside, my new agent explained that the oil business was in a slump right now, but he had arranged meetings for me with representatives of the oil companies. He would take me to see the heads of Shell, Chevron and Texaco. If there was work for my vessels he would help me find it. I wondered what the oil execs would make of him. I wasn't sure I'd buy a used car off the guy.

Linda wanted to stay in town for a few days. 'What's the best hotel?' she asked.

'I will take you to the nicest place in town,' the agent said. 'The Palm Court – and I will see that they give you the Presidential Suite.' He took us right there. It was far from impressive, and the 'Presidential' part referred to the fact that we would have an indoor toilet. Linda whispered, 'Maybe he thinks we have no money. Tell him we can afford a nice hotel.'

I laughed. 'This'll be the best Warri has to offer,' I said.

As the agent left he told us, 'Go to Auntie's Kitchen for your dinner. All the expats eat and drink there. And the owner is married to a Scottish man.'

We went there by taxi. It looked nice enough – a wooden kind of bungalow, surrounded by trees draped with fairy lights. Linda held onto my arm, all smiles and anticipation. We ducked under the awning and went inside. It was gloomy in there, but as our eyes got accustomed to the light I could see that as well as being a watering hole, a café and a meeting place, Auntie's Kitchen was also a whorehouse. I had my hand on Linda's back and I could feel her start to shake. Sweat was oozing through her blouse. I whispered in her ear. 'Stay calm and stick close to me.'

First thing I noticed was that there were a lot of white faces. The place seemed to have attracted a cross-section of foreigners who sat talking at the tables, while the girls – all of them black – mostly hung out at the bar, sitting on high stools, legs crossed, smoking, making eyes at the guys. Everyone was staring at us.

We went up to the bar and I ordered a Star lager and a coke. I soon realised that having Linda with me was going to be useful. People were looking at us and getting up to order fresh drinks. One or two introduced themselves. Pretty soon we were the centre of attention, surrounded by a circle of expats. There was a Yank or two, a couple of

Germans, but mostly it was Brits. They'd already heard the
rumours of the guy with two beat-up old ships and a beautiful woman on board. They wanted to know how we'd
ended up in this shithole.

Linda smiled at them. 'It's my honeymoon,' she said,
and that got everyone relaxed and laughing. They couldn't
believe a guy would drag his bride halfway around the
world in a rusty old supply vessel, and they loved hearing
about our adventures on the journey from Singapore. I
stood to one side and watched her talk. These guys were
putty in her hands. They would've paid to hear her read the
damned phone book. Over at the bar, the girls pouted and
took out little mirrors to fix their hair. One of them started
painting her pal's toenails.

We sat ourselves down at a table. There was me, Linda
and maybe another seven or eight people. I got talking to
some British guy, bought him a beer and told him I was
looking for work for my boats. He shrugged. 'Things are
pretty quiet at the moment,' he said.

I nodded. 'That's what I heard.'

'My best advice is to try the oil majors,' the guy said. He
stubbed out a cigarette and added, 'but I don't fancy your
chances, to tell you the truth – not with crude selling at $18
a barrel.' He thought for a moment, then said, 'And whatever you do stay away from the Nigerian companies.'

'Oh,' I said, 'why's that?'

'The buggers never pay, that's why.'

'And what about fuel?' I asked. 'Someone told me you
can buy it unofficially, get a better price.'

'Don't know nothing about that, mate.' He looked away,
more or less dismissing me. A couple of girls from the bar
had come over and were sort of listening in – either that
or sniffing around for a possible transaction. That was the

excuse he wanted. He drained his glass, patted me on the shoulder and took off.

I struck up conversation with another guy, putting the same questions to him, and noted that one or two of the girls were listening in again. This guy was less evasive. He laid it on the line. 'Listen,' he said, 'you need to know it's not a good idea to talk about these things. Especially in a public place.' He glanced around, then leaned forward. 'I could lose my job. Any of us could. You could even get arrested.'

I got the hint and joined Linda, adding a few exaggerated details to her stories about the storms. They were lapping it up, but I was already anxious to leave. I'd drawn a blank here and needed to try some other avenue. When we got up from the table we had a struggle getting through the crowd that had gathered round. I'd always been aware of that with Linda; everywhere she went men wanted to be close to her, even if it was just for a minute. A smile, a word or two, they craved that. I felt a hand touch mine. One of the girls was shoving a piece of paper at me. I tried to shrug her off – what did I want with a hooker? But she whispered, 'This is the man that you have to see.'

We took a taxi to the hotel. Back in our room I looked at the note, half expecting to find the girl's name and a list of her services, but it was as she said, a man's name, a Nigerian by the look of it. There was an address too. Could be interesting.

Next day I went back into Warri. I told Linda I had some business to see to, and left her sunning herself by what had once been a pool but was now a slimy scum-filled pond. I hooked up with the agent, who was as good as his word, taking me to visit the oil companies. Being expats, the people I met were all happy to talk, but they all had the same story. Work was slowing down and as soon as the contracts ended for the ships they had on hire they were going to get rid of them. They didn't think work would pick up for a couple of years.

I thanked the agent and then told him I would do a little sightseeing on my own. I took a taxi to the address the girl had given me. My cab driver wanted to know whether I'd been in Warri before. He told me he'd grown up there. 'Bet you've seen some changes,' I said.

'Yes,' he said, 'a lot of things have changed.' He was silent for a while as he leaned on the horn and accelerated towards an oncoming truck, missing it by inches. He told me he used to be a farmer – growing enough to feed his family and a bit extra to sell at market. Then a spillage from a pipeline buried his crops. There was no compensation. That was when he moved his family to town.

'You make a good living?' I asked.

The tyres squealed as he swerved around a woman carrying a child across the road. 'I supplement my wage,' he said.

'With?'

He laughed. 'I "wheel and deal". Is that the expression?'

I wanted to ask him more, but at that moment I saw someone lying on the edge of the road. 'Jesus,' I said, 'that's one dumb place to take a nap. What is he, drunk?'

He shook his head. 'That one? No, he is dead. He was shot this morning.'

'What, and nobody's picked him up?'

'Nobody has the courage to do that, not even his family – if he has one. Maybe the police will remove him later.' We were out on the edge of town now and the road was clearer. As he picked up speed he said, 'But maybe it was the police who shot him.' He turned to look at me and added, 'It is a commonplace incident in this town. You touch a dead body and people think it is yours. Or maybe you are now a suspect in their eyes.' He shrugged. 'So you do not touch. You walk on by. Then at night it disappears. Maybe the family take it. Maybe it is the dogs.'

We were out near the airport now. The cabbie pulled up outside the address I'd given him. It was a small bar. I gave him a decent tip. Immediately, I was surrounded by a gaggle of children, some of them as young as 4 or 5, some of them almost naked. At the door of the bar I put my hand in my pocket: I wanted to help them. The kids pressed in, expectantly. Just then a man appeared beside me and sent them scattering with some harsh words in a local tongue. Then he touched my arm. 'Mister Stone?' he said.

'That's me.' I wondered how come he knew who I was.

'I believe you want to see me.'

He had one of those unpronounceable names. When I tried to say it out loud he cracked up. 'Just call me Lucky,' he said, 'It will be easier for you.' I didn't know what tribe Lucky came from, not at first, but what struck me was that this guy was seriously black. He had the darkest skin I'd ever seen. His face bore a number of scars, but they weren't from fights; they were the kind that are made on a kid's face when he's young, like a sort of tribal ID. To start with, I was wary of him. He was taller than me, broader than me and he made little attempt to hide the top of the revolver that he had poked down through his belt.

As he pushed the door open, a couple of other guys got up from a cane seat and followed us inside. They were standard issue heavies: sleeveless vests, bandannas, chunky rings on their fingers – knuckledusters, more like. They had huge biceps and they never spoke. Behind their dark glasses they were watching my every move. I'd met their type many times before – in Miami, Bimini, New Orleans – but these guys made me a little nervous.

Lucky led me inside. The heavies followed, letting the door swing shut behind them. It was cooler and quieter in there. We went down a corridor to a small room where a ceiling fan turned lazily. There was a big old fridge, sounding more like a small truck. Lucky took out a couple of beers, booted the door shut and offered me one. 'So what is it that you are looking for?' he asked.

'Fuel,' I said. 'I need fuel, and I'm not a rich man. I can't pay the international price.' I laughed. 'That's for suckers, right?'

'That is what they tell me,' he said, and took a couple of swallows from his bottle. 'And what do you want this fuel for, Mister Stone?'

'I have two ships,' I said. 'Big thirsty ships. I am going to Brazil. They'll want a thousand tonnes.'

He looked at me and smiled. 'How many gallons in a ton?'

It wasn't exactly the question I wanted to hear. 'Roughly 250–300 gallons,' I replied.

'So, 250–300,000 gallons then?' I nodded. 'Yes, I can supply you, at a price you will like. But it will take time.'

I wanted to know where and when – and how much. He shrugged off my questions and changed the subject. 'Warri is not a good place for your woman,' he said. I wondered how come he knew about Linda, but then I figured: a blonde woman in Warri? She'd be the talk of the town already. 'Take her to Lagos,' Lucky said. 'Put her on a plane to your home and return to Warri. Check back in to the Palm Court Hotel. I will know when you return.'

I took a taxi back to the hotel and told Linda to pack up, as we were heading back to the boat. We took a taxi to the speedboat dock and hired one to take us back along the river to Bennett Island and the *Rig Mover*. On the way I told her the good news, that we were going to leave Nigeria

– and that she was to go home to Scotland instead of heading to Brazil on the boat. She looked at me. She had her hair combed back and tied in a sort of bun. The schoolmistress effect. 'That sounds appealing,' she said, 'but what about you? What are you going to do?'

'Gonna fill the boats up with fuel and take them to Natal.'

'Fill up with fuel in Warri, am I right?'

'Where else?'

'Are you seriously going to attempt to do business here? Those captains said that you have to buy fuel at the official price. Is that what you will do?' I didn't answer. 'Promise me,' she said. 'This is a dreadful place. You told me yourself, they're all corrupt.'

'I can live with that,' I said. 'When guys are on the take at least you know where you stand. Listen, I can't get these boats over to Brazil without fuel, and plenty of it. If it turns out I can get a discount from some guys, I will. If not I will pay the official price.' Linda didn't like it, and she said so. I told her not to worry. 'I'll take you to Lagos, we'll get a hotel and I'll book you a flight home.'

'You just want me out of the way,' she said. 'Then you'll get on with whatever it is you do and nobody will be here to question you. That's right, isn't it?' I didn't answer. As far as I was concerned, there was my marriage and there was the world I operated in. They weren't connected; they couldn't be. Maybe I figured that one day I'd have enough money to get out of my world and move into hers. Then I could live the kind of life she'd approve of. But, in my experience, people who lived her kind of life never had any money – not serious money – unless they were born to it, or they were educated and looked to higher things. I was neither of those. I was lucky I'd got out of Toronto with my ass in one piece.

We flew to the capital next day and put up at the Eko
Holiday Inn on Victoria Island. It took me a day or two to
get Linda a flight. By then, she couldn't wait to get home.
Her 'honeymoon' had gone on long enough and she'd had
enough of Nigeria. I was about to enter a world where she
didn't belong, one in which even I might find myself out of
my depth.

After I'd seen her off at the airport I took a taxi to Lekki
Peninsula, where the big oil companies had their headquarters – I mean firms like Chevron, Texaco and Mobil. I spoke
with a number of people over there, Americans mostly.
They were happy to receive me, but all gave me the same
story. They didn't have work for a brand new state of the art
oilfield service vessel, never mind a couple of 20-year-old
rust buckets like the ones I had. As soon as their boats came
off long-term contracts, the big companies like Tidewater,
Zapata and SEACOR Marine were sending them back to
the Gulf of Mexico. Over there, at least, the industry was
picking up after the mid-eighties slump in prices. They
simply confirmed what I'd been told in Warri. I guessed it
was time to get out of Nigeria.

Dispirited, I went to the airport to get a flight back to
Warri. There, I got my first lesson in the etiquette of boarding a plane, Lagos style. It was only a little shuttle flight,
and there can't have been more than a couple of dozen of
us standing beside the runway, where various aircraft were
taxiing. A guy in uniform pointed at a particular plane and
shouted, 'That one!' and suddenly it was like I was back in
school and morning assembly, except it was grown-up guys
with briefcases. The last one in got the shittiest seat. Later,
I learned to bribe the guy to point at the wrong plane. That
way, once the scramble started I could saunter across the
tarmac and claim the front aisle spot with the extra legroom.

We ran into some heavy weather en route. As we came into land, the rain was coming down in sheets. We hit the tarmac, the plane skidded, made a 360° turn and came right off the runaway into the mud. I was sweating, but nobody else seemed bothered. Just disembarked like nothing had happened.

I took a speedboat out to the *Rig Mover* and the *Adnil*. If this guy, Lucky, was going to come good, the ships had better be ready. The first job was to get the crew off their asses and clean the tanks. Next was for them to prepare a list of supplies. Natal was a long haul; we needed plenty of food and water.

Once I'd got the crew organised, I gathered a change of clothes, went back to Warri and checked into the Palm Court – the Presidential Suite again. Then I headed downtown to the telephone exchange. It's hard to imagine now just what it took to make a simple phone call back then. It started with the taxi ride. I flagged one down, walked up and grabbed the door handle. It came off in my hand. The driver leaped out and told me I had to pay for the damage. 'No fucking way,' I told him. A cop materialised out of thin air and immediately took the driver's side. Like an idiot, I argued. Then I paid for the damage and the fine, both of which had probably gone up by the minute. I was learning that, in a place like this, you rolled with the punches.

Inside the cab I found a clean bit of seat to sit on, then settled back to enjoy the view – of another 'go-slow'. It was scorching hot and the windows were down, which meant that as we crawled along there was a forest of hands reaching in, begging for money. Here was another choice: I could ignore them, pay them, or wind the window up – always assuming the mechanism wasn't screwed. In this case it worked. The Lord be praised. Only thing was, in that heat and with no AC, I was soon frying.

There was no relief at the telephone exchange. It was like an oven, it seethed with people lining up to make calls, and it stank. Good God, it stank. I asked a guy how long a wait he thought I'd have. He said an hour, maybe more. When I finally got to the desk I gave the number I wanted to call, estimated how long, and paid my deposit. It was Doug I was calling, in Natal. I barely understood half of what he was saying, thanks to the din in the waiting area and the static on the line. Still, the main point of the call was for me to update him, and he seemed to be getting it reasonably clearly. 'Listen,' I shouted, cupping my hand around my mouth in case people were listening, 'I need you to spread a little kindness around.'

'Sure,' he said. He knew what I meant.

'When we come into port I don't want anybody taking too much notice of the cargo. Ya got that?'

'Consider it done,' he said. I knew I could rely on him. We'd been buddies a long time.

Back at the hotel, I soon got bored waiting for Lucky to contact me. And worried. What if he was just screwing me around? I figured I should maybe think about alternative plans, so I went back to Auntie's Kitchen a couple of times for a beer and some food. Maybe I'd learn something. But without Linda I couldn't seem to attract any attention. People were much cooler than they had been. I got to know the owner of the place, a huge fat Nigerian woman who'd married a skinny little Scot called Wally. He'd been in Warri for years. He was a great source of local knowledge, but untaxed fuel? 'Nae, laddie', he knew nothing about that.

Just when I was starting to think I was wasting my time, I showed up at my hotel after lunch one day and there were

the two heavies waiting for me. Lucky was ready to negotiate. We met at a bar he claimed to own. He told me he
had twenty tankers and barges lined up, all ready to deliver
the fuel. 'And what sort of price do you have in mind?'
I asked him.

He clasped his hands and stretched his mouth into a
grin. 'That fuel I can let you have at 1 naira per gallon.' He
paused, then added, 'Delivered right to your ships.' I wondered where else he might deliver the stuff, then considered
his price. One naira ... that wasn't a bad price, at all.

'You thieving sonofabitch,' I said. 'You're paying a twentieth of that.' I got up from my seat and turned towards the
door. 'That's a week of my time you've wasted.'

'You do not understand,' he said. He'd gone kind of quiet.
'You white people ...' he began, 'I could get shot for trea-
son for what I'm talking about here. For me to supply you
it has to be worth my while.'

I sat back down. Maybe I'd gone too far, but I was already
starting to see how things worked here. If you got someone
so mad that they wanted to kill you, you'd got one hell of
a deal. Catch them smiling – even the hint of a smile – and
you could bet the bastards had ripped you off. We batted
it back and forth and I got him down to four gallons per
naira. I was pretty happy with that, and he had to be – the
price he was buying at, he'd be multiplying his investment
five times over.

Even as we wound up the negotiations, I was making
calculations in my head. At roughly 5 naira per US dollar
this was costing me 5¢ a gallon. Say 40 gallons to the barrel,
making $2, and 7.5 barrels per metric tonne. That was $15
a metric tonne, or $15,000 for the full load. Even if I took
off the fuel we'd burn getting across the Atlantic, at the
Brazilian price – $320 a tonne – I was saving myself ... shit!

– $300,000. And the cream on the cake? I could cash in my US dollars on the local black market at a rate of 6 or 7 naira before I paid Lucky, making it even cheaper.

So, when we shook hands on the deal and I saw that tell-tale smile of his, I grinned right back at him. I guess each of us was pretty sure we were screwing the other.

Of course, there had to be a catch. He wanted the money up front, whereas I wanted to see the fuel first. I was adamant I would not give him any money before I saw the tanker loads. We haggled, but this was more of a play fight than the first one. We were starting to like each other and we agreed I would give him $1,000 up front.

So now it ought to have been plain sailing. No, not in Nigeria. It's never plain sailing. When I went to see Lucky's 'tankers', what did I see? A bunch of 1,000-gallon containers on wheels that had to be loaded onto a rusty little barge. But the barge didn't have an engine, so it had to be towed out by speed boats to where my ships were waiting – 250 trips, minimum. I huffed and puffed and called Lucky a lot of bad things, but I knew I had no choice. 'Okay,' I said, when I'd run out of expletives, 'you may be a Mickey Mouse outfit, but round here you're the only outfit. Let's get to work.'

For the first load, two of Lucky's men guided us to a rendezvous, way out in the swamps. They were thugs, and heavily armed 'for our protection'. We made that run at night. It was pitch dark, and whatever animals they had out there kicked up a racket to strike fear in a guy's bowels. I was in the hands of people I didn't know and I had no choice but to trust them. All I had was my wits and a strongbox full of cash. It wasn't a great feeling. One thing was for sure – the pilot knew what he was doing. There were no buoys, no navigation beacons, but this guy could tell from the flow of the current, even the surface ripples, where the channel was. As to the mosquitoes, they were so dense you could cut a path through them with your hands.

I'd told Lucky I would pay for each load as it was transferred and I monitored every damned delivery in person. Sure enough, as we went on, I started to find that one tank would be full of kerosene, the next one water. 'What the fuck is this?' I shouted, grabbing hold of the tank.

Lucky peered over the top of the dented galvanised tub. 'Ah, I think the guys must have got them mixed up,' he said. 'I will make sure it doesn't happen again.'

'Please do,' I replied.

Later I figured I'd start checking them at the onshore end, make sure of what I was getting. That's when I saw what I was dealing with here. Lucky had committed to getting me 1,000 tonnes of fuel and was having trouble finding places to buy it. He wasn't geared up to operate at this level, so his people were stealing it. First they started siphoning it from cars and trucks. That was way too slow, so somebody had the bright idea of drilling into a pipeline. That certainly sped the process up, but when they'd filled their containers they weren't too bothered about sealing the hole, so the damned stuff was spilling out onto the ground. It was a free for all. Total frigging mayhem. Women were running to the tankers with pails of fuel, one in each hand, slopping it all over the place. There were men in rubber boots, and kids. I even saw a little boy running along beside his mother with a bowl in his hands, as if he were off to the store to buy a few pounds of rice.

After several nights of this we'd got the vessels fully loaded. In fact, we were now sitting in the water with the load line submerged. 'Jesus,' I said, 'the coastguard are gonna see that as soon as we break cover.'

My chief engineer had the answer. 'What if we paint another line?' he said.

'Do it,' I said. It wouldn't have passed close scrutiny, but through a pair of binoculars, from shore? Yeah, that would work. He painted it 3ft higher than the official one. Crazy, but as far as I was concerned this was a one-off deal. The sun was shining and I was damned well going to make myself some hay.

We cast anchor and set off down river, picking up our pilot on the way through Bennett Island. As soon as he came aboard I could see him sniffing the air. He could smell the fuel that had been spilled over everything. He even skidded as he walked across the deck, but I put some ballast in the guy's pocket and he never stumbled again. Then I made a big show of berating the crew for failing to clean up properly.

A few hours later, we dropped the pilot off at the mouth of the Escravos and turned our nose out into the broad Atlantic. Next stop, Natal.

5

Natal, Brazil, July–August 1988

Three thousand miles is no great distance by air. Mainland Europe to New York? It's a hop. West Africa to Brazil? Likewise. Even in a cruise liner it's no more than a leisurely five or six days. But try it in a world-weary anchor-handling supply vessel, tugging another rust bucket in its wake, both of them so rammed full of fuel that the slightest wave engulfs their bows. Key in the pull on the towline and the constant stretching out and you can see why you end up with a cruising speed, on a good day, of 6 knots. That's like an old man taking a run in the park. Heading for Natal at that speed, it was going to take three weeks. I felt I could've got there faster by swimming it.

Despite the slow rate of progress, however, I felt good. After all the hassles of dealing with Lucky and his ragtag crew, as well as all the tensions involved in making sure that it was genuine fuel they were dumping in our tanks, not the contents of the Niger River, this was a chance to unwind and enjoy the thing I love to do: navigating the world's

oceans. I'd dreamt of this when I was a kid, reading about
the great explorers of the past. Drake, Magellan, Columbus:
they were my heroes and here I was, about to cross from the
eastern hemisphere to the west, from northern to southern
latitudes, at the helm of my own vessel and plotting a course
by the sun and the stars. Sure, my life so far had been about
making a pile of money, but it had also been about control-
ling my own destiny. That's the thing that came first. The
rest followed. I knew I was feeling good when, for the first
time in weeks, I got back into my daily workout routine.

Up on the bridge of the *Rig Mover* I sat on the big swivel
seat. I had the throttles within reach, but I hardly needed
them. The real work was navigation, taking a sighting with
my sextant, verifying the result against the GPS, then log-
ging our progress on the chart – and that didn't take all day.
Otherwise, I kept one eye on the compass, making sure the
autopilot was keeping us on course, the other on the radar,
making sure the horizon was clear. Just as the law of the sea
says that steam gives way to sail, so it says that a powered
vessel must alter course to avoid collision with anything
towing a load; but that's not much comfort when you see a
giant container ship knifing through the water at 20 knots
and the crew half asleep over a hand of cards. That was one
game of chicken I wouldn't want to engage in, ever.

Generally, though, being on the bridge was a relaxed
business. I had time for reflection, time to soak up that sense
of absolute freedom you get as the ocean unfurls before you,
constantly changing colour and shifting into new patterns.
Hour after hour I sat there watching the horizon, my parrot
perched on my shoulder. At times I couldn't stop myself
from grinning. This wasn't the life that fate had mapped
out for me had I stayed in Canada, no way. I don't know
what the gods had in mind when they dumped me in that

miserable little home in southern Ontario, with a drunken father and a psychotic mother, but it wouldn't have been sailing around the globe with a suitcase full of money in the safe, a beautiful wife back in Scotland and a highly success-ful fishing business down in Brazil. No sir!

So, had I done something bad in a previous life like those poor kids rummaging through the trash in Warri? Or the dead man on the roadside? Or the scrawny, barefoot women staggering through the mud with buckets of fuel that would fill my ships and line my pockets? Or had I done something good? Why the sudden change of fortunes after I slugged my high school teacher, packed a bag and took off for the sun without even writing a note to my mother? I was 15 years of age. Things could have gone badly wrong. So was it luck? Or was it some guardian angel taking pity on me?

Charlie, my New York attorney, who in reality had turned out to be more of a father to me than my real dad ever was, said it was 'the good spooks looking after you'. He reckoned people who were connected to you in some way and had died made it their mission to look after you. Whatever. The way I saw it, my circumstances now were nothing more than a fair reward for all the hard work I'd put in, saving up for my first snorkel and flippers and diving 40ft down to spear fish and hook lobster while my lungs screamed for mercy and my fingers bled into the salt water of the Bahamian reefs, just to put delicacies on the rich man's plate.

And what about the years I welded pipelines together on the bottom of icy seas around the world? But then, if we're talking about rewards and punishments, what about all those runs I did, 70mph across the Grand Banks with bales of Colombian pot on board, heading for the Keys or Fort Lauderdale? Hell, that was as good a time as I'd ever had – and big money too. Surely I deserved a kick in the balls for all that fun? But hey, so far so good. I wasn't complaining.

When Felipe relieved me, I took a towel, a book and my ghetto blaster and went up to the top deck above the wheelhouse. I lay in the sun for an hour or so, luxuriating in the warmth. Sun was another thing, like money, that I could never get enough of. I'd earned it and I was going to grab all I could get. In this life, you never know when your luck's going to run out.

I lay there, basking, listening to the thrum of the engines far below and the swish of the bow cutting through the tropical sea. Occasionally I turned over to feel the sun on my back, or went below and got myself a diet coke. I could have used an ice cold beer, but I had a strict rule that there should be no alcohol on the ship while we were at sea – and what was good for the crew was good for the captain. I lazed away the time while my watch ticked around to early evening, UK time. Then I went down to my stateroom, cranked up the single side band and called Linda. I could tell something was up the moment she answered. 'There's been an accident. Have you heard?'

'No. What's happened?'

'God, it's dreadful.'

'What are you talking about, honey?' I was thinking it might be something she'd seen on the road – or maybe a plane crash. She always got upset about those.

'In the North Sea. They're saying there's over 100 dead.'

As soon as she gave me the name of the rig I felt a shudder run down my back. Piper Alpha. Jesus, I'd worked on that. Laid the pipelines that connected it to the onshore facility. Most likely there were guys on there I knew, guys I'd worked with. She told me it was an explosion, that the whole place went up. They were looking for survivors, but they weren't hopeful. 'Poor fuckers.' That was all I could say.

You're always aware of danger in the oil industry. You know that accidents are going to happen. They're bound to. You just hope you aren't around when it's the turn of your particular field. In my career as a diver I'd been one of the lucky ones, and I knew it.

I came close often enough, like in 1976. We were salvaging the *Odeco Margaret*, a rig that had gone down on the lower Mississippi, at Avondale Shipyard. I was about 35ft down and starting to burn off the last section of a steel wall that supported the drill floor. I struck an arc into what turned out to be a tank full of fuel. The force of the explosion hurled me clean out of the water. I was unconscious for three full weeks, but when I woke up all I'd got was two busted eardrums, a few broken ribs and a face that was bruised so bad I looked like an eggplant.

My luck was in, I guess, and when I decided I'd done enough ten-month trips offshore, with back-to-back stretches of sixty to seventy days locked in saturation chambers, I was able to pack my bags, count my money and look around for another way of making a living while my body and mind were still intact. All told, I spent over 2,000 days in saturation conditions. That's close to five years of my life locked into a 40ft long tube with an 8ft diameter. A couple of dozen times I got the bends. Nothing serious – pain only. It could have been so much worse. Paralysis, for one. So, if there was one place I was glad never to be going back to, it was the North Sea. That was one dangerous place. Twenty-nine divers died in those dark, cold waters between 1973 and 1979 alone, three of them close friends.

I was aware of Linda sniffing on the other end of the line. 'Listen,' I said, 'why don't you fly out to Brazil, meet up with me?' There's nothing like bad news to make you feel mortal, and I suddenly wanted to see Linda, remind myself of who she was. We hadn't exactly parted on the best of terms back in Lagos.

'Can't do it, I'm afraid,' was her answer. She had a marathon to run and a couple of other races. Then she added, 'And my grandmother's ill. I need to be around.' I don't like to admit it now, but that bothered me. Maybe it even annoyed me. I'd never had to use family as an excuse to miss anything. I'd never had anybody to worry about. I had no ties, so I couldn't really understand her reasoning. As soon as the call was over, I put her to the back of my mind once more and started thinking about Douglas Kane and the business in Natal. I knew I should be talking to him sometime soon, see how the business was doing without me.

We had twenty-seven vessels fishing the waters off the coast of Brazil, with our own dedicated processing plant in Natal. We were shipping huge quantities of fresh fish – 150,000kg a month – to our distribution centre in New Orleans. It was tuna mostly, along with swordfish, all caught on the longline method, and it was like printing money. I was making more, and faster, than I ever did running marijuana across the Caribbean. And the good part? Every cent of it was legal.

We were no more than a couple of days out from Natal when I radioed Doug. We'd rigged up our own private line with a special frequency. It was simple enough and it usually worked. We each cut a length of wire to the same precise length. Those were our antennae, and what they meant were that, in theory, we would be the only people capable of tuning in. 'Listen, man, we should be in dock forty-eight hours from now, okay?'

'Got ya.'

'So you'll line up a pilot, right?'

'Done. Anything else?' Doug and I made a point of keeping our conversations short.

'Yeah, just to let 'em know we're in transit to the States. Both vessels.'

'And fuel?' He was prompting me, just in case someone was listening in.

'Just carrying what we need to get us home.'

Doug was my right-hand man. I trusted him. Hell, I'd known him long enough. Met him down in New Orleans back in the early 1970s. He came from a good family. His dad owned a construction outfit and his mom had health studios. Between them they made plenty, so why Doug took to crime I couldn't say. It wasn't like he needed to. Most likely he did it for the thrill of it, I'd guess, because what we did, smuggling pot, was one hell of a lot of fun. Fast boats, easy money, good-looking girls. What else could a young guy want? When we weren't chasing girls together we would go deep-sea fishing. Later, he married the daughter of a Yugoslavian guy who was big in oysters. It was a good connection to have. You always wanted to be on the right side of those mothers.

Doug started out selling dope around the city, by the pound. He was already making good money when I introduced him to Brett Eastwood and that was the beginning of our smuggling the stuff into Louisiana – a business that started great, but didn't end so well. Load after load came in without a hitch, until the guys on this particular freighter thought they saw the coastguard. They torched the damned thing and opened the sea-cocks. Suddenly there's a huge blaze lighting up the sky all across the Breton Sound as the ship burned. That was mistake number one. Number two was the dumbest thing I ever saw. They failed to take into account that they were sitting in 20ft of water, so when the boat went down it sank only a few feet, then rested on the bottom. When the coastguard finally showed up to see what was on fire they found the vessel in flames, burned out with bales of weed floating in the hold.

That blew the lid clear off the entire operation – and that's when I got the hell out. Packed my bags, went to Aberdeen and started diving again. Muscles went to the south of France and then to Brazil, Jack to Colorado and a couple of the other main men went to ground. As to the rest of them, 120 went to jail, Doug included. He kept his mouth shut tight about me, which is why I owed him, why I asked him out to Brazil with me when we started the fishing business – and that was why I knew I could trust him to take charge while I was away. He was like a brother to me.

Before we got to within sight of Natal harbour, I put the first mate, the engineer and a couple of seamen onto the *Adnil* and disconnected the tow. She would come in under her own power. It was safer that way. Less suspect too. As we approached the quayside we had to manoeuvre past a few of my own boats, converted shrimpers waiting to unload their catches of tuna. On the quay itself a party had broken out. A bunch of my employees had got the steel oil drums out and were battering the life out of them to a samba rhythm. Others were singing and dancing. My chef, Odee, had come up and was staring at the scene below. 'Brazilians,' I said, 'I love them. Maybe that's what I was in a previous life. A samba king.'

We tied up. I was looking for Doug, not a guy you would normally lose in a crowd. He was 6ft 2in and weighed 200lb. I soon spotted him, coming out of the office in a loud Hawaiian shirt, his ponytail longer than ever. He was followed by Customs & Immigration officers, which

I expected, and police, which surprised me. He looked distracted, possibly worried. When he caught my eye, I could've sworn there was a momentary flash of something there – animosity, anger, I couldn't tell. He walked over to the staff, thanked everyone for turning out and told them to get back to work. When he came aboard and hugged me he was all smiles, whispering in my ear, 'All okay, man.'

Next thing, Doug introduced me to the officials and I showed them all into the galley where my first officer and the rest of the crew were waiting. Odee had brought us mugs of coffee. The Brazilians pulled faces. They were used to little cups of espresso. I explained that he came from the Philippines and thought that more was better, and that kind of relieved the tension. Thirty minutes later, all the documentation was in good order and we were free to land.

As the officials disembarked I went up to the bridge for a few moments to take it all in. I'd been away six months and needed to adjust. I sat there at the wheel and checked the calculations I'd made when we were in the Niger Delta. Yep, it still added up. Getting the fuel in without hassle from the officials had saved me around $300,000. I rose from my seat and looked down to where the converted shrimp and lobster boats were offloading their catch.

These were good vessels and I'd got them ridiculously cheap. Steel hulled, they were 25m long and 8m wide. Fully loaded with ice, fuel and water, they drew 3m. I'd got hold of them when the local lobster and shrimp industry collapsed. The owners were desperate to get something for them, anything. It was their own damned fault, the fix they were in. They'd fished the waters out. I offered them 10¢ on the dollar and they couldn't grab it fast enough. The fact that I could pay United States dollars, cash, made them even keener. As they took my money, they shook their heads and told me I was crazy. Nobody had ever fished longline for tuna or swordfish before, not off the coast of Brazil. They looked me right in the eye and told me I was going to fall flat on my face. 'Yeah?' I said. 'Just watch me.'

Longline fishing had been used by the Japanese for many years. They probably invented it. It's very selective, not an ugly business like gill nets, for instance, but still rapacious. In fact, it rapidly depletes the stocks wherever you try it. But by the time that happens you've made your fortune and you're onto the next thing. You leave the sea to its own devices and in time it recovers. I'd been reading up about this business, same as I did every venture I undertook, all my life. My hunch was right about the Gulf of Mexico and I figured that maybe there were enough stocks in the waters between Brazil and Africa to support a business. I was hoping to catch tuna – yellowfin and bluefin – and sword-fish. Big bucks if I was right – and I was. Super right.

I equipped every vessel with 10 miles of line. I got hold of radio buoys, three for each line: one at each end and one in the middle. They would give a constant beeping signal. Then I had six radar-reflecting buoys that would go every mile between the radio beacons. After that there would be large, round, inflatables that would attach to the line every 500ft between the radar buoys. Finally, 500 hooks, each one baited with a big squid. Then I stuck glow sticks 10ft above the bait. Each vessel took on provisions for seven crew for two weeks. When that was all organised, we had them fuelled up, filled the hold with ice and were ready to go fishing.

There is a current that runs alongside the equator. It feeds in cooler water. And for some reason, wherever you have this mix of temperatures you'll get gatherings of bait fish, which attract the predators. All we had to do was find the current and lay out the line alongside it. There were other factors, of course, like setting the depth right and cutting your buoy lines to a certain length – in our case 50–100ft. The captain would sail out and locate the current, then the crew would attach the main line to a radio buoy and throw it over the side. Then the deckhands would bait a hook with squid, attach a light stick, throw it into the water and snap it onto the main line, and so on, until the whole 10 miles was laid out. It took them eight, maybe ten hours, after which they would sleep, taking turns on watch.

Next day, they'd start picking up. There might be rows and rows of empty hooks, but every so often you'd find a catch. A 2 per cent success rate and we were in profit. It might be yellowfin and it might be shark or swordfish. The yellowfin would weigh in at anything from 100–400lb. In amongst them you'd find the odd bluefin and everybody would start yelling. This was serious pay-dirt. They weighed anything up to half a tonne and, boy, do the Japs love them. They love them so much they'll pay through the nose. I once sold a single fish at auction in Japan for $72,000.

The guys had a small crane on board with a gaff on the end to pick the big ones out of the water. First thing they did was bleed the fish by cutting off its tail. Then they cut the head off and gutted it, before packing it down below in the ice.

Any sharks, which accounted for about 50 per cent of the catch, had to be stowed separately, on account of the strong ammonia smell they give off, which would contaminate the rest of the fish. The fins were hung out on the rigging. When they were dry, they'd be bagged up and sold to a Japanese buyer from São Paulo. The city has the biggest population of Japanese expats in the world. The shark's meat was sold in Brazilian supermarkets. Those two products alone covered our Brazilian expenses. The tuna and sword-fish were pure profit. The whole operation came down to a ten- or twelve-day cycle for each boat. Putting out the line, sleeping, hauling it in and repeating until you'd got a full load. And, day by day, I was piling up a fortune.

From the bridge of the *Rig Mover* I watched the graders on the dock. They were mostly Japanese. Anywhere I have been in the world where there is fish for sale the main grad-ers have always been Japanese. I watched as they inspected each fish individually, inserting a hollow tube about ¼in in diameter and a couple of feet long and taking out a section of the tail to examine for colour and fat content.

Once graded, the fish were put into boxes which were filled with frozen gel packs. An average two week catch for all the boats would be 100–150,000lb. We had trucks waiting to take the boxes to the airport. There, a sched-uled Varig airliner would fly it to my distribution centre in New Orleans, via Belem and Miami. And here's where I seriously worked the system: according to the official bills of lading, my company, Pescado de Brasil, was exporting it at 25¢ per lb to another company I'd set up in the Caymans – this part would be taxed, but I could stand that. The Cayman company then sold the yellowfin tuna to Ocean Harvest (my US company) for anything from $5–20 per lb, depending on the market price on the day and the qual-ity. That way, just about all the profits remained offshore, untaxable and virtually untraceable. Who needed the mari-juana business?

I climbed out of the bridge and went ashore, passing through the crowds of workers, embracing the men and hugging the girls. In the offices, Doug was waiting to update me. I asked him about the police presence. Had there been some problem?

'Nah,' he said. 'They came into the office for their money just as you put in, that's all.'

'So, how's that wife of yours?' I asked him.

'Jacqui?' He shrugged. 'She's gone home, stateside.'

'Oh?' I didn't ask him why, but he told me anyway.

'Thought I was paying too much attention to the Brazilian girls.' He looked at me and his face split into a big grin.

'Why change old habits?' I said. He didn't answer. He had some figures printed out on his desk. I looked them over. I couldn't believe how well we were doing. I'd really found a niche here. Question was, how long would the stocks last? Doug interrupted my thoughts.

'Listen,' he said, 'I had a visit from Jack.'

'Yeah? What was he doing here?' I asked. 'On vacation or what?'

Doug shook his head. 'He's got it all figured.'

'Got what all figured?'

'Another shipment, man. He's got it all ironed out. He has enough backers for a 12-tonne load. All he needs is a fucking boat.'

'Jesus Christ!' I said. 'What do I want to get involved with him again for?' I picked up the sheet of figures Doug had shown me. 'We're making money faster than you could print the fucking stuff.'

'Yeah, but 12 tonnes man.' Doug had lowered his voice. He went and closed the door. 'That's one helluva – '

'Yeah sure,' I said, 'but aren't you forgetting one little detail, buddy?'

'What's that? What am I forgetting?'

'Jack and his band of fuckwads had the *Rig Mover* and the *Adnil* for a full year and didn't get a single joint on board, never mind 12 fucking tonnes.'

Doug laughed. 'Yeah, that's a fact – but this time it's going to be different, he says.'

'Jesus Christ, Doug, see the fucking light. Look, this business – we ain't breaking any laws. We can't be touched for this. Doesn't that feel good to you?'

Doug sat down and lit up a joint. Sometimes I wished the guy would leave the stuff alone, but he'd always done it, ever since I first met him. Used to try to persuade me, back in the fast-boat days, but I was never into consuming the product. 'Yeah, I know,' he said, 'this is easy and it's legal. Just … I don't wanna let the guy down, ya know?'

'How much did he promise you to talk me into it?' I asked. I saw right away I'd hit a nerve. 'Look, Doug, I'm running a legitimate business. Jack can do what Jack's always done, but I'm not chasing his fucking dreams – or yours, if that's where your head's at. Not with my money. Ya got that?'

We left it there. Doug was pissed off, but I wasn't going to move on this one. No way. I went to my own office to cool down, picked up the phone and tried Linda, on the off chance. I was in luck. When she picked up I told her I'd arrived safely. 'That's good,' she said. She didn't sound too thrilled.

'So,' I said, 'when you coming over, hon?'

She hummed and hah-ed a bit, then said, 'I've got a lot on just now. Let's see how things are in a couple of months, shall we?'

'Whatever,' I said, and slammed the phone down feeling even more pissed off. I had to make a physical effort to stay calm. Take a deep breath, I told myself. I gave it a couple of minutes, then went outside and walked across to Doug's office. I put an arm around his big broad shoulders and said, 'Hey, sorry I blew up, man. Been a long trip, y'know?'

'Yeah, sure,' he said. 'So what's on your mind?'

'Right now,' I said, 'this sailor needs some R&R. How about you and I head into town, get us some cold beers and hot girls?'

'Now you're talking,' he said and we went outside and jumped into his car.

6

Brazil, New Orleans, Brazil, August–November 1988

Despite her apparent coolness on the phone, Linda flew out about a week later. She'd quit her job. I'd wanted her to stop work for some time, ever since that day in November 1986 when the Chinook helicopter she was supposed to be on crashed, killing forty-two out of the forty-four people on board. It had happened on a routine North Sea run – one that she was scheduled to be on, until she switched shifts to come see me while I was doing a salvage job in Mexico. After all the years she'd put in as a hostess on those things she wasn't sure how much longer her luck could hold. Maybe she was already thinking about starting a family – although I guess it was more likely she was thinking about getting her husband straightened out first. So she quit and got a flight over to Natal and I picked her up.

We spent a month or so together, kind of vacationing – by which I mean Linda took things easy and I did my best to spend some time with her. In the early hours of the morning I'd be on the phone, chasing up crew for the fishing fleet, monitoring sales and shipments and talking to Doug over umpteen cups of coffee. Then we'd get changed and go out to exercise. We'd leave the *Rig Mover*, run a mile or so through the streets surrounding the harbour until we got to the sea, and then do 7 miles along the Ponta Negra beach. At the far end we'd run up Morro do Careca, a 500ft-high sand dune, which earned us the right to walk down, get a *coco gelado* and sip the ice-cold milk from the young coconuts through a straw. After that, we'd take a taxi back to the boat, shower and head for a late lunch at one of my favourite restaurants.

When the sun went down we'd visit some of the local clubs and enjoy dancing into the night. On the surface we were having a good time, but deep down she was simmering. Brazil is full of gorgeous women and they're pretty uninhibited. If they like the look of a guy, they let him know. I was used to getting a fair bit of attention. I'd always been in good shape, I was a casual but classy dresser and I carried myself well. And I'm a happy kind of guy. I smile a lot. When I'm on my own and a beautiful woman eyes me up and down and flashes a grin, she gets one back and maybe a wink, too. If a girl comes up to me in a club and wants to dance, my attitude is, why not? We're all here to have a good time, right?

I soon got an answer to that question. The girls in Brazil don't care if you have a woman with you or not. They think you're attractive, they let you know – and they're not too subtle about it. We were in a club by the beach, a nice place with lots of locals and a great band. We'd eaten barbecued shrimp and lobster tails and had a few *caipirinhas*. Linda seemed to be in a good place. We stepped out on the floor and were dancing to the rhythms, really into it. After a couple of numbers, a girl came over and tapped me on the arm, crooked her finger and started swaying her hips at me. She was a mover, a real peach. I shook my head at her, and then gave a 'Hey, what can I do?' kind of shrug to Linda. Wrong move. Linda shoved me away. 'You bastard,' she said, and left me on the dance floor, pushing her way to the exit and knocking aside a waiter with a loaded tray of drinks. That brought the owner rushing over to see what the hell was going on.

I guess what you're supposed to do in these circumstances is sit down and figure out what went wrong. Talk it through like they do in the soaps. Apologise – even if it's not your fault. Not me, not at that age. My attitude was, screw it, what did I do? Besides, I had a plane to catch next morning and I was going to catch it, even if I did have to sleep on the sofa. At that stage in our relationship, I was happy to leave Linda to cool down while I headed to New Orleans to visit Ocean Harvest and my distribution team.

I'd also arranged to meet up with the shipwrights who were working on my 'labour of love', as I liked to refer to it. Everyone else I knew called it a wreck. This was the fancy yacht – the remains of a fancy yacht – that I'd hauled up from the Mississippi mud. Every time I heard the progress report from Clyde, my shipyard manager, he gave me the same story, 'another six months', and frankly I was getting sick of hearing it. They were spending my money – bucket loads of it – and I wanted to see what they were doing with it.

The 'SS *Neversail*', as Linda called her, was renamed the *Caledonian*. She had started out life in 1933 as the *Explorer*, a steel-hulled luxury yacht, 33m long, topsides all varnished wood and polished brass. She had belonged to some long-dead oil executive whose trustees had managed to let her sink in a bayou on the border between Mississippi and Louisiana. She had been lying there for a decade. I paid

$25,000 to General Electric Finance for the privilege of taking her on, but that was only the start. The restoration project that I'd thought would take six months had taken three and a half years. Every time I picked up the phone to ask how we were getting on it seemed there was another delay, another request for cash.

On this occasion, I arrived to find the guys had made some real progress. They'd managed to gut the interior, but now they were sitting around awaiting a delivery – in the case of the engineers it was parts, in the case of the shipwrights a consignment of Honduran mahogany. They couldn't proceed without it, they told me. 'Meanwhile, where's our salary?'

I've never been a great believer in good luck and bad luck. The way I see it, shit happens to everyone, indiscriminately, or it doesn't. You simply play the hand you're dealt. But looking back, it seems as if the problems with the *Caledonian* marked a tidal shift in my fortunes.

I'd only been in the Ocean Harvest office in New Orleans for an hour. I was talking things over with Doug's brother-in-law, Mark, when a call came in on the radio from my captain on the *Coastal Servant*, one of the two vessels I had still fishing in US waters. He told me he'd been arrested.

At first I was alarmed. 'What the fuck for?' I asked him, and before he could respond, my concern had turned to deep suspicion. 'C'mon, Wayne, what did you do?' Wayne was another guy from my past. He smuggled three boat-loads in from Colombia on a converted shrimper called the *Northern Breeze*, got caught, served two and a half years and never said shit, even though he'd been working on behalf of Jack. I trusted him. We all did. But if he'd been attempting to smuggle a load on my boat I'd feed him to the fucking fish, and I told him so.

He knew what kind of mood I was in. 'Hey, cool it,' he said. 'I got officers from Wildlife and Fisheries on my vessel – yeah, they're standing right beside me.' He paused and said, 'It seems we don't have a bluefin permit.'

I shouted back at him. 'You tell them we got every single permit they give out in the state of Louisiana and the state of Texas too!'

'They appreciate that, Rob, but it seems we don't have a federal permit. Jesus, they can seize the vessel … and I can get five years in federal prison.' There was another pause before he said, 'Right now they're escorting us to the docks. You need to get some lawyers out to meet us. Please.'

By now it was obvious that the Fisheries guys could hear the entire conversation. I did my best to sound calm. 'Okay,' I said, 'Tell the officers that we will rectify the problem. We honestly tried to do everything by the book, right down to the letter of the law. Explain to them it's a new industry and we're very sorry. Give them all the co-operation they require. Ya got that? Good. Over and out.' Soon as I was off I screamed, 'cocksuckers!' and slammed my fist on the desk. I looked at Mark. He looked back at me like he had something else to say. 'What, you got more?'

'More bad news, yeah. You ready?'

'Sure, go ahead.'

He inhaled deeply and I automatically braced myself. Mark didn't go in for dramatics. 'Okay,' he said, 'here's what it is. The company is being sued for 250 large.'

'Sued? Who the fuck's suing us? What have we done?'

'Remember the guy – the crewman – who speared his finger with a hook?'

'Yeah, course I do. We picked up his hospital bill and then we paid his goddam wages for four weeks 'til he was fit to go back to sea. What's the ungrateful prick suing us for?'

Mark was nodding his head. 'That's right, we did all of that. But it seems his girlfriend's real pissed off. His finger's never quite healed up and she's the one suing us.'

'You're losing me, Mark. What the fuck are you babbling about?'

Mark sighed. 'You ain't gonna believe this. She's found herself a smart-ass lawyer and told him it was, like, *her favourite finger*.'

'You're fucking kidding me!'

'No, they're claiming we ruined her love life.'

'So tell her to go fuck herself.' I laughed at my own joke in spite of myself. Couldn't help it.

'Yeah, very funny, Rob, but let me tell you, this lawyer's one clever sonofabitch. Our guys have known him a long time and their advice …' He paused.

'Go on, what is their advice?'

'That we settle with her. Otherwise it's gonna cost us big.'

'What, even when we win?'

'We won't win, Rob. Not according to our lawyers.'

I could squeal all I liked, but I knew I'd have to cave in – and I detested that. It was like being shafted and agreeing to it. It took me a day or two to get it out of my mind. I could picture the damned bitch finger-fucking herself, and the lawyers, and the fisherman – and his brother, just as soon as she got the money.

So, a run of bad luck. And it carried right on. It was during those two days that I got the call from Linda, reminding me I'd forgotten her birthday, something I'd never done before. I apologised, naturally, but she wasn't in the mood to accept it. Two days later, she was back on the phone to say her grandmother had finally died. I commiserated as best I could, but the fact was, I'd never met the old lady and I had other things on my mind. And she could tell it.

As if the lawsuit and the bluefin licence thing weren't enough, I got a call from Jack. He needed to meet up. Had something important to discuss and wouldn't do it over the phone. We met in the French Quarter, one of those little bars they have down there. They had a blind man playing boogie-woogie on the piano. He was damned good. Jack told me that he and his crew had cooked up another plan. 'Jesus Christ,' I said, 'you guys cost me close to a million with the money I spent on the *Adnil* and the *Rig Mover*. Tommy spent a year trying to get loaded and all he got was a dose of clap from those Thai hookers. Then Barry Sangster goes and torches the engine room on the *Adnil* – and forgets we don't have insurance.'

Jack nodded, but ploughed ahead. 'Listen, it wasn't all our fault what happened in Thailand,' he said. 'And the fire – that was an accident. One of those things, man. Look, I've raised all the money from my guys.' He meant the doctors and lawyers who would give him money for a run and get a fourfold return if it succeeded. Respectable guys who loved a gamble – and got a vicarious thrill. 'Everything is prepaid. We got some serious Thai weed being grown – right now. There's acres of it and they're taking extra care to make sure it's all buds. No seeds, man. Just like that sensimilla we used to get from Colombia.' He nudged me in the ribs. 'Barranquilla, remember? Listen, just find us a boat that'll get us from Thailand to Alaska and we'll cut you in. You'll make a bundle.' He snapped his fingers. 'Just like that, man. A finder's fee of a couple million and you hardly have to get off your ass.'

I was trying to be respectful. I waited a few moments before replying. 'Jack,' I said, 'we go back a long way, but we've headed in different directions. My answer is no. Has to be. I can't afford to take a risk like that. I got too much to lose.' Jack was seriously pissed off and I guess I could see why. I knew how to get a ship and was in a position to help him out – but I wouldn't.

'Okay,' he said, 'have it your own way. But if you change your mind, gimme a call. I'm your buddy, remember?'

'Okay, I'll do that.' But I knew I wouldn't. No way. I flew back to Natal. Doug picked me up off the plane and broke the news that Linda had gone home. 'That's fucking great,' I said. 'Why didn't you call me?'

'Because she told me not to,' he said.

'And you take orders from her now? Is that it?'

'Rob, she made me promise.'

'Well, fuck the pair of you then.'

I was sore as hell with Linda and mad at Doug for not keeping me informed. To me, at that time, your first loyalty was to your buddies. Always.

However, I didn't have time to dwell on it. That very afternoon, as I sat in my office overlooking the dockside, I got two visitors. They were Americans. I thought they were cops until they gave me their cards. They were from some seismic outfit called WesternGeco. They had a small survey vessel up in Fortaleza that they needed to get across the Atlantic to West Africa. It was mostly used in the swamps and no way was it seaworthy for an ocean crossing. What they wanted to know was, could they hire the *Rig Mover* to tow it to Nigeria? 'Whereabouts in Nigeria?' I asked, wondering out how much I could charge them.

'Place called Warri,' the guy said. 'Warri, Nigeria. You know it?'

'Sure,' I told him. 'I heard of it.' Soon as they left, I clapped my hands together and burst out laughing. After all the shit, here came the sun again.

I drove up the coast to Fortaleza and met the guys at the shipyard. When I saw the survey vessel I realised there was no way we could tow it at sea. There was a lot of high-tech shit on board, very sensitive. The only way she'd go to Nigeria was if we lifted her up and stuck her on the *Rig Mover*'s deck. That way we could get her across the ocean in twelve to fourteen days and by the time she arrived I would have had a chance to fly out and look up my old pal, Lucky. If we could load up with fuel again – boy, this would be a nice little money maker.

While I was with the guys, I had to work out what I was going to charge them. There are a lot of people who'll take hours – days, even – to price a job like that. I figured it out my usual way, which took about two minutes. First, what it would cost me to do it? Fourteen days over, four-teen days back, making twenty-eight days at \$2,000 a day. Double it for contingencies, add 20 per cent, then round it out –\$140,000 – there's my price. And as fast as I added it up they agreed to it. You beauty!

It took a few days to load their vessel on the *Rig Mover*, after which I took the crew out to dinner. We had a great night out and next morning I was on the dockside to wave goodbye. See you in a couple weeks in Warri, guys!

As I drove back to Natal, it occurred to me that I should make some time to go have a visit with Muscles before heading over to Nigeria. A little R&R. God knows I needed it. The next week, I booked a flight and went down to Rio.

I'd known Muscles since 1972. I know I can't have been more than 16 years old. It was only a year since I'd left Canada and set up home in Andros Island, Nicholls Town. Home? The first night, I actually lived under an upturned boat on the beach, eaten alive by sand flies.

Muscles was a speed junkie. Race cars, power boats, any-thing that would go fast. He stood 6ft 4in, weighing about 250lb. Boy, was he tough. Solid muscle, head to toe, and fit with it. Always working out. He'd been a wrestler; he'd done a tour as Captain USA on some pro circuit.

I met him as a result of a ride I'd got from friends of his from Nicholls Town to Bimini. The Bahamian immigration was coming to arrest me and these guys gave me a lift out of there. We were flying along about 70mph when we crashed into a wave, knocked a few things loose and broke the compass. But, using the hands on my watch and the sun – which I'd read about in a book – I got us to our destination. When they were told it would be a week before a replacement could be flown over, I steered the boat to Miami, hitting the entrance to Government Cut on the money. That impressed the hell out of them. They didn't realise how easy it was. As far as they were concerned I was a regular genius and they couldn't wait to tell Muscles about me. Next thing, he sent a message. He needed a navigator for a race, Nassau to Key West. His own man had gone AWOL. Later I learned he'd been arrested. Anyway, was I interested? Fuck, yeah man.

That was one absolutely wild ride, skimming over the water at 70–90mph on his 39ft cigarette boat, *The Long Shot*. We won and that was it. I was hooked on racing. He tried to give me a grand, but I turned it down. 'No way, man. I owe you,' I said. 'I should be paying you a grand for letting me be on board.' It was the right thing to do, I guess. He's the guy who arranged my first job in the pot smuggling business – on the salvage boat.

The thing with Muscles was, as well as all this showman stuff, he just loved smuggling. It was a thrill thing – him against the authorities – and once he knew what I could do he wanted to get me on board. We certainly had some times together. Made a lot of money, fast. He said smugglers were born, not made. 'You and me, it's what we were put on this earth for,' he said. Later, when I set up in legitimate business,

Muscles was disappointed. 'Each to his own,' he said, 'but
you should stick to your roots, Rob. You wanna go busting your balls, that's your decision.' Turned out he called it
right, the smart-ass sonofabitch.

Muscles had gone to France after the crew fired that boat
in Breton Sound, exposing the huge smuggling operation
we were involved in. In fact, it was me who arranged for
him to get a fake Brazilian ID and move to Rio. Among the
people he hung out with was Ronnie Biggs, still on the run
from the British police. Muscles had a big swanky place in
one of the city's most exclusive neighbourhoods. Built a dry
moat around it and had a bunch of pit bull terriers running
around the perimeter on wires. When I showed up from the
airport, he was stretched out on a sun lounger lobbing steel
weights into the pool. 'What the fuck ya doing? This your
new workout regime?' I asked him.

Muscles laughed and pointed to the water as one of his
pit bulls broke the surface, front legs working like pistons
and a 5kg weight gripped between its teeth. 'I'm teaching
these bastards to dive,' he said. I laughed. It was good to
be there and, after recent events, I felt I needed to relax
in the company of a guy who wanted nothing from me, a
guy I could be honest with. He was the nearest I'd got to a
shrink, I guess. I gave him a rundown of my situation and
he laughed. 'Busting your balls, man. Like I always said. All
that legitimate business – that ain't for us. We don't fit the
mould, man, and that's the truth of it.' He looked me up
and down and frowned. 'When was the last time you really
worked out? You don't look like you could press 250. You're
getting scrawny.'

I stayed a couple of days up at Muscles' place, relaxing. I
got some sun, drank a few beers and ate good food at the
rodizios. I was packed and about to head to the airport to

catch a flight to Nigeria. I was waiting for a taxi to take me to the airport when I got a call from Doug. I was expecting to hear him report the *Rig Mover*'s arrival in Nigeria. I was wrong. 'We got the DEA on our asses, Rob. The Brazilians.'

'What the fuck do the Brazilian DEA want with us?'

'I'll get to that. Thing is, man, they dumped an entire shipment on the tarmac and –'

'Whoa, where was this?'

'Belem. An entire plane-load of tuna – 70,000lb of it. Tipped the lot and chopped up every last fish. They were using machetes, man. It's done, fucked, kaput. All cut in little pieces and thrown back in the boxes. By the time it arrived in New Orleans – nothing but cat food.'

'Doug, tell me you're making this up. I mean, why the fuck would they do that?'

'They think we're using the fish as cover. For a drug-running operation.'

'Drugs?'

'Yeah, cocaine.'

'Well what the hell put that in their minds? That's a fucking crazy idea.'

'They figure there's no way we could be making so much money, expanding so fast.'

I was struggling to get to grips with what Doug was telling me. I thought it over for a moment. It just didn't make sense. 'Okay,' I said, 'I'm on my way.' I sent the cab away and cancelled my flight to Nigeria, but it was too late to fly to Natal.

By morning, I'd calmed down some. Muscles and I decided this had to be a shakedown, a heavy-handed attempt by the Brazilian authorities to get themselves a slice of the cake. Yeah, if that was it we could surely sort it out. But then I started to doubt my own reasoning. If that really was the case, why bother to destroy several hundred thousand dollars' worth of perfectly good tuna? Why not just threaten us?

I was drinking my first coffee of the day when Doug called again. He had more bad news. The US authorities had got in on the act. Stopped another plane in Miami and another in New Orleans. Unloaded it and 'inspected' the catch. They meant 'trashed', but that's not what they put on the documents. Like the Brazilians, of course, they found nothing incriminating and had to compensate me. That's when my devious plan – billing the fish at 25¢ per pound to save paying income tax in Brazil – came back and bit me in the ass. I'd lost 500,000lb of fish, but instead of being reimbursed its true value – around $5 million – we would receive $125,000. It wouldn't even cover the cost of the shipping.

And now, just to twist the knife in the wound, the Brazilian banks had frozen our accounts. Doug had got my lawyers on the case, pronto, but they didn't have to tell me that once any government agency was involved, the whole process was going to be slow – slower than molasses.

With no access to my own funds and a labour force demanding their wages, I called Mark, who worked as my general manager in New Orleans, and told him to bring $350,000 down to Natal, in cash. The last thing I said to him was, 'Make sure you declare it, Mark.'

He was on a flight within hours – or would've been if the feds hadn't stopped him at the gate in Miami and arrested him. The charge? Trying to leave the country with undeclared funds. Asshole.

I was still reeling from this latest piece of incoming news – it must have been sometime that afternoon, because Muscles and I were by the pool, taking a break – when

Doug called. 'Rob, put your TV on – now. Channel 9. Move it.' The tone of Doug's voice told me all I needed to know about how serious this was. I dashed into the house and switched on. Muscles was beside me. There was a sort of jazzy current affairs show on called *Aqui Agora* – 'Here and Now'. They did a lot of investigative reporting – a real sensationalist, tabloid type of show. They exposed slum landlords, corrupt officials, white slavers. I sat down on the edge of the sofa with Muscles. It wasn't some handcuffed conman I saw staring out at me as the picture formed. It was Muscles' mugshot, then Doug's, then mine. As the images registered, they cut to a shot of my catches being hacked up with machetes, then flashed us up once more as the voiceover described us as fugitives from justice, drug lords, gangsters.

Doug was still on the line. 'What are they fucking talking about?' I shouted. 'This is insane.'

'Fuck knows,' he said, 'and tell ya the truth, I ain't about to try and find out. We need to get our asses out of this damned country, and fast. Call me when you can, man.' I slammed down the phone and started to throw a few things into a case. Money, mostly. And a false ID. Muscles did the same. We got a cab out to the airport.

You look around for something positive in these situations – or, at least, that's what I do. Sitting on the plane watching the runway flash past, I had an overwhelming feeling of relief. I was out of there, thank Christ, and on my way to Lagos. As long as I was free I could work something out. As I thought things over, my mind seethed with the injustice of it all. I was worried about Doug. It would be a few weeks before I heard from him again and I was besieged with questions about why this was happening and who was behind it. But at least I was free. I looked out of

the window and saw the Brazilian coast slipping away from
me, the Atlantic Ocean far below, dotted with white caps.
Here and there I could see an occasional craft ploughing
through the choppy waters. I wondered idly how the *Rig
Mover* was getting on. Then I slept.

7

Warri, Nigeria, December 1988

It was the voice of our pilot that woke me. The sound system in the aircraft was crackly and at first I couldn't make out what he was saying. I reached up and gave the little speaker a whack, then looked out the window, expecting to see thunderclouds, but there was nothing there, just a drab, biscuit-coloured haze. Then the pilot's voice came into focus, telling us that we'd run into the *harmattan*. I didn't mind it when I was travelling at 8 knots in a ship, but 600mph in a jet that was sucking sand into the turbines – that was a little disconcerting. The pilot warned us that we might have to change course and land somewhere else. I shifted my seat to upright and took another drink from the passing trolley. What the hell. Right now the atmospheric conditions were just a footnote to a great long list of worries.

As the stewardess moved on down the gangway, I sat there twirling the ice around in my crystal glass. I thought over the events of the past few months. Something was niggling at the back of my mind, but I couldn't work out what.

In any case, there was the bigger question: why had everything suddenly collapsed this way? Who was behind it? If
I was looking for someone to point the finger at, someone
who maybe wanted to see me go under, I could've drawn
up a list of suspects without too much trouble. In a place
like Brazil, if you're making money, you're most likely
making enemies too. For every winner there has to be a
loser. People get jealous; they feel you're crowding in on
their space, taking what's theirs, and on top of that I was a
foreigner. I was still seen as a young upstart – a cocky bastard who always dressed a little too sharp.

But set against that, I'd created work for a bunch of
people, hundreds of them, and I'd always made a point
of paying over the going rate. It suited me to have good
employees, and contented ones. Why had they celebrated
that way when I arrived back in Natal? Because they liked
me, that's why. So, who had I upset? Who was so pissed off
that they would try to bring me down?

Just then the pilot came back on to tell us that, despite
the dust, we were going to land in Lagos. That surprised
me. Looking out as we approached the runway, it seemed
to me conditions were pretty difficult. We got down okay,
but half an hour later when I went to the transfer desk I was
told there was no onward flight for me. The airport at Warri
didn't have any instrument landing capability, so it was
closed until the dust cleared. Might be hours, might be days.
These north winds, they said, they can go on a long time.
I went across to the taxi desk. It took me a while and it cost
me plenty, but I finally fixed myself up with a driver willing
to take me to Warri.

An hour later, I wished I hadn't bothered. The drive was
a nightmare. Most of the way we could barely see 50 yards
in front of us, and every so often we ran into a cloud of

smoke and had to edge past yet another car that had crashed
and caught fire. Naturally the riot police were out in force,
setting up roadblocks and exacting a fine from anyone foolish enough to be out in such conditions. No matter that
they were out there breathing in the dust and fumes, they
weren't about to let a good money-making opportunity
slip by.

When we finally arrived in Warri I directed the driver to
the Palm Court Hotel. It was a dump, but it was a familiar dump. I checked in, showered off the dust, got a taxi
and made my way to Auntie's Kitchen. Night was falling.
I noticed along the road that, if anything, Warri had become
dirtier and more decrepit during my short absence. Or was
it that I was now seeing it more clearly, despite the dust?

I walked in to the sound of laughter and clinking glasses.
I turned to see the crew of the *Rig Mover* gathered round
a table with a bunch of local girls, all drinking and eating.
I walked over and asked them, 'So when did you guys get in?'

They hadn't been expecting me. They fell silent, looked a
bit embarrassed. 'Hey,' I told them, 'relax, enjoy yourselves'.
I bought them a round of beers, had one myself, then said,
'Okay, guys, I'll catch up with you in the morning.' For a
moment I was tempted to update them on the situation
back home, then I thought better of it. Why spoil their
night out?

I left them to it and got a cab to Lucky's bar. At first
I thought I was in the wrong place – or that it had changed
hands. It was kind of jazzed up. There was new decor, new
furniture, lots of nice mirrors on the walls. Even the hookers at the bar looked like they'd been spruced up – or traded
in for a new lot. The whole place had been refurbed – and
all on the back of that one deal. Christ, they even had a
big picture behind the bar, an African wildlife scene in

lurid colours. Below it sat two of Lucky's minders. They recognised me straight away. They slid off their stools like alligators entering a swamp. 'Mister Stone, take a seat please,' one of them said. The other one snapped his fingers and the guy at the bar straightened his bow tie like he was still getting used to wearing it. A moment or two later he arrived at my table with a jug of iced water.

When I was called to enter Lucky's office I had to try not to laugh. Lucky looked like some ghetto kid who'd won a world boxing title. His hands were covered with gold rings. He had a gold chain around his neck and a jewelled wristwatch the size of a small mantel clock. He had the girls too – four of them draped around him like they were fur coats. He jerked his chin and they melted away, wobbling across the room on their high heels and squeezing onto an upholstered seat made for three.

Lucky was on his feet and coming towards me with his arms spread out. He was grinning. He'd put on weight. 'Rob!' he shouted. 'It is good to see you again.' He clapped his hands on my shoulders and embraced me. 'You look very well,' he said. Then he stood back, took a deep breath, held his stomach in and said, 'And what about me? How am I, eh?'

'You look fantastic,' I said, and glanced around once more. 'The whole place looks fantastic.' He beamed with pride.

'Rob my friend, I must tell you that, thanks to our dealings, I am doing extremely well. Sit down, sit down. What can I get for you?' He opened a drawer at the desk. 'I have imported malt whisky from your adopted homeland. The genuine article,' he added. I laughed, remembering how he'd recycled the expats' empty bottles of Glenfiddich and Jura, filling them with local rotgut and passing them off as the real thing. 'I have chilled beer at the bar as well.'

He pointed across the room. 'And I have some beautiful young girls.'

'Sure,' I said. Then, as he beckoned towards the settee, I smiled and added, 'I mean the beer, man. Just the beer.' It was good to see the guy, but I wanted to get down to business. Before I had a chance to tell him about the *Rig Mover* he told me that he had heard of its arrival. 'So, do you want me to allocate some staff?' he asked. 'Tell me how much fuel you want and I will provide the manpower. We can do it more quickly this time.'

'It's not going to be ready for a little while,' I said, 'but yeah, I'm not planning to sail home empty.'

I wasn't sure I wanted to tell him what was happening in Brazil. I would have preferred him not to know just yet, but I was going to have to alert the crew to the situation, and once I'd done that it would be all over town. So I filled him in – just gave him the barest details. His whole demeanour changed. This was a major let-down for him. Up 'til that moment he'd imagined he was going to supply my entire fishing fleet for the foreseeable future. He'd done his calculations and made plans for all the money he foresaw coming his way as he supplied my fleet. Now I was telling him there was no fleet. This trip was a one-off. Unless something happened, I'd have no reason to come back.

I left Lucky's place, went back to my hotel and tried to sleep, but the wind had got up and kept rattling the windows. Early next morning, I got a cab across town to McDermott's yard. The *harmattan* still hadn't cleared and by the time we were halfway there I was covered with dust and had a vicious headache. The taxi driver was honking his horn incessantly as he battled through the go-slows. I was in such a foul mood I was sure that if I'd had a gun in my hand I would've shot him. At the yard, I looked around for the

Rig Mover and soon spotted her, berthed next to a derrick barge. It cheered me up to see the old lady again, although she did look weird with the WesternGeco boat perched on her like some giant parasitic bug.

The crew were on board, cleaning up as well as they could with the dust still flying. I gathered them together and broke the news about the business in Brazil. I explained the situation as well as I could, but the whole damned thing was still a mystery to me. I was slowly realising what it meant, though: Pescado de Brasil and Ocean Harvest might be washed up. The crew realised it too and they were worried. They had families to support back in the Philippines and Indonesia.

While I was talking, a little fat guy came up – not a Nigerian, but a brown-skinned fellow in a white linen suit. He looked like he didn't have a worry in the world. He was smiling. He wanted to speak to the captain. I introduced myself as the owner and asked him who he was, what he wanted. He told me his name was Habib. Something about him immediately appealed to me. He had none of that ingratiating air that some of the locals put on when they were trying to impress you – and just to see a happy face kind of cheered me. 'I am McDermott's representative in Warri,' he said, 'their agent. The firm are hoping to charter your vessel for a week or two.'

The phrase 'manna from heaven' was on my lips, but I shoved it back in. 'Okay,' I said, 'we might be able to arrange that.' I turned to the crew and asked, 'How d'you guys feel about staying in Nigeria and working for McDermott?' You could see the tension leave them.

'Happy to, boss,' was the reply. Work was work and Warri was no worse than many of the ports they ended up in. Besides, as Odee pointed out, the girls there only charged 50 naira – which translated as $10, give or take a few cents.

'Right,' I said. 'Each to his own, eh?'

I went and had a coffee with Habib. I asked him where he came from. He told me he was Lebanese, that he was a native of Beirut, but had got the hell out of there some years ago. 'So what's your arrangement with the company?' I asked him.

Habib grinned. 'I am their Mister Fixit,' he said. 'When the company want something done that involves local businesses, they come to me.' Then his mouth straightened. 'But since the slowdown in oil, there hasn't been much to fix – as you can imagine.'

'Yeah, I see where you're coming from,' I said. 'Listen, right now I need as much work for the *Rig Mover* as you can get. What are McDermotts paying – for the hire, I mean?'

'They will pay $2,500 a day, maximum.' My heart was bumping double time. I'd been planning to open the bidding at $2,000 and go down to $1,500 if I had to.

'Okay,' I said, 'I reckon I can go with that.' I looked him in the eye and laughed. 'You look like a man I shouldn't haggle with,' I added. 'So how about I cut you in – 1 per cent of the daily rate – for as long as this lasts?'

Habib perked up right away. 'You mean you'd like me to keep her busy?' I nodded. This was looking extremely promising. 'Make it 2 per cent,' he said, 'and I'll keep her working for many months.'

After leaving Habib, I went to town and called Doug to find out what the hell had happened after I took off from Muscles' place. He told me the police had raided it just a few hours later. Next day, the newspapers had headlines about Muscles and Doug, alongside photos of the Pescado de Brasil offices and maps showing the routes our boats were supposed to be taking between Africa and Portugal. Then, a story about them loading up with cocaine and returning to Brazil to pick up fish. They had planes flying money to the States. If it had been happening to somebody else I might have found it funny. In a paperback thriller I would have laughed it off as ridiculous. But it was happening. To me.

This was a runaway train of disasters and I was powerless to put a brake on it. As to the plant, the police had swooped on that too, surrounding it. No workers from outside had been allowed in. Those still at work were strip-searched and questioned. All our boats were impounded and every last ounce of our precious, perishable fish was being thrown out of cold storage onto the hot concrete docks and chopped up.

'So what's happening now?' I asked.

'I'll tell you what's happening,' he said. 'The fuckers found exactly what we knew they'd find. Nothing. Diddly squat. How the fuck could they? So that's the good part. There are no charges. Only thing is, nobody wants to work with us anymore.'

'Jesus.'

'Right, suddenly our name stinks – and all because some-body started spreading lies to the cops, the DEA, the press, the media.' There was a pause, then he said, 'So the plant's shut down. I mean ...'

'Yeah, sure,' I said. 'What else could you do?'

'So what next? Any ideas?' I thought for a moment. Fact was, I was fighting back tears. This thing was supposed to be setting me up for life and here we were taking it all apart piece by piece. I spent some time chewing things over. Maybe I needed a break, time to lick my wounds. I had a whole lot of figuring to do and I could do that better in the comfort of my own home. I told Doug I'd call him from Scotland and hung up.

I got a Pan Am flight that left Lagos late in the afternoon of 21 December, due into Schiphol, Amsterdam, next morning. Exhausted by the events of the past few weeks, not to mention the broken nights at the Palm Court, I had a large glass of malt whisky and managed to sleep most of the way. First class was virtually empty and the girls had turned the lights down for me almost after take-off. When I woke up, it was to the sound of the stewardesses sobbing and comforting each other. It seemed a sister flight had gone down over southern Scotland, some place called Lockerbie. Wiped out everybody on board.

In Amsterdam, before I changed planes for Aberdeen, I tried to call Linda, tell her to expect me, but there was no answer. So when I arrived I just hopped in a cab. Her delight in seeing me turned to anger when she realised I'd travelled Pan Am. 'My God,' she said, 'that means – that means if you'd been on the flight that came down I wouldn't have known a thing about it until the airline called me. Why didn't you tell me?'

I apologised and calmed her down. So why was I home, she asked. I couldn't even think about explaining it all to her at this stage, so I bullshitted. Told her things were fine and I just wanted a break. It was only the next day, when she drove me into town, followed me into the bank and saw me withdraw a pile of cash – several hundred pounds of it, all in coins – that she realised I was up to something. 'Now I get it. You're going to be calling those gangster friends of yours.' She was seething with anger as we left the bank and went back to the car. 'From public call boxes. That's what this is all about, isn't it? You're planning something – something secret, something outside the law.'

'Linda,' I said, 'you don't understand what's happening right now.'

'No,' she said, 'I don't. And would that have something to do with the fact that you never tell me what you're up to?' I hated it when she got mad at me. Especially when I knew she had every right.

'Look,' I said, 'some bad shit has happened over in Brazil. Seriously bad. The whole business could be washed up, far as I can see.' I sat her down in the car and told her what had happened, in outline.

'So what's your next step?' she asked. She was a lot calmer now.

'No idea,' I said. 'Tell you the truth, I haven't a clue what to do. Guess I got to talk to some people – and this', I pointed at the bags of coins in my lap, 'this is just in case the DEA or somebody's tapping our phone. I don't want those bastards on my case, not over here.' Then I looked her in the eye and said, 'You got to understand, Linda, the Brazilian business was clean. All down the line. We were 100 per cent legal. These accusations, Christ knows where they're coming from. This was me trying to do the right thing. And doing real well at it. And look where it's got me.'

She ignored that last bit. She had no time for self-pity. 'What I don't like,' she said, 'is how you're always chasing the big money, the big pay-out. Why do you have these fantasies? Why not just – you know, have a job and earn a decent income and be satisfied with that? Like normal people.' She was silent for a moment. I didn't say anything either. Then she said, 'Maybe this is your chance to break free of those influences.'

I had to chew that one over for a minute or two. 'Tell you the truth,' I said, 'it never occurred to me that that was an option. But you know I haven't been on anyone's payroll since – hell, since I worked on the construction sites, back in my schooldays. Even when I was diving in the oilfields

I was self-employed. And trust me, Linda, when you work for yourself there's no safety net. You're out on your own. Every month you got to generate a pay cheque. So you aim high, against the day when the walls cave in.'

I don't know whether she ever really understood that part, but she seemed willing to let it go. I drove home with her, then set off in the car to make my calls. I used a whole series of phone boxes, some in town, others way out in the country, but never the same one twice. The system was simple enough. Me and the old gang, we had a ten-letter code word, and each letter stood for a digit from 0 to 9. It might be 'SCOTLANDUK', for example. I'd check the number of the call box, dial whoever it was and give a brief message, 'Call me back on LLCLNDNLTLKS.' Then I'd hang up and wait for the phone to ring – give them time to get out of where they were and find a payphone of their own. The idea was to leave no record, no bills that could be examined – and make sure there was no chance of anybody listening in.

First person I called was Doug, back in Brazil. 'Okay,' I said, 'better send word to the attorneys. You listening?'

'Sure I'm listening.'

'Okay, sell the fishing boats. All of them.'

'You serious?'

'Doug, they sit there in the dock they're only gonna rust. Tell them to get what they can, then wind up the business.'

'Then what? I mean, what do I do?'

'Send the *Adnil* over to Warri, then go over to Nigeria and manage the boats there. I met this guy, Habib. He's a fixer. You need to be in touch with him. He'll keep you right.'

'And you?' he said. 'What are you gonna do?'

'Me? I'm staying home 'til after Christmas. And then …' I didn't want to tell him what I had in mind, not at this stage.

'Yeah, after that,' I said, 'I got something lined up. Tell you more when I catch up with you, but it'll take a chunk of time. Maybe six months. And listen …'

'I'm listening.'

'If I don't make it back, I want you to promise me …'

'Promise what, man?'

'Promise me you'll make sure Linda gets half of whatever's left to us.'

There was a long silence. Then he said, 'Jesus.' I waited for more, but he didn't say a thing.

'Okay,' I said, 'you send her half and you take the rest, okay?' Half. That's how much I trusted the guy.

Soon as I'd hung up I drove to another box and called Jack in Aspen, Colorado. 'Call me in twenty minutes,' I said, then gave him the coded number and hung up. Right on schedule he rang back. 'Okay,' I said, 'I changed my mind.'

'Changed your mind about what?'

'About what you mentioned when we last met. I'm in.'

'You are? Why, that's fucking great news, man.'

'Yeah, I want in. But there will be conditions.'

'Name them, my friend.' He sounded pretty charged up. Tell the truth, I could feel my pulse starting to race too.

'Okay, number one – and this is the only one that matters right now: I'll be in charge.'

'Hey, I can live with that. You always were *numero uno*, man.' Jack was laughing. I'd clearly made his day.

'I just don't want any more of those screw-ups,' I said. 'I can live with my mistakes. Can't live with other people's.'

'I get you. No, I got no problem with that, whatsoever.'

'Okay, we'll meet where Tony Bennett left his heart, sometime in January. By then I'll have a crew together.'

'The old "Over the Hill Gang", right?'

'Right. Them. And pal?'

'Yeah?'

'I'm going to want more than a fucking finder's fee, right?' I didn't wait for an answer. After I'd made some more calls I drove home. This was the bit I didn't like. I knew I was going to have to lie to Linda, straight to her face. And the sooner I did so the better. 'Honey,' I said, 'everything's going to be okay.'

'You mean you've sorted out the Brazilian business?'

'No. I don't think that can be fixed. But we won't starve. I've got myself a job down in the Gulf of Mexico. Means I'll be away a while, but it's what I do best. Diving again and safe enough. Gonna last five or six months. Pays enough to put us back on our feet, then I'll come home and we'll start planning something new.'

We got through Christmas and New Year, but I never felt right. All the time I was thinking, what would she do if she knew? As the time drew near for me to take off for the States, I felt worse. She was so happy that I was giving up all my dreams and settling down, she even cried when she talked about it. And all the time I was lying my sorry ass off, riding back into action on a wave of anger and defiance. When she waved me off at the airport that snowy January afternoon, her face alight with hope and love, I just had to turn away to hide my tears of shame.

8

Gulf of Thailand to Alaska, April–May 1989

The clouds sagged so low you could almost reach out and touch them. They were full of rain. You got the feeling that all you had to do was poke them with a sharp stick and it would cascade down onto the blue-grey swell of the South China Seas. The monsoon season was about to break and the instant I stepped outside the air-conditioned wheelhouse my shirt was sticking to my shoulders. The only good news was that the satellites weren't going to spot us. No way. Not through this.

I wiped the sweat out of my eyebrows, raised the binoculars and scanned the horizon one more time. The fact that nothing had changed in the last five minutes didn't make me feel any better. Same haze, same dangerous waters, same bearing. I was heading north in the Gulf of Thailand, easing along the coastline of Vietnam in a 200ft anchor handling tug supply vessel. Only thing was, we weren't handling anchors and the only tows would be my fictional entries in the ship's log.

Three months after kissing Linda goodbye, I was doing the very thing that would have had her scanning the *Yellow Pages* for a divorce lawyer if she got to hear about it. I was waiting to take delivery of a shipment, a shipment of the best damned marijuana ever produced in south-east Asia. It was a crop whose cultivation I had supervised, at first remotely, later in person – everything from preparing the ground, selecting the seed and planting it, to watching over it and ensuring that we harvested at precisely the right moment, when the buds were packed with resin. It was good husbandry – and it yielded us 27,000lb of a product that would give millions of Americans what they needed: a really good feeling. As to the value? Hard to say precisely 'til it got out there, but $100 million wouldn't be far off the mark.

This was the project Jack had been talking about all that time, the big one, the one he'd asked me, pleaded with me and badgered me to get involved with. And in the end, like a weary old rodeo rider looking for one last pay day, I climbed aboard. I did it for one reason and one reason only: because the DEA, the IRS and all the rest of them had fucked me over. Robbed me of everything I'd sweated for. So screw it.

It had been a lengthy and meticulously planned operation. My part started with a flight to Norway. There I chartered the vessel I was now on. I told the owners I needed it to tow a barge from Singapore to Mexico. That was okay with them, so long as I was willing to deliver the vessel back to them in Rio. I shook hands on it and flew to the States, where I met up with my crew, the 'Over the Hill Gang' as Jack called them, and got them organised to come to Singapore to help me get the ship ready.

After that, I spent a long time up in the Golden Triangle with the soldiers and farmers, all of them in our pay, watching over the precious crop and harvesting it safely. It was the most lucrative and the most dangerous shipment I'd ever had anything to do with. I supervised the transport from the jungle down to the coast, making sure every bale was loaded onto the Vietnamese fishing boat. After that it was down to Singapore to board the *Deep Marianas*, the vessel in which we'd take our harvest halfway around the world to rendezvous with Jack's men off the coast of Alaska.

Only fly in the ointment was some damned ship called the *Exxon Valdez* – or should I say her drunken captain – ploughed into Bligh reef and dumped her load of oil, just a few miles north-west of the spot we were supposed to rendezvous. That sparked a massive air- and sea-borne invasion of the area by coastguard, navy and air force – not to mention press, scientists and environmentalists from all around the world. The skies, and the seas, were going to be buzzing with activity. First thought was to call it off. Then I thought it through. Maybe this would work in our favour. Who would think of a massive shipment of dope showing up in the middle of that circus?

Right now, though, I had to make contact with my man from Vietnam. Nervous? You bet I was. There were naval vessels all around these seas, in particular American and Thai. If those fuckers caught us we wouldn't see home again, ever. A tourist trying to sneak a few bags of dope through customs will get life in most Asian countries. For what we were doing, it'd be the firing squad, no fucking question. Better than rotting in one of their jails for the rest of your life, I guess, but that wasn't going to be much consolation if we were caught.

Even assuming there was no naval presence, there was still a huge question mark over the delivery boat. Would it show? The last one – the one Tommy had gone to meet in the *Rig Mover* a couple of years earlier – had disappeared. At first we figured it must have been captured. But as the weeks went by, there was no news story, no reports of any trial or executions. So, had the crew tried to resist arrest? Had the interceptors decided to cut through the red tape and blown the poor bastards out of the water, to save themselves the cost of a trial? Or had the crew just shafted Jack, taken the load for themselves and got clean away? Jack kept a watch on the men's families for months afterwards, but no, all he ever saw was grieving widows and orphaned children.

I went back into the wheelhouse and checked the radar once more. Nothing new – only the one vessel that was shadowing us, just out of sight over the horizon. Looking up, I saw my reflection in the gantry window and caught my breath. Jesus, I was jumpy. I stopped and stared for a few moments, then shuddered. You look at yourself long enough and what you see is a stranger. My eyes were glaring back at me, like sharks' eyes do as their jaws open and they roll to take a bite out of you. Black as coal, but with a fire in them I'd never been aware of before. Is this what people see when they look at me? I wondered. Maybe that explained the fear they sometimes showed in my presence. I blinked to see if I could break the spell. It didn't work. Christ, when you start to frighten yourself it's not a good sign.

I shifted my gaze to the radio, willing it to crackle into life. But the only sounds were the thrum of the engines, the slap of water against the blunt prow, the low creaking sound of a ship riding a swell. Come on, when was I going to get the call from the fishing boat? I looked at my watch and swore. It was looking like they'd missed today's window and that would mean waiting another twenty-four hours. Had something gone wrong? Or was the guy struggling with the call sign?

The beginnings of a smile tugged at the corners of my mouth. 'Yellow Rubber Duck' – that's the call sign I'd allocated to the Vietnamese fisherman. It might seem like schoolboy humour, but I had sound reasons. This wasn't a business I'd joke about. If the pronunciation came over clear and I could understand it, chances were it wasn't him at all and we were being set up. People in this part of the world really do have a problem with their Rs and Ls. Just like in comic books and cheap films.

I caught my reflection again in the darkening glass and the smile faded as quickly as it had appeared. God knows I loved smuggling, but this had to be the last hurrah. Surely. After this, man, I was through. Hell, with a personal pay-off of something that should be around $10 million, I surely didn't need to risk my life all over again. Just take it easy with Linda, enjoy our future together. Start talking about a family – because that's what she wanted.

Back on the open deck it was like a steam room. I could smell lightning in the air – it gave me a coppery taste in the back of my throat. On the bow, Dean, who was acting cook and deckhand, was just cleaning up his paint brushes. He'd been hanging over the side renaming us. *Deep Marianas* now read *Deep Maria*. If there was a rat on the fishing boat they'd be reporting a non-existent vessel.

Darren, my chief engineer, had come up from his engine room and was leaning on the rail below me, peering out at the horizon. I liked Darren. I'd known him for years and trusted him. He was solid as a rock. I called down to him. 'Problem?' He lit a cigarette and took a lungful of smoke.

'Engines are fine. Everything smooth down below.' He spat out a stray fragment of tobacco and looked out to sea.

'Thought I saw something a while ago when I came up for a piss. Just wanted to take another look.' He removed his New Orleans Saints baseball cap and wiped his forehead, then nodded at the horizon. 'Something just sittin' out there, kinda movin' with us.' He put the cap back on. 'I don't know, hard to tell.' He glanced up at the sky. 'Light's startin' to go.'

I went inside and looked at the radar. Then I came back out with my binoculars, a new Fujinon pair I'd bought especially for the trip. I took a good, long look. 'Darren, that boat you saw out there?'

'Yeah?'

'It's a navy patrol.'

He paused, the cigarette halfway to his mouth. 'Jesus. Fuck, Rob!' The cigarette dropped over the side as he turned to me, his face a picture of fear.

'Looks like it's Thai as well.'

'Aw, fucking hell. Whadda we do now?'

Poor Darren. I couldn't keep it up. I started laughing. 'Don't worry about it, kid.' I gave him a wink and rubbed my thumb and two fingers together. 'Necessary expenses. Those boys are on our side.'

The vessel he'd spotted was a Vietnamese Navy patrol boat. And I'd paid them to be there. They were our insurance against pirates, and with luck it'd keep the Thai Navy from snooping around us. Not foolproof, but as good as I could get at the price.

'You are a sonofabitch, Stone, a certifiable sonofabitch.' Darren was lighting another cigarette. He came into the wheelhouse and grabbed the bins from me to check for himself. He was laughing as he went back below, but he was shaking his head at the same time.

I spent most of the night on the bridge. There was no way I was going to sleep until our fisherman had contacted us. Dawn was breaking when I finally heard the call sign. It was faint and coming from some distance. 'Yerrow Lubba Duk, Yerrow Lubba Duk. Come in prease.' I was shaking with relief as I gave our position, then handed the wheel to Eric, my first mate, and went below for some breakfast.

It was a little after noon when the old fishing boat came alongside. I held my breath as the captain grabbed the tarpaulin and pulled it back, but there were no guns pointing at us, no DEA agents jumping out to flash their warrants and cuff us all. Just the grey-haired skipper baring his gums in a toothless grin. Everything was the way it was supposed to be – every 60lb bale precisely the way we'd stacked them on the deck a week before, all 450 of them.

I turned to Darren and Eric, put my hands on their shoulders and whispered, 'Fucking fantastic.' Everyone was smiling now, laughing out loud. We all shook hands, slapped each other on the back, then stripped off our shirts and started humping the bales up onto the deck. We got into a good rhythm. Bend, grab, throw, catch and stack.

In a little over an hour, the job was done. As we stowed the last of the bales into the refrigerated containers on deck, I saw our Vietnamese guardian angels slide over the horizon and out of sight. Cheers, fellers! Money well spent.

Darren set the controls on each container to keep the cargo at ambient temperature. When it's packed up tight marijuana will warm up, like hay or silage. Satellites, coastguards and DEA spotter planes are equipped with thermal imaging cameras that identify a suspect cargo instantly. If you want to play this game you have to stay a jump ahead. The devil's in the detail, as they say.

We said goodbye to our Vietnamese captain and set our course to the south. It would take us four weeks to make our way to Alaska. Through the Gulf of Thailand and the

South China Sea, between Taiwan and the Philippines, we battled through some heavy seas and two typhoons. But those troubles were just a prelude to what lay in store three weeks later.

Even in spring, Glacier Bay can live up to its name. Barely 100 years ago, it had lain unseen under the ice. Since then, the weather's warmed up some and the glacier has receded, exposing about 40 miles of coastline. Now it's a magnet for kayakers – but that's in summer. We got there early in May and it was still winter. Snow was falling, a cold wind blowing from the north, and there was ice in the sea. It was here that we were to meet the *Klondike V* and tranship our cargo.

Doing the transfer wouldn't be easy. The second typhoon had messed with the ship's gearing. Darren and Jimmy had tried over and over to resolve the problem, but they hadn't really fixed it. We could steam forwards on full power, or do the same in reverse, and we could turn the boat on a dime, if we wanted, but we couldn't idle. We couldn't sit still in the water unless we cut power altogether, and when you're transhipping a massive consignment of illegal drugs you want to be ready to move at a moment's notice. The opinion from the engine room was that we could just about get away with it if we applied varying degrees of thrust to the boat's power outputs, running them in opposition to each other. That way we might just hold a steady position. How this would work in practice when the fishing boat came alongside to take on the cargo remained to be seen. Still, as Eric said, 'If it was easy, everyone would be doing it.'

There was also a brief panic when a coastguard helicopter pilot came on the radio wanting our name and destination. This was the moment I had dreaded. Depending on how I responded, things could go badly wrong from here. I bullshitted. 'This is the *Deep Maria* out of Singapore,' I told them. 'We're heading up to the Valdez terminal, see if there's anything we can do to help. Over.'

It turned out they had Vice President Dan Quayle on board. The guy came on and thanked us in person, and away they went. Probably the biggest gaffe he made during his tour of duty as VP! Eric had come up onto the bridge and heard the call. 'Always good to have the White House rooting for ya,' he said.

Transferring the load to the *Klondike V* was the most dangerous manoeuvre of the entire trip. I talked over the options with Eric. The coastline, and our rendezvous point, was obscured by a thick bank of fog. Once we steamed into that we'd have to rely on our radar alone, but the upside was we were unlikely to be spotted. When the *Klondike V* finally appeared through the murk, both vessels slowed to a crawl and manoeuvred themselves onto parallel courses.

This is where the size of our harvest gave us a headache to match. We discovered that the transfer vessel simply didn't have room to take it all. We still had one full container to unload when they told us they were full. No more room. Getting the *Klondike V* to make a double trip to shore was out of the question. It would surely attract attention, involving as it did another rendezvous with a truck which would transfer the cargo to a remote airstrip, from where it would be flown down to the States for distribution. No way could we go through that procedure twice.

On the plus side, all the bales of dope were vacuum-packed and watertight. What if we sank the remaining container, noted the co-ordinates and came back for it when the heat had died down – maybe in a year or two?

We decided that was the way to go. As the load went over the side I took the co-ordinates, then went below and took out my Hans Hass and transferred them to a blank page at the end of a chapter. I closed it, put it in my trunk and smiled to myself. The smile was short-lived. Hearing a shout from up above I went to see what the trouble was. It was the container. Damned thing wouldn't sink. In order to weigh it down, I had to enter the icy waters in a skimpy old wetsuit and attach the spare tow cable. Looking back, I guess it was a damned foolish thing to do, but there were incentives. The container held close to 4 tonnes and would be worth $30–40 million if I managed to secure it. If it didn't, it would alert the coastguard that a major smuggling operation had taken place – and they'd surely start their investigations with the *Deep Maria*.

The fact that the operation almost killed me didn't seem to matter at the time. I was in sea water at 28°F for half an hour before I got the job done. By that time I could barely move a limb, let alone grab hold of the ladder I'd gone down. It took two crew members, one on each arm, to drag me back aboard. 'Get him inside, quick.' I was barely conscious of the voices, just vaguely aware of my teeth clattering together and somebody – Jimmy, maybe Darren – saying, 'If we don't warm him up we're going to lose him.' At the same time, he was shouting to Eric in the wheelhouse, 'We got him. Just get us the fuck out of here!' They dragged me below, peeled my clothes off, rubbed my blue flesh with towels and shoved me into a hot shower.

I let the steaming water pound onto my head and shoulders. From time to time, I blinked through the fierce downpour at the dull-grey bulkhead and asked myself, why? Why put myself through all this? The answer, of course, was money, and even in the haze of shock brought on by my immersion in the icy waters, I could feel a deep satisfaction, not only in the apparent completion of the transfer but in the fact that there, under the ocean, we had a little pot of gold buried away for a rainy day. Some days later, as we steamed into warmer waters, I took out the Hans Hass book. Inside, I found the page that had the precise co-ordinates of the spot where we'd dumped the container. I wanted to make sure I hadn't imagined that.

9

Mexico, New Orleans, Bermuda and Europe, May 1989–January 1990

Large sums of money are like certain women you meet. They look great, they sure as hell make you feel good, but there comes a time when they're a pain in the ass. Then try getting rid of them. My big problem now was disposing of the cash the trip would generate. Before you even think about where to stash a sum like that, you have to figure out how to transport it. One thing you sure as hell don't do is carry it on a commercial airline. Security staff are trained to spot those things as your bags go through the X-ray machines, and if you're dumb enough to have a case stuffed full of paper currency, don't be surprised if you're taken aside by the police and asked to explain where you got it. I would soon have a huge amount in my possession and it was rarely out of my mind. I comforted myself with the thought that it was the kind of problem most people would die for.

After sinking the container, we sailed south. The warmer weather soothed my aching bones and slowly dispelled the memories of my immersion in Arctic waters. Instead of heading straight towards our destination, which was the Mexican port of Manzanillo, we continued until we were about 300 miles due west of it. We then turned hard to port. That way, it looked as though we were arriving from Singapore, which was the port of origin in the ship's log. We'd doctored that, of course, to show that the towing of the fictional ship had gone according to plan and to record us handing it over to another tug the day before entry. All the charts we had used to get to Alaska and down to this latitude were burned on the back deck. At the same time, we sent a painter down the side of the boat to rechristen us *Deep Marianas*. In Manzanillo we hired a regular crew to take her through the Panama Canal and down to Rio.

Darren, Eric, Jimmy and I left Mexico on separate flights and reconvened in San Francisco. Jack and Dominic Stopani were there as well. From them, we heard how the pot had flown off the shelves at 30 per cent above what we were expecting, the higher price effectively wiping out the loss we'd taken by sinking that final container. My take was to be $7.5 million. I was anxious about how they would get it to me. Turned out they'd chartered a Learjet and hired two former Israeli fighter pilots. The money was in good hands.

We had a big party to celebrate our success and next day I flew down to New Orleans where I caught up with Mark, the guy who was caught trying to leave the States with undeclared funds. He was out on bail and knew nothing about what I'd been doing the past few months. As far as he was concerned, I'd been away, diving, trying to earn some money. He brought me up to speed on Doug, who had wound up the business in Brazil, sold the fishing fleet and was already in Nigeria setting up a yard and an office from which we might operate. At this point, I wasn't sure what the operation would consist of, but even running two boats I needed somewhere to fix them up. And whatever else we got into, we'd surely need a good-sized base. So that was good news.

I told Mark that next time Doug called in he should say hello from me and tell him that I was back from my diving job, but he'd be on his own for a while yet. I had a few things to tidy up in the States, after which I needed to go home to see Linda. He didn't need to know the details.

My first job was to de-flag the *Coastal Servant* and re-register it in Panama. That would derail the lawsuit that the fisherman's girlfriend had brought against us for his chewed-up finger. That whole episode had seemed like a joke at first; it was now a serious pain in the ass. Okay, I thought, so let's see how they like suing a Panamanian company. I had a sort of sentimental attachment to the *Servant*. She was already 20 years old when I bought her, back in '85. I'd earned a lot of money with her, loading her up with fuel at US prices for Nicaraguan fishermen, then trading it for their shrimp and lobster catches, which I sold at a huge profit back in the States. Later, I took her out on my first attempts at longline fishing. We had history, the *Servant* and I – and I get sentimental about history.

While I was at it, I also de-flagged the *Mistral*, formerly known as the *Northern Breeze*, another vessel I had a soft spot for. I'd acquired her from Jack McBain. He'd been using her for his Colombian smuggles and I had wanted a lucky boat that I could fit out for my treasure hunting expeditions off Florida. She had proven to be perfect. We found the wreck of a Spanish vessel that had sunk off Fort Pierce, Florida, in the seventeenth century. We also found some of the treasure she contained – 849 pieces of eight, a half dozen gold chains, a chalice and a few other artefacts that we never declared to the feds. That was another boat that shared a part of my past.

So, I re-registered both in Panama and sent them over to Nigeria. I was sure we could find work for them. They had to do better over there than sitting at the docks in New Orleans.

Meanwhile, the *Caledonian* renovation project was nearing completion and I registered her in Port Vila, Vanuatu. Why Vanuatu? I'd got into the habit of using offshore accounts and corporations to hide my assets. I had a number of Isle of Man companies with nominee directors, which owned a bunch of Gibraltar companies with nominee directors, and they, in turn, owned the shares in the Vanuatu company that also had nominee directors. These companies each cost $10–15,000 a year to maintain, but it was a price worth paying. If any government investigator wanted to figure out who owned what, or where, let 'em try. They'd soon get a sore head as they hit the stone walls.

With those jobs out of the way, I figured it was time I called Linda and brought her up to speed. I told her that my big diving job was done, that I'd been paid off handsomely and was ready to take a break. That seemed less of a lie than the big one I'd told her when I left Aberdeen – or maybe I was just getting used to telling lies and they didn't seem such a big deal any more. I bought her a ticket and told her to fly down to meet me. 'Got a surprise for you,' I said. I meant the newly refitted *Caledonian* that she was always making jokes about.

Then I went to the travel agent, as you did in those pre-internet days. In the excitement of the moment, I screwed up. I bought her a one-way ticket, which got the INS all hot under the collar when she flew into New Orleans. Why was she on a one-way? Was she planning to go home, or was she going to stay stateside and try to settle? Had she got a job to go home to? She was horrified at the very idea of staying in the USA, and told them so. It's not a stance I would've adopted in her shoes, but then I was never going to dazzle the officials with my looks. They let her in. What else were they going to do with her? Very few people ever stood in her way for long.

Before Linda arrived, I bought a safe and installed it on the *Caledonian* – under the bed in the master stateroom. Shifting that thing off the back of a truck and into the living quarters was no easy task on my own, but I was very security conscious, and needed to be. Even so, as I grunted my way across the dockside, worked it onto the deck and down below, one step at a time, I realised that Muscles had called it right: I needed to work out more.

I stashed $6.4 million in the safe. With the other £1 million, I bought gold in the form of krugerrands. Now all I had to do was find a home for them. I had a long think about this and finally did the sort of thing that crooks, kings, misers and plunderers have done with their treasure since the dawn of civilisation. I dug a great big hole and buried it. The only difference was, I excavated this hole under a building that I owned, just across Lake Pontchartrain, in a town called Mandeville. Doug's younger brother rented it from me and ran a health studio from it.

Early on a Sunday morning I went in with a sledgehammer, a pick and a shovel. I'd already bought a safe and put the coins in it. I moved a desk, rolled back the carpet and then broke up the cement floor. I made the hole good and deep and lowered the safe into it, along with the final hundred grand in cash. I was never sure why, but I just thought it might come in handy. Then I backfilled the material into the hole and tidied up. I badly wanted to write 'X marks the spot' on the wet cement, but resisted the temptation. I just prayed I wouldn't one day pick up a newspaper and read how some utility outfit had come to repair a pipe and stumbled upon a stash of gold coins.

I was now able to focus on the trip I'd planned, taking the *Caledonian* over to Europe, where I could live on it from time to time. When I broke the news to Linda, she nearly exploded. 'Rob, we were at sea four months on that … that *Rig Mover*. Don't you remember anything about that? Anything at all?'

I thought for a moment, then said, 'I remember you got a real good tan, honey.' But even as I spoke I was ducking out of the way as she swung her arm at me. 'C'mon,' I said. 'This'll be different. That rust bucket was an old slapper. This girl – this girl's a supermodel.'

My joke didn't go down well. 'Don't give me your bullshit analogies,' she said. 'I was sick as a dog, Rob, day after day. I always get sick at sea. And now you drag me all the way over here just so that I can spend a few more weeks being tossed around the ocean. And where did you say we're going?'

'Palma de Mallorca.'

'That's terrific, Rob. Do you know how long it takes to get to Palma from home?' She didn't wait for me to answer. She was fuming. 'Two hours,' she said. 'I could hop on a flight and get there in the time it takes you to – to splice the bloody main brace, you idiot!' I shouldn't have laughed, but I did.

I took it all on the chin and carried on planning. Tried to pass the whole thing off as a big, family style holiday. I thought if I invited her father it would smooth things over. He was up for it. He loved the sea and was actually excited by the idea. Then I called my mother, for the first time in years. Told her it would be a chance for the two sides of the family to get acquainted with each other, a chance for me to get to know her new boyfriend. I never expected her to take me up on the invitation, but she did.

Of course, this wasn't something I would normally have done and, frankly, I couldn't have cared less about family relations. But there were more important things at stake. When you boiled it down, the trip was just a part of an elaborate money laundering operation. I had to get that cash to Europe and put it somewhere safe – safe and anonymous. I'd got to know a couple of private set-ups when I'd assisted Muscles years ago, one in Switzerland, one in Lichtenstein and another in Austria. So the trip was all part of the cover-up. If we happened to be stopped by the US coastguard, what would they see? A big extended family taking their vacation. Baggage everywhere you looked, swimsuits drying on the rigging. Throw in a seasick Linda and one half of the party not talking to the other half and it would look just the way it does in real life.

As we continued the preparations, I did my best to placate Linda. I gave her the job of keeping an eye on a young lad we had on board, a kid called Michael. He was the son of Ronnie Biggs, the British train robber and celebrity fugitive who'd been living in Rio for the past twenty years or more. Michael was only 15 and I had him on board as a favour for his dad, who wanted the boy to see something other than Rio. Apart from him, my chief engineer Darren and his girlfriend, the rest of the crew were strangers to me. I had hired them from an agency. Darren had been on the Alaskan trip, of course. He was solid and totally trustworthy.

We set sail down the Harvey Canal, out of the Mississippi and into Breton Sound. Along the way we passed the burned-out hulk of the MV *Noordekron*. That was one weird experience. I remember Linda's dad looking at it and asking me whether I knew how it came to be there. I said

I'd heard stories about it, that it was known locally as the dope boat. I told him I'd read about it in the newspapers, how it was found ablaze with bales of marijuana floating in the hold. Obviously I couldn't tell him I was involved, knew the smugglers personally, that I'd supplied half of them with fake IDs and passports, nor that a bunch of my best buddies were rounded up and sentenced to jail on the back of the investigation that followed the fire.

Our first destination was Key West. It was no great distance, maybe a forty-eight-hour trip, and I'd been hoping for a nice smooth passage. No such luck. First night we ran into a storm which threw the vessel every which way and made everyone except Darren, Linda's dad and me seasick as hell. Linda was worse than she'd ever been. When we made port, a day late, half the crew decided they'd had enough and wanted to quit. With the exception of Linda, the 'tourists' also wanted to leave, but I talked them all — except Michael — into staying until we hit Bermuda and were outside of US waters.

In Bermuda, we prepared for the long stretch over the ocean to the Canaries. We re-crewed, provisioned, refuelled and then had to wait two or three weeks while the hurricane season passed. Before my mother left, she convinced me to buy a farm in Ontario, Canada. She knew a place with a beautiful home and 55 acres, going for $250,000 Canadian. I could buy it in her name, but it would always be mine and I'd be able to hand it down to the children I would someday have. I wasn't keen, but Linda persuaded me to agree. The trip was going pretty well, everyone starting to get along. I guess I momentarily forgot all the bad stuff and agreed. I would wire her the money when I was in Europe.

Once the weather had settled, Linda wanted us to get to our destination as soon as we could. We sailed right on into the Mediterranean and put in at Palma de Mallorca. While the crew went about making the vessel bright and shiny again, Linda rested up. She was a lot happier now we were out of ocean waters. Me, I had business to attend to on the Spanish mainland.

I went to visit an Irish buddy who lived just outside Malaga. I'd known him for some years, a real useful contact who could supply me with UK passports. Once he got up-to-date photographs he would need three weeks to complete the process. I said I had a couple of friends who would also need some new 'books'.

I wasn't gone long, but I returned to find Linda's mood had swung around 180 degrees. The trouble was that Doug had flown up from Nigeria. What the hell was I still doing with him, she wanted to know. I just smiled and said, 'Let's see, eh?'

Doug had good news. The boats had arrived safely in Warri and he'd immediately found regular work for them. They were making $75,000 a month. Not bad for two rusting hulks that had cost me $50,000 in total. We then got together with Muscles. He'd rented a big house on the north of the island. His girlfriend and Doug's wife, Jacqui, were there as well. Now Linda was really pissed off. She'd met them before and decided they were dangerous. She said I ought to stop associating with them, that their criminal backgrounds were going to hurt me one day. 'Fly with the crows and get shot for a crow' was the expression she used. I told her I had no intention of ditching my oldest friends.

Besides, I needed their help. I told her not to worry; she didn't have to put up with them for much longer. She was okay with that – until I told her I was leaving with them. We all had business to see to. Linda would go with the yacht to Cannes and when I was finished I'd meet her there.

She wasn't crazy about that idea at all. But right now I had nothing better to suggest. All that was on my mind was getting rid of the cash that was in the safe.

Before we took off, I thought about what Doug had told me. It seemed pretty clear to me that my best prospects for a future business were now in Nigeria. The fish business was finished. No way could I start that again, and to hell with smuggling weed. I would start up a new business, the Coastal Shipping Company.

Doug, Muscles and I took a ferry to Barcelona and a train via Paris to Zurich, where the guys got passport photos taken, two sets each. Doug then flew back to Nigeria. I spent a couple of days visiting my bankers. I set up a series of numbered accounts and a password for each one. The idea was that I would be able to send anyone to access my money, as long as they had the account number and the password. These were simple enough, but hard for someone else to use. For example, if my password was the number 3, I would say 'three' and get my money. If I sent a runner they would be asked to spell it out. That was the coded part – the use of 'threee': three 'e's instead of two. It would work the same with the number 8, which would come out as 'eightttttttt'. Very simple, but it worked. I put half a million in cash in each account. I also wired the $250,000 to my mother to buy the farm. From Zurich, I went up to Vienna and set up a couple more – same method – until all the money was deposited.

Back in Zurich, I helped Muscles move all the money that he had in various accounts. It amounted to almost $20 million. After that, we headed back to Barcelona. He went on to Majorca and I went to Malaga to drop off the photos of him and Doug and to pick up my new passports. Then back to the yacht which, by now, was in Cannes.

I was glad to have the banking business completed. Relieved, too. The money was now spread around a number of safe locations. It was a good feeling to know that, whatever happened, I had a stash of money in Europe as well as the gold down in Louisiana. In that relaxed frame of mind, I spent a couple of months on the yacht with Linda. It was a proper vacation, and with none of my shady friends around we were able to enjoy each other's company without any arguments, followed by a few months home in Scotland over Christmas and Hogmanay.

Then I dropped the bombshell. I was going to return to Nigeria. Linda all-but exploded. She told me she knew it was too good to be true, a leopard never changes his spots. I can't remember how I did it, but I dare say there was a strong whiff of bullshit in the air as I placated and reassured her while I booked my flight to Lagos.

10

Lagos, Warri and Up-country Nigeria, January 1990

I arrived in Warri wondering what I would find. Had Doug been exaggerating? No. The situation there was good. In fact, it had moved on. I went over to look at the yard he'd managed to rent. Picture 20 acres of scrubby land on the bank of the Forçados River, old bulldozers and trucks scattered here and there in a jungle of weeds and exotic tropical flowers grazed by a small herd of nanny goats and a threadbare, stinking billy. As soon as I walked into the place, it tried to charge me and I had to kick it away. A bunch of local guys were working in a half-assed way. They wore faded overalls and shirts bearing the logos of various oil companies.

To one side of this compound was an office building, built of concrete with steel bars over the windows and big steel gates over the main doors. It looked like a damned fortress. There were warehouses, too, half-round sheet metal things like Quonset huts. Leaving the goats out of it, the place looked okay. On the banks of the river the guys had stored the cement and mud tanks they'd removed out of the

Adnil, the *Rig Mover* and the *Coastal Servant* to make way for
fuel. The first two were gone, busy with McDermott, but
the *Coastal Servant* was idle at the dock, as was the *Mistral*.
I couldn't see a use for her. She was nothing more than a
converted fishing boat, albeit one that was beautifully fitted
inside. My friends called her the 'Gucci Shrimper'.

I hadn't been back more than a day or two when Habib
came to see me. He was all smiles. His 2 per cent had
brought him peace of mind and prosperity and he wanted
to share it with me. 'Come to my home and meet my wife,'
he said. 'And my daughters.'

Habib had a small but elegant home laid out on one level,
surrounded by an acre of well-manicured gardens. His wife
was from the Itsekiri tribe. She was a very large woman,
but that's the way some of these Middle Eastern guys like
them. The bigger a man's wife is, the more it says about
how well he's looking after her. This woman had on a vividly coloured floral dress to honour my arrival and a scarlet
turban of some kind. She smiled as she served kola nuts on
a golden tray, ice-cold gin and tonic for me and a soda for
Habib. When we moved on to the dinner table she brought
out a succession of Nigerian specialities such as *banga* soup
and *ukhodo* – a dish of yam and unripened plantain served
with poultry and fish.

As we cleared our plates, Habib rubbed his stomach,
smiled at me and said, 'You see how happy a man can be on
a small regular percentage?' I agreed that he did indeed look
the picture of contentment, but I knew he hadn't invited
me round simply to show me what a difference I'd made to
his life. He waited for his wife and the girls to retire, then
told me what was on his mind. 'Nigeria is a special country,'
he said. 'It's made of many small … kingdoms, you might
say. You know some of the history?'

'No,' I said. 'I didn't spend too long at school.'

'It's like this,' he said. 'Until the British came, there were many small kingdoms here – hundreds. And although the British put a line around them and called this a single country, Nigeria, most of those little kingdoms still exist – and so do their kings.'

'What's this got to do with us?' I asked.

'I'll tell you. These kings, as they are called, are only kings of their locality by consent. Think of them as – let's say they're godfathers. Men who are given power and standing by their people but are expected to look out for their interests and see to the community's welfare.'

'I get it,' I said. 'So you mean – ' Habib cut me off before I could complete the sentence.

'My wife is the daughter of such a king. She is the daughter of the Olu of Warri.' I was suitably impressed. Okay, so the Olu probably had twenty daughters, but she was still the daughter of a very important man. 'If we are going to expand our operations here,' Habib continued, 'we need to meet some of these people. Without their co-operation we cannot succeed.'

'So what do you have in mind?' I asked. 'You gonna bring 'em in and have a meeting, or what?'

Habib laughed. 'That's not the way they do things here. No, we will visit them. Call it a goodwill mission. We will arrive bearing gifts. And if we have to kiss their feet, that's what we'll do.'

'I got you,' I said. 'An old-fashioned charm offensive.'

Habib laughed. 'Charm offensive. Yes, you could call it that as well.'

Over the next week or two, we visited a whole bunch of villages in the Delta region. I had to hand it to Habib, he'd been doing his prep. He'd put out the word, and everywhere we went it looked like we were expected. Each place we showed up there was a reception committee and each of these so-called 'kings' received us in his palace. When I say palace, think 'biggest building in the village'. Some of them had the grand look, with colonnaded entrances, and, in one case, a pair of alabaster lions – most likely a remnant of colonial rule. Some were richly furnished and beautifully cared for. Others had the look of those dying motels you get on the Louisiana back roads – at least from the outside. In some of them you'd get random animals walking through the grounds and in through the doorways. I mean livestock, like goats, cows and chickens.

The kings varied too – between the young and the old, the seriously rich and the genteel poor. One or two drove big cars, but not so much flashy as elegant. I mean, vintage Rolls-Royces, that kind of thing. But as varied as these kings were, they had a number of things in common. They were all dressed up in colourful robes and headgear, with necklaces or beads, and they all sat in some kind of throne to welcome us. Some were made of ornate, carved wood; some were covered in animal skins; in contrast, one or two of the kings had nothing grander than an old easy chair with a beautiful homemade throw over it. Most of them had a sort of guard of honour flanking them as they sat to receive us.

The kings were all calm, self-possessed and, I would say, dignified. They made me feel a bit of an impostor, being so young and obviously western, but even so we were welcomed with grace and courtesy. We had a deal to make, a deal that could benefit both sides. When we arrived, we generally had to bow low, almost to the floor. We addressed each host as 'Your Majesty' and thanked them for inviting us in. After the formalities were over, everybody relaxed and we were served drinks, fruit and kola nuts by a bunch of women. Later, they would serve up a feast. They looked to me like they were royal wives and daughters, but maybe I was wrong on that. Hard to tell, and it wasn't a question I was going to ask.

Habib generally gave a little speech introducing me as some kind of oil magnate, after which I handed over the gifts I'd brought. I'd brought with me a number of jewellery boxes, ornately carved, and in each one I put ten $100 bills, wrapped in coloured tissue paper. When the kings talked, I was impressed straight away. These were smart cookies, urbane, intelligent men who, in most cases, had been educated in England. In fact, they were by far the brightest men I'd met in Nigeria so far, way more clever than any military or police officers I'd come across. Those guys had got where they were by brute strength, by cunning, or by family connections. The kings were there purely because their people respected and honoured them. It was like they'd all assumed a great responsibility for the welfare of a community, and they wore it with calm assurance. We let them know I was starting up a business and they promised to be of any assistance they could. They all wanted to make sure I hired men and women from their village.

After we'd done the rounds of these various kingdoms, I spent a few days visiting the oil and service companies around Warri, even outfits engaged in seismic surveys – anyone who might have work for my boats. They all seemed interested to meet me but, in the end, I guess it was only curiosity on their part. Word had reached them that there was a new entrant in the field and they wanted to know who they might be dealing with. Who was this new kid with the ponytail? Where had he come from? As to finding work for my boats: no, they had no need of another vessel. Not now, not in the foreseeable future.

One thing about me – I don't give up easily. I took a flight up to Lagos and started on a round of the companies located there. I had pretty much the same result I'd had a copule years earlier. I was starting to regret my enthusiasm. Maybe I'd just wasted my time setting up Coastal Shipping. The two boats that Doug had found work for, maybe that was nothing more than a stroke of good fortune. So should I quit, or should I dig in?

I'd been thinking about Linda and our future together. Somewhere down the line we would have a family, I figured, and there was this new feeling in me, that I wanted to leave them something they could be proud of – something that might set them up for life, a legitimate business they could take over one day. I'd talked this over with Muscles when we were in Europe seeing the bankers. He laughed it off. 'Whaddayou want to do that for?' he said. 'I mean, you? Going back into business? Get to fuck, man. Listen to your old buddy, Rob. You got money in the bank. Enjoy it. I'm buying me a 90ft motor sailer – a Jongert. Gonna sail away with my girl. Eat tunny fish and caviar, buddy – 'til the sun sets.' Then he said, 'Be true to yourself, ain't that what the wise man said?'

'What are you trying to tell me?' I asked.

'That you're a smuggler, man. Born to it. And the best I've ever known. You got enough money. Be careful with it, live easy. But if you need more, do another smuggle. Jesus, don't go back into business. Look what happened to your fishing company.'

'But I want to be respected – by my family.'

'Sure you do, man. But I'll tell you one thing right now, old buddy. Those motherfuckers you got to deal with in the oil business – sure, they'll be all over you while you're making money for them. They'll smile and shake your hand

and all that shit, but behind your back? Behind your back they'll be waiting to fuck you over. You aren't one of them. You count for nothing. So once they've got what they're after – man, they'll feed you to the sharks.'

At the time I laughed it off and told him he'd been watching too many movies. But after two weeks of beating a path to all the top men in Warri and Lagos, I was starting to wonder whether he'd called it right after all, that I would've been better off just staying home and relaxing.

Then, everything changed. I met Fraser White.

I was staying at the Eko Holiday Inn on Victoria Island. I was in the casino, just me and a glass of whisky. Maybe I was on the brink of drowning my sorrows – because life was bringing me plenty of grief right then. I even had a few chips on the table in front of me, which was unusual, because I've never been a gambler – leastways, I only gamble on things I can control. The fact was, I'd called in for a drink or two and bumped into an old friend, a guy I'd known way back in the 1970s in the Bahamas. He was with his father, who was connected to the Chicago mob and used to run the casino on Paradise Island for them. Now the pair of them were running this joint. I wanted to know what was behind that. 'I mean, what did you do and who did you guys piss off to end up here?' I asked.

They just smiled and shrugged but, before they could answer, another expat joined us. They introduced him as Fraser White, an American here on business. Of course he's here on business, I thought. This dump? What the fuck else would he be here for? Not a vacation, that's for sure. 'So, where you from?' I asked, trying to sound like I gave a shit.

'Texas,' he said.

'You in the "Earl Bidness"?' I asked, trying my damnedest to sound like I was a fellow Texan.

'Sure am,' he said. 'Got my own company now.' He fished out a card and handed it to me.

'Offshore Construction, Inc.' I read the words aloud. I'd never heard of them. Plenty of folk down there were trying to scam the Nigerians and the most impressive thing about them was usually the business card. 'New outfit?' I said.

'Newish,' he answered. 'We bought the offshore division of Brown & Root.'

I laughed. 'Hey, really? I know those guys,' I said. 'Boy, do I know 'em. Used to dive off of their barges with Taylor Diving. In the Gulf of Mexico, down in Thailand, over in the North Sea.'

'No kidding?' he said. 'I used to be a diver for McDermott.'

Suddenly we were buddies, trading stories from the old days, remembering guys we both knew – some alive, some dead – and buying one round of drinks after another. Fraser told me the story of how he floated on the stock exchange and bought the company the same day, after which he won a bunch of contracts in Nigeria to lay and bury pipe. Only problem, he said, was that for every contract you win, somebody else loses – and that somebody will be sore as hell. 'Yeah,' he said, 'I been too damned successful. Made enemies. It was all going real smooth 'til they stabbed me in the back.'

'What happened?' I asked.

'I'll tell ya what happened,' he said. 'Those sonsabitches at McDermott and Bouygues got to work. I mean, they were pissed at me for underbidding them – seriously pissed. So they decided to get back at me. Used their political muscle to block the fucking fuel supplies.' He banged a fist on the table. 'I've spent the whole of this week seeing everybody in town, but they just take my money and close the door. Man, I hate this goddam country. My barges are going to run out of fuel any day.'

'So you're ... what?' I asked.

'Whaddayou think we are? He spelled it out one letter at a time. 'F U C K E D. I got a whole bunch of barges lined up out there and one by one they're going to shut down. If I don't get hold of some fuel pronto ...' He threw his hands up. 'That's it. I'm outta business.'

'How long does the pipe-laying contract run?' I asked.

'Couple years,' he said. 'Maybe longer if it goes well.'

It may sound like a cliché, but I could feel my heart thumping inside my chest. This was an unbelievable break. I leaned towards him and whispered in his ear. 'I can get you your fuel. No ... fucking ... problemo.'

'You serious?' he asked. 'And how the fuck can you do that?'

I laughed at him. 'I just can.' Then I said, 'Listen, I can make this work for both of us. But I got to demand one thing of you.'

'And that is?'

'You tell nobody what your source is. I do business with McDermott and if they find out what I'm up to with you guys, I'll be out.'

'Yeah, I can believe that,' he said. 'Don't worry, my friend. You come up with the fuel and you're saving my ass. Count on me.'

My biggest fear at this point was that Habib would get wind of what I was up to, but right now I had to go to Lucky and get him to kick-start the operation. I told Fraser I could bring him 500 tonnes a week to start with, at a cost of $350 a tonne. This was above current international rates, but he wasn't going to argue. The guy was desperate. His entire business was dangling by a thread. I added that he would have to charter a vessel from me, permanently, and that it would cost him $3,000 a day. He agreed, but when

I asked for the money up front he drew the line. I was pushing my luck with that, and I knew it. Instead, he agreed to pay me by wire transfer upon delivery.

After we'd agreed that, we did the old-fashioned thing – we shook hands. That's how I've always done business when I can. I've seen too many deals where people crank out a ton of paperwork and then dump on each other. Then there's a feeding frenzy for fat cat lawyers. Fraser was old-fashioned, like me. You gave your word and that sealed it.

Soon as I got home I called Darren. He was still in Cannes with the *Caledonian*. I told him to drop everything and get his ass to Nigeria, pronto. First thing next morning I flew down to Warri to meet Lucky. 'Got your men ready?' I asked him. 'Because I need fuel. Hundreds of tonnes of it. Thousands.'

His first response was to throw his head back, open his mouth wide and let out a lungful of laughter. It was more of a yell. The guy was exultant and it echoed around the walls of his bar and out the windows. People came from the surrounding buildings, wondering what all the noise was about. He wanted to get out the champagne.

'No,' I said. 'Forget the celebrations for now. Just get to work. We can party some other time.'

He got the message, told me he was on the case, and I left him to it. I roused the crew of the *Servant* and told them they were going to be working round the clock. We all were. Then I hurried across town to the telephone exchange, paid off everybody in the line in front of me and started calling my contacts in New Orleans. 'Listen,' I said, 'I need you to find me a couple more supply vessels. Gotta be cheap, but they need to be in running condition. When do I want them? Right now.' That was all I could do: ask and see what turned up.

Darren arrived the next day, as I knew he would. He was 100 per cent reliable, every time – straight off the plane and down to work, getting ready to take the *Servant* to the swamps and meet the barges, then transfer their loads of fuel. Of course, Darren didn't know the estuary, but I'd already hired a local captain called Sam, born and raised on the river. I needed locals for this work. There was no other way.

It took Lucky a full week to get the first 500 tonnes to the *Coastal Servant*. And that meant Darren had a real baptism of fire out there in the swamps, bitten to pieces by mosquitoes and having to face armed guards on top of barges full of fuel. The guy had to stand up to them when they tried to cheat on the figures. I'd briefed him about this.

'You gotta monitor every transfer of fuel,' I told him. 'Those bastards will try every trick in the book. They'll give you kerosene instead of diesel, they'll add water, and if you query the content they'll produce false sounding-tubes. Take your own and do the sounding yourself. You don't trust any fucker. Use my pumping meter,' I said. 'And only that. It's the fucking law. If it says 98,970 litres, that's what you sign for and that's what I'll pay for.' Of course the locals argued. They even threatened to shoot him, but every time he stood firm. The guy had balls of steel. 'We pay what the meter says and that's it.'

After loading up, Darren sailed out down the river as bold as brass with a false load line painted on, right past the navy base and out of the Escravos River. On the way to Fraser's barge he would be in full view of the Chevron base, and I dare say he gave them the finger just for the hell of it.

Fraser had insisted he was running seriously low. I hadn't realised just how bad his situation was. No sooner had Darren unloaded the first consignment onto OCI's Lay

Barge 347 than they were screaming at him to bring the next lot – now, if not sooner.

This was going to be better than I'd ever dared dream. I rushed back to the phone centre to check that Fraser had transferred the payment to my account and also to get some cash brought down to me. I walked out of the building wearing the biggest, widest grin. Suddenly life was a beach and I was lying in the sun, soaking it up.

At least I was until I heard a screeching of tyres and saw a blue van pull up beside me. I was standing there with my mouth open when three cops jumped out, grabbed me and bundled me inside.

11

Warri, Rio, New Orleans, January–July 1990

I was on a narrow bench, wedged between two big, sweaty guys in uniform. They both stank of cigarette smoke. As the driver threw the van around the streets of Warri, horn blaring, I was thrown this way and that, my spine jarring at every pothole, then slamming against the steel side. Each time it looked like I would be hurled off the seat I was brought back in line by a sharp kick, or with the tap of a rifle butt. Tap? I mean whack. Nobody said a word and I knew better than to ask questions, let alone protest. These guys were carrying out orders. It would all become clear soon enough. Stealing a glance at the guys' uniform, I felt a little more hopeful. This was not the cops, but the navy.

We arrived at their base, which overlooked the Warri River. I was turned out, blinking in the sunlight. They marched me into the main entrance, up a set of stairs and took me through a door with some lieutenant's name on it. He was sitting at a desk, hands clasped together, like he'd been waiting for me. I was ordered to stand in front of him.

He dismissed the two guards who'd brought me in and waited for them to close the door behind them. Then he offered me a seat.

'Mister Stone,' he began, 'it has come to our attention that you have been buying fuel on the black market.' I nodded. There was no point denying it. Whether I was or wasn't trading was not the point of this encounter. He had his sources. This was going to be about making a deal. About cutting him in. I knew that. It was just a matter of waiting for him to get around to naming his price. So I stood there while he went through the whole pantomime of reading me the riot act. 'What you have been engaged in, Mister Stone, is a treasonable offence under the laws of Nigeria. Do you realise that? You are guilty of stealing the nation's wealth. These are serious matters. Your actions represent corruption – corruption of the highest order.'

I was working hard to keep a straight face. This guy was full of shit. Corruption was what kept the damned country going – and kept the public sector, guys like him, in pocket money. Paid their damned salaries, and they knew it.

He got out of his seat and walked to the window, parting the blind with his fingers and looking outside. Then he turned and stared at me. 'What you have been doing,' he said, 'is a crime.' Down came his fist on the table and I sort of jumped – mainly because that's what he expected. 'A terrible crime,' he continued, 'that undermines the very moral fabric of our nation.'

That was the toughest one to swallow without grinning. I tried, but I guess I failed. He got madder than hell and started to rant about the high standards expected of every citizen and official and how distasteful it was to see people like me – foreign opportunists – making money from the nation's irreplaceable natural resources. 'You do realise that your crimes are punishable by the ultimate sanction? By execution?' I didn't answer. 'Do you understand me? That you can be hanged by the neck until dead?' He leaned forward so that his face was up against mine. His eyes were wide and his lips were wet with saliva.

'Yes. I understand that.' That was what he wanted to hear. As soon as I said it, he got off his high horse and came to the point, and I was able to relax.

'However, this is your first offence and I am prepared to be lenient with you,' he said. I smiled and nodded. Come on, you grasping little fucker, what's the deal? How much do you want? 'Seeing how much you stand to gain by these illicit transactions, I think it only right that you contribute something to the Nigerian economy, don't you, Mister Stone?'

'Oh sure,' I said. 'Absolutely.'

'So, for each tonne of fuel that goes past my base here, you will pay me the sum of … what shall we say, $5? I think that sounds a reasonable amount, don't you?'

'Very reasonable,' I said. 'In the circumstances.' Meaning I had no frigging choice and he knew it.

'Good. For the 500 tonnes you delivered last week to Barge 347 you owe me $2,500. I will arrange a suitable method of payment and let you know how the money is to be delivered.'

'I will have to pay you in naira,' I said. 'I don't have anything else.' I was damned if I was giving him US dollars, which he could then sell at way over the official rate.

He accepted that fact. 'That will be suitable for me,' he said. He got out of his chair. Clearly, I was now free to go. The mood was suddenly much more relaxed. As he opened the door to let me out I got a smile and a hand-shake. The guy even agreed to arrange a lift back to the telephone exchange, and this time I got to sit in the front of the van on an upholstered seat.

I concluded my business in town and returned to the Palm Court Hotel, where I got in the shower and inspected the bruises on my ribs and arms. Exhausted, I went to bed. It must have been late afternoon, because I remember having to pull the blinds against the low sun. I got two, maybe three hours' sleep before I was awoken by a hammering sound and a voice bellowing, 'Open the door!'

It was the navy guys again. Or their buddies. They told me I was going down town. I protested and they hit me with their rifles. I threw on some clothes. They handcuffed me and took me out onto the street and into a waiting van. I kept trying to explain how I'd sorted everything out with their lieutenant, but all I got for my trouble was more pain.

Back at the base, they marched me up the same steps and took me to the same office I'd been at earlier. Inside, seated at the desk, was the guy I'd struck the deal with that very afternoon. I wondered what kind of shift system they worked to – or was he putting in a spot of overtime to conduct his unofficial dealings? 'What the fuck is going on?' I asked him. 'I thought we'd got this all straightened out. What are you doing, dragging me back here?'

'Mister Stone.' The guy was back in official mode now. No smiles, no favours. 'Mister Stone, my further investigations reveal that two ships registered in your name left this country last year carrying full loads of fuel. Pirated fuel.'

Oh fuck, I thought. Here we go. It was clear he'd known about this when he pulled me in the first time. 'There is a fee payable on such vessels, as I am sure you understand.'

I nodded. 'Yeah.' I understood okay. 'Why don't you just tell me how much?' I asked. 'I need to catch up on my beauty sleep – since your guys tattooed my ribs.'

The sonofabitch was enjoying every minute of this. He laughed. 'They are like caged animals. If they don't get their exercise they will get frustrated and angry. But you mentioned the fee. The fee, Mister Stone, amounts to $2,500 for each vessel. And, as agreed, you can pay me in naira.' I wondered who the hell was telling him the amounts of fuel I had on board. There was a rat in the woodpile, of that I was sure.

I agreed to pay him, in cash, later that day, but if I thought that was it, I was sadly mistaken. I was taken back to the Palm Court, where I slept for several hours. Next morning, before I'd even shaved, I was arrested again. This time I was taken not to the navy base but to the police station, where I was brought before a sergeant, a weaselly little bastard who admitted that he had nothing on me – yet. However, he told me, with a sly grin, that he'd heard the navy had hauled me in and wanted to know why.

This was the start of a series of weekly arrests, each one coinciding with the *Servant*'s deliveries to Fraser White's vessels. And they followed a pattern. Each time I was treated with a little more civility and each time I was interviewed by a higher ranking officer. And each time, of course, the price of my freedom went up.

Meanwhile, I had Fraser White yelping for more fuel. Every day with him was a crisis and I was the guy he came running to. I put the squeeze on Lucky, who took me to his 'father', way out in the country in his own home village. His 'father' reminded me of a black Al Capone – short, pugnacious and supremely confident in the power he had within his narrow domain. We were out near a place called Abraka. There, I met the group of men who had taken it upon themselves to organise the fuel supplies for me. Now I found out what was actually happening. They'd been hijacking road tankers at gunpoint and had built up a fleet of vehicles.

Lucky seemed proud of his achievement and I could see he was respected in the village for bringing this opportunity to his people. But these were tough hombres he'd rounded up, the kind who stare at you and say little. I wondered how much control Lucky actually had over them. There was I thinking of him as a wannabe gangster, but beside these guys he was more like Mother Theresa.

His 'father' told me there was a growing problem with supplies. The trucks were being sent in convoys with armed patrols. That hardly surprised me – it's what anyone with a grain of sense would have done. So what were they planning to do, I asked. Simple: they were going to divert the flow of a pipeline and refine the fuel themselves. I just nodded when they said that, anxious to conceal my total scepticism. They added that they would organise more regular supplies for me. They were inventing fictional trucking companies that would supposedly use all this fuel. I had to hand it to them: they were pretty damned imaginative – ambitious too.

'And the price?' I asked. 'I can only give you what I've been paying up to now.'

'No, we need twice that,' they said. I turned to Lucky, who simply shrugged. He wasn't in charge of these people and there was nothing he could do.

'They say it's a dangerous business,' he explained. 'They could be arrested and put in prison.'

'Right,' I said, 'and I could end up on the end of a fucking rope. I can't pay what they're asking. I gotta pay the police in Warri – and the navy.'

We negotiated back and forth for some time and in the end I got them down to 50 per cent on top of what I'd been paying up to that point. 'And you can tell them right now I'm not having any of that cheating shit. Water in the tanks – kerosene – they know what I mean. They try that and the whole fucking deal's off. Got it?' I could tell by the way they laughed that I'd been ripped off. But then we were all doing that, weren't we, so what the hell?

The deal meant that, with bribes to the navy admiral and police, I was now paying $100 a tonne. Against that, I reckoned I had a more reliable supply chain – and I was charging OCI $350, plus $3,000 a day for the boat. At four trips a month I would be netting over half a million, and I still had the other two boats at McDermotts making me $150,000 gross. Hey, this wasn't such a bad deal after all. I drove back to Warri with Lucky, dropped him off at his club and went to my hotel.

When I climbed the stairs and opened the door I found someone sitting in the chair waiting for me. Jumping Jesus Christ!

'Today is the tomorrow you worried about yesterday, my dear Robert.' Habib wasn't pissed off at me. He was, he told me, sad. 'Yes, I'm sad that you didn't trust me enough to tell me what you were doing.'

'Listen,' I said, 'you know how it is here. Things are moving fast and White's been putting me under pressure, big pressure.'

'I can see that,' he replied, 'but let me tell you something. Working with street gangsters like Lucky …' He shook his head. 'You won't last long, my friend. These people are dangerous.'

'But they can get me the fuel I need,' I said. 'You got an alternative?'

'Yes,' he said. 'I have. I have thought about it and I have a plan.'

'Go on, let's hear it.'

Habib seemed pleased with himself and when he spelled it out to me I could see why. It was truly audacious. 'I can introduce you to the man you really need to be dealing with.' He paused. I would've done too if I was about to deliver his next line. 'The head of the refinery,' he said. His idea was that I should bring my tanker directly to the refinery to fill up. Cut out the middle man and secure clean supplies from the most reliable source.

'My tanker?' I asked. 'But I don't have a tanker. You know that.'

'Of course I do. And in any case, you cannot take your vessels there. They would be too obvious. And besides,' he got out of his seat and walked across to the window, 'they only take 500 tonnes each. My man will not risk his life for small amounts. No, Robert, you must buy a tanker.'

'And where do you fit in?' I asked him. 'What do you get out of all this?'

Habib smiled at me and rubbed his stomach. 'I will get $10 for each tonne,' he said.

I looked at him. I liked the guy. I'd met his family and eaten at his table. What was I going to do? This was his big chance in life. He agreed that it would take a while to source a tanker – until then I would keep getting supplied by Lucky's mob. 'I see. Something for everybody,' I said. 'Okay, let's see how it pans out.'

Of course, this was all another huge scam, this time involving the head of the refinery. The procedure was that I would pay the official Nigerian rate for half of all the fuel I collected. For the other 50 per cent I would pay the head honcho the same rate in cash and he would divert the flow through non-metered lines and fix the records. What was required of me was to alter my own logs to show that my vessels were burning all this fuel. There was only one way to do that and that was to buy more vessels. There was no way the *Servant*, *Adnil* and *Rig Mover* could use even 500 tonnes in a week, unless I put them out on the high seas, raced round in circles 24–7 and then torched them. That might do it.

What was working in my favour was that Fraser White's outfit, OCI, had just won another big contract. They'd have four more barges coming any time now. Each barge in a pipe-laying operation has eight anchors, two at each corner, and as they lay pipe they pull themselves along, letting out wire behind and picking up the slack on the front. As they move along the line of the new pipe so the anchor handlers (AHTS) come in, pick up the anchors and drop them ahead of the moving barge. Depending on the speed of the pipe lay – or it could be a dredging operation – the vessels will sometimes run to port to pick up more supplies, or a barge full of fresh pipe. So in theory I could have six, maybe as many as ten, vessels working for them. Of course, the other shipping companies would want to bid for this work, but I had OCI over a barrel here. If they didn't take my ships they wouldn't have any fuel. Simple as that. The other companies were publicly owned, American outfits, squeaky clean – or keen to appear so. There was no way they would dip their toes in the waters I was swimming in. That was for sharks.

After meeting with Habib I made some calls. I found out there were four AHTS vessels lying idle in Rio. They were owned by the Z Group, one of the world's largest tanker owners. Sometime previously they'd formed a partnership with a rich Brazilian kid of Chinese origin. He'd started up a company which had folded after a year or two. He went back to what he was best at – playing polo with his buddies – and left the ships tied up in Porto de Niterói.

I called Darren and told him to pack his bags for a trip to Rio. We flew down and inspected the vessels. They were beauties, 7500bhp, 200ft long and only a few years old. Better still, they were ready to work. I sent a telex to the owners in Monaco. Were the boats for sale? They came back and confirmed that they were – but at a price. Name it, I said. $1 million, they said. Each. I said I'd think it over.

I remember sitting down with Darren in a bar overlooking the Copacabana that afternoon. It was a beautiful day, the girls were promenading to and fro in their tiny bikinis and the sun was blazing down. Paradise. 'Four fucking million,' I said. 'There's no way I want to pay that, Darren, boy. I'm used to bargain basement shit, picking up rust buckets at fifty grand apiece.'

'Yeah,' Darren said, 'that sure is a heap of money. Any way we can bring 'em down, d'you think?'

I'd been working on it, but I couldn't think of one. We sat and talked it over. We ordered another drink and talked some more. We looked out at the girls, graded them one to ten – damn, they were all nine and upwards, every last one of them – then ordered more drink and tried to figure out a way, any way, of bringing that price down.

I don't know how much of that Brazilian punch we put away, as afternoon turned into night and the girls started coming into the bar in ones and twos followed by all the horny young hustlers, nor what was in it, but whatever it was I blame it for the plan we finally came up with. Because it was a sheer fucking genius. Twisted, sure, but fiendishly clever.

First thing next day I telexed the Monaco guys. Told them I'd pay market value for the four ships, subject to an independent surveyor's report. If it was $1 million each, so be it. They were fine with that and said they'd send over a company rep to verify the surveyor's findings.

While Darren went off to recruit a team of engineers, I paid a visit to the head of security at the yard where the boats were laid up. For an agreed sum he would allow us access to the vessels – and find a good book to read for a few hours. After that, it was like stealing candy from a baby. Darren and his boys went in with their tools, removed all the turbo chargers from the engines and drove off. There were two turbos per engine and they cost about $250,000 each. We spent the next day on the beach while the surveyor went to the yard and ran his inspection. He pronounced the boats deficient. In his opinion it would cost about $4 million to fix them. Sold as they stood, they might be worth $150,000 each. Now we were getting towards my price range.

I have no idea what the Z Group guys thought when they got the survey report, but I concluded they were suddenly glad to see the last of the vessels and doubtless spent a lot of energy cussing out the Chinese kid for being a feckless sonofabitch. I offered them $500,000 cash for the four, the offer valid for twenty-four hours – take it or leave it. They took it, I paid, and as soon as the paperwork was done I slipped the security guy another brown envelope. Darren and his crew went back and replaced all the turbos and I went looking for crew to sail the vessels to Warri.

Hiring good crew was becoming more and more of an issue. Most of the crew in Nigeria were locals, of course, but I was running two shifts already – four weeks on and four off – and needed an expat captain and chief engineer for each. There were only a few Nigerian captains with the skill and experience to run supply ships and anchor handlers. I hired as many as I could find and put a few more into first mate positions to learn the ropes. American officers didn't even come into the equation. They were simply too soft – too spoiled to work in Nigerian conditions – and I knew damned well that they wouldn't tolerate conditions on my old ships.

My ideal, Brits or Germans, were in short supply now that the industry was taking off again. As for Brazilians, I'd worked with plenty of them and they were capable enough, but right now, despite the fact that I was in Rio, I couldn't seem to find any who were ready to pack up and fly. Then I remembered the time I'd worked in the Gulf of Mexico, the Bay of Campeche, for an outfit called PEMEX. A lot of the supply boat captains and engineers were Honduran. Those guys wouldn't give a damn about a bit of rust and the odd leak. They were tough cookies and great crew. I put out the word that we were looking and left it to the bush tele-graph. We soon had more enquiries than we could deal with.

While all this was happening, I relaxed in my penthouse in Leblon. I'd bought the place off Muscles when he went on the run again after all the negative publicity from my fishing company. In fact, I'd bought the company that owned it. I liked it there.

Leblon is the most prestigious neighbourhood in the city, more so even than Ipanema. I could sit by my pool and look out to sea over the top of the Intercontinental Hotel. I could be on the beach in minutes, swimming or taking an evening run. To one side of me was Sugarloaf Mountain, to the other, Corcovado (that's the one with Christ the Redeemer on top). Sitting in my apartment at night look-ing out at the statue, all lit up, I invariably found myself thinking about Linda. I wanted her to be with me, but she had just told me she was pregnant with our first child and there was no way she was going to fly over. She found Brazil dirty and disagreeable.

Once I'd got crew hired for my new acquisitions I flew out to New Orleans, where I bought some more bargain basement vessels, repossessions, mostly from finance companies. These people would always listen to a halfway sensible offer. Some of the craft were in a shocking-looking condition, but mechanically very sound. I had them brought over to my yard on the Harvey Canal, not far from downtown. There, I had them painted bright orange to hide the rust, crewed them up with my Honduran recruits and sent them to Nigeria. As soon as they arrived, Doug got them work on the spot market for Chevron, Texaco, Bouygues, Mobil and, of course, Fraser White's OCI. Working in the spot market meant there was no contract. The contractors simply worked them until they had no further use, then sent them back. It was perfect for an outfit like mine, since they paid a premium rate. The big shippers wouldn't get into that kind of work as it was too irregular, too unpredictable. They would have seen it as prostituting their ships. So maybe that made me a pimp, but with the money we were making, hell, I could live with that.

12

Cannes and Abraka, Nigeria, August–December 1990

Before I went back to Nigeria I wanted to see Linda. We needed some time together and decided to have a week in France, on the yacht. But even that didn't work out as I'd hoped. The problem was all those French beauties strutting around looking like suntanned sex goddesses – as if they could help it. As I pointed out to her, they were suntanned and they were raised to try and be sex goddesses. The fact that I thought she looked even more beautiful since she'd got pregnant didn't cut any ice with her. The expression 'throw away the shovel and back away from the hole you're digging' came to mind. She simply hated being there.

It occurred to me that there was no point having a yacht with a full crew on it sitting in Cannes while I was living in that dump of a hotel in Warri. Why not have the yacht down there and live in comfort? When I broke the news to the crew, I nearly had a full-scale mutiny on my hands. Good job they didn't yet know the full horror of the Forçados River.

I talked Linda into flying down to Nigeria and spending a couple weeks with me there. I wanted to show her what I was doing. I also wanted to show her that there was more to this country than pollution and corruption. I gave her the hard sell. I'd got my eyes on a place that Lucky's godfather had shown me, out near Abraka, a university town just a few hours along the Sapele road from Warri. It was the cleanest, most beautiful part of Nigeria I had seen, by a mile. All natural surroundings, with the Ethiope River, spring-fed and crystal clear, running through it. It would be perfect for a vacation trip.

So that's where we went, by car. Of course, there was no such thing as a simple car journey in Nigeria. We were barely halfway to our destination when we hit the inevitable road block. 'What's this?' Linda asked, as one of the police officers walked over and told me to open up.

'Don't worry,' I said. 'It's just the riot police. I'll deal with them. You sit still and put on your innocent face.' Fat chance. They did the routine search of the car. There was one guy at the tailgate, poking through our baggage. The only thing that interested him was Linda's stash of diet cokes, and he just helped himself. She went nuts.

'Hey, what do you think you're doing?' she shouted. Before I could restrain her, she'd opened the door and stomped around the back of the vehicle. I followed her and could only watch in silence as she snatched the can out of the officer's hand. She stepped forward and eyeballed him. 'And where are your manners, young man?' I was nearly crapping my pants. These were guys who would kill you as soon as look at you. I stepped forward, but was stopped in my tracks as she continued to berate the guy. 'If you want a drink, you can ask. But since you hadn't the good manners to do so, I'm sorry. The bar is … closed.' And with that she slammed the rear door shut, almost taking the guy's hand off.

I stepped forward and put my hand on her arm. 'Darling,' I said, 'I think it would be better if we were more – polite to these valiant officers of the law. Y'know, they're only trying to protect us.' She calmed down some, but I could sense her rage as she watched me stuff a bundle of naira in the guy's hands. Moments later, we were back in the car and through the barrier and she was ripping into me for colluding in a corrupt transaction. 'Yes,' I told her, 'I colluded. I am a bad person, but we're on our way – and we're alive.'

When we got out to the resort area I figured it might be fun to tube down the river. The locals thought I was crazy and in hindsight, well, maybe I was. But people have often said that about things I do and that's when I ask myself the question, would I rather be living my life or theirs?

Linda wasn't that good a swimmer. She was also four months pregnant, but I figured she'd be fine. Floating downstream in a great big inflated truck tyre: what could go wrong? At the beginning she loved it, drifting along in the tepid water with dense jungle on either side of us, monkeys chattering as they swung from tree to tree, vividly coloured parrots flitting from sunshine to shadow and back into the light.

Then we rounded a bend and the current swept her slap bang into the mangroves. Linda freaked out, convinced she was going to drown, sucked dry by leeches and eaten by crocodiles. She panicked big time and tried to swim back against the current. I was talking to her, trying to calm her down, but she was way beyond that, thrashing around and struggling to keep her head above the water. Finally I shouted, 'Just stand the fuck up, will you?' That shocked her into doing as I said. With her feet on the riverbed she realised she was little more than waist deep in the water. She stood there, glowering at me, her hair plastered all over her face. I cracked up. She went straight into the tears and 'you don't love me' routine.

She soon got over it and I did what a guy has to do, apologising profusely. We waded back into the main stream and carried on drifting. Only difference was, this time she had hold of my leg and wouldn't let go, her grip like a vice. Two weeks later, after she'd flown home, I still had a reminder of her visit in the shape of five neat bruises on my calf where her fingers had dug in.

You don't travel far in those parts without coming across a village, and sure enough we soon heard, mingled with the chatter of wildlife, what sounded like the screams and laughter of a bunch of kids. At first there was nobody to be seen. Then, as we rounded a curve, they came into view, lined up on a rickety wooden bridge that spanned the river. There were about a dozen of them, mostly boys. We didn't need to understand their language to realise they were running to the shore and back, shouting to everybody to come see the crazy white people. I can't imagine they had too many tourists floating by at that time, and we must have been one of the weirdest sights they'd ever seen. They jumped up and down, pointing and laughing, the bridge wobbling like crazy.

The one big disadvantage of tubing is you have little or no control over your movements. You go with the flow, quite literally – and the kids knew it damned well. As we approached the bridge, those that had trousers on opened their flies. The rest just stood, legs apart, and took aim. A dozen streams of hot piss cascaded down on us.

I liked this area so much I decided it would be ideal for some kind of private resort, a weekend getaway. I approached the local prince and arranged to lease a piece of land on the riverbank, just a couple of acres. Like all the country around it, my plot was raw jungle, a chaos of trees, tropical shrubs and wildlife. I hired a few villagers to cut down the brush, leaving the taller trees to provide some shade. Then I got them to put up a 12ft-high wire enclosure and plant bamboo 10ft deep on either side.

I built an A-frame house with a bedroom and balcony looking over the river. Outside, I had a generator installed in a soundproofed shed. If I was going to have weekends in the jungle, I wanted natural, ambient sound, not the puttering of diesel engines. I built a big barbecue and set up picnic tables with awnings over them. The villagers planted banana, mango, papaya, lemon, lime and orange trees, along with a bunch of flowering plants. They dived into the river and filled up wicker baskets from the river bed with the whitest of sand, spreading it over the land until the whole compound was like the Copacabana. We then built a wooden deck that extended from the shore out over the river where there was a deep spot we could dive into. The current on the river was a nice, steady 2 knots or so, which meant you could jump in the hole, surface and swim against the flow for as long as you liked without actually leaving the compound.

I decided that if I was going to invite oil execs and the like for barbecue weekends, I was going to have to provide decent meat. Whenever I sent a ship over from Rio, I had a reefer container filled with Brazilian beef, far superior to what was available locally. I had whole sides of it butchered in Brazil and only shipped the finest cuts.

Once I'd got that up and running, every Saturday and Sunday I would organise a big barbecue and shrimp boil. I'd invite a handful of the expats I did business with – or hoped to. I invited their wives and families, most of whom were too frightened to leave their company compounds, so this was a real treat for them. We organised a convoy of cars and paid the navy or the riot police to escort them back and forth along the Sapele road. When the guests showed up, we'd have music playing. We'd play boules or swim, eating and drinking all day and into the night.

My little resort paid for itself 100 times over in terms of the contacts I made and the deals I was able to strike. One weekend, I was out with a bunch of guys from the various seismic companies. Some of them were belly aching about Nigeria and the endemic corruption, when this other guy cut in and said, 'You think this country's bad? You wanna try running surveys in Indonesia, man.' I asked him what he meant. He told me that their survey boats ran cable sets that trailed 4, 5, 6 miles behind the boat. They were plagued with fishermen running across the lines and cutting them. It was costing them a fortune in damages and they had to hire chase boats to keep the locals away. I didn't say anything at the time, but filed it away in my memory. It sounded to me like here was a chance to put at least the *Mistral* to work.

First thing the following Monday, I tracked down the owner of one of Nigeria's largest fishing companies. I told him I thought he was being too damned polite to these foreigners with their fancy seismic gizmos. Hell, I said, whose sea is it? He soon got my drift. For a modest payment he would order his fishing fleet to rough things up a bit – but not until I gave him the word. At the same time, I ordered two dozen big blue revolving police lamps and sirens from Brazil.

Next up, I went to the admiral. He was the navy guy I now dealt with; I mean, he was the man I paid off for my oil transfers every week. The lieutenant who'd arrested me that first time, he was history. I talked to the admiral about the situation with the survey vessels. I laid it on with a trowel, how the fishing fleet was in danger, how it might cause a loss of income for the villagers. I told them that there were reciprocal problems for the seismic survey crews and their precious equipment, and asked him to consider the likely costs of any delays to the oil acquisition programme – and what that might mean to the Nigerian government. 'So what do you suggest?' he asked me.

I made a big show of chewing it over for a while, then said, 'Well, if the fleet needs protection it can't be right that the fishermen pay the bill, can it?' He agreed, grinning from ear to ear. He knew damned well where this was heading. 'So,' I said, 'how about if it was made mandatory for all seismic vessels operating in Nigerian waters to have a chase vessel on duty at all times? No,' I corrected myself. 'How about two? You got to take these things seriously.' The admiral was loving this. I promised I could give him specifications, which were pretty much standard for all offshore supply vessels – and threw in the requirement for sirens and flashing blue lights. I could even wire him some extra funds to assist with these 'logistics' and pay for the extra work. We shook hands on it and parted company.

I waited 'til my chase boat equipment arrived, then packed up a huge sack full of naira notes for the owner of the fishing fleet. At the same time I started a series of telex messages to the heads of all the seismic companies, offering them my services should they see the need to protect their vessels from any interference. Almost to a man, they told me there was no need for chase boats, but they would keep me in mind if the need arose.

I made damned sure it did, and soon. Once that bag of naira landed on the desk of the fishing fleet owner there was chaos at sea, with the boats running right across the lines from all angles. It was mayhem out there and my phone was red hot. Could I help? Well, sure I could, but they had to understand there was quite a demand all of a sudden. But we need help now! Well, okay … I'll do my best. Naturally I was able to charge a premium price. This was an emergency, right? Other companies tried to get in on the act, but failed. They were not equipped with the legally required blue flashing lights and sirens. Flushed with success and this huge boost to my income, I sent the admiral a large Christmas bonus, then boarded a flight back to Scotland for the birth of our first child.

13

Rio, West Africa, Louisiana and Europe, January 1991–February 1992

I was home in Scotland for a couple of months. It was a magical time and the joy of seeing the birth of our first child, a son, stays with me to this day. Being a father stiffened my determination to build a business that he might one day take over from me. When my old man had left home in an alcoholic fog, he had left behind nothing but a lot of bad memories and a psychotic wife, who dished out beatings on an almost daily basis. I was determined that, for my newborn son and heir, it would be a different story.

When it was time to return to work I flew, not to Nigeria, but down to Rio, very much the nerve centre of my operations now. I had a banker and financial fixer living in the city, a fellow named Cristiano. To make life easier, and to save me from having to commute through Rio's anarchic traffic, I'd turned the bottom floor of my penthouse into an office from which I ran the communications, banking and travel side of the business. We even started our own travel agency in order to get a better deals on the tickets. I put a couple of our secretaries in charge – I needed to – because we were spending $50–100,000 a month flying the ships' captains and engineers, along with other expat managers and crew members, back and forth between Nigeria and their various homes in the UK, USA, Honduras and Brazil. It was pretty neat having our own travel agency. It earned us commission from the airlines and a few other perks, such as first-class tickets at economy prices.

The secretaries occasionally found they had time on their hands and they put it to good use. They were soon advertising their 'See Rio with Ronnie Biggs' tour that brought in tourists from the UK and Germany to party with 'The Great Train Robber'. He threw himself into it with enthusiasm and took them around all the sleazy dives he'd got to know over the years. He got them drunk and he got them laid. He posed for photographs with them and played the part of the alternative celebrity to the full. Ronnie was always stone broke from paying off the Brazilian cops, so this was a nice little earner for him.

I had arrived in Rio in late February, when the carnival was in full swing, so for a couple of days I relaxed and enjoyed the party atmosphere. There was no point in doing anything else. At carnival time the business of the city is partying – and they take it very seriously down there. Everything else just grinds to a halt.

Once things got back to normal, I called on Cristiano. One of his jobs was to take the money we were generating from the ship and fuel business in Nigeria and wire it to my accounts in Gibraltar, Switzerland and Austria. When I needed cash in the form of US dollars, I would get the funds from him even when no one else in the country could. When runaway inflation panicked the government into freezing all the bank accounts in the country, he still managed to find all the cash I needed. It turned out he had a friend in the Catholic Church – although for every transaction he had to cough up a 10 per cent 'donation' or 'exchange rate fee'. It seemed the Catholics were always open for business.

Cristiano was a great asset. I had accounts all over the world and he played them like a shell game. He claimed that no one could follow his movements, least of all the tax people. The guy was a regular financial wizard and he did it all for 3 per cent of gross.

My office was now busy enough to require a manager. I hired an American guy called Tony to take charge. He was living in Rio and understood the shipping business – and ships. Also, he spoke Portuguese and Spanish. He knew nothing of my past, except that I had been a diver and used to run a fishing boat or two. He assisted with black-market money deals, of course, but everyone in Brazil was involved in that and he knew that I was trading in black-market fuel. He needed to, since he handled a lot of the calls from OCI and other people I dealt with in Africa. Otherwise, I kept him in the dark.

Ever since Habib had outlined the refinery deal to me, I'd had agents searching for tankers, but even with the admiral's help we'd only found two and they had been seized down in Cameroun. I flew over to Doula and soon found out what the problem was. It was nothing new: the owner of the two tankers, a Belgian, hadn't paid the crew, so the crew had stolen money set aside for port dues and the ships had been seized for non-payment. It was a familiar African scenario.

I found the prison where the owner was being held and paid him a call. He was in bad shape, very bad. He was emaciated, bruised and bloody, like something out of Belsen. He'd been beaten by other inmates, robbed of whatever was worth taking and was practically starving to death. In these African jails they don't feed you. You have two options: either some-one brings you food because they care about you, or they bring it because you pay them. There is a third, of course – you starve. This guy was desperate, gripping my arm with a hand swathed in grimy bandages, pleading with me. 'You get me out of this place,' he said, 'and those ships are yours.'

I told him I'd think it over and promised him I'd get some food sent in. Then I called Darren in Nigeria to come down and inspect his vessels and went to the port authori-ties to get their take on the situation. I was told there was a stack of money owing on the ships – for wages, port dues and accumulated fines. I was given the name of a French lawyer who had been in Doula for years and was well con-nected, as you needed to be. Within a few days he'd tracked down the paperwork on the Belgian guy's vessels. Now we could add up how much was really owed and, more impor-tantly, who we had to bribe to clear a path through the administrative jungle. I was pleased to see that both ships were registered in Liberia. That would be a help with any future deliveries down there.

By the time the lawyer had completed his enquiries, the total sum outstanding added up to around $800,000. It would take a little time to work this deal. As ever, the oil companies were dragging their heels over payments due to me and now our fuel sales had slowed. I had bought over a dozen ships in the last year alone and paid to get them to Nigeria. At the same time, I had my own staff to pay. Suddenly cash flow was an issue. I had all these assets but I was running out of money; all the money from the Alaska trip was spent.

There was only one practical solution and that was to fly over to the States and take a trip to Mandeville, where I'd buried the krugerrands. Boy, was that health studio owner pleased to see me. This guy was Doug's brother. His business had been doing real badly, but every time he threatened to shut up shop and sublet the place, I was down his throat telling him he couldn't do it, that he needed to persevere. Suddenly I show up and tell him he can board it up as soon as he likes because I'm going to put the building up for sale.

Doug's brother didn't need any further urging. He put up the closed signs and moved out within hours of my arrival. I hired the biggest power drill I could lay my hands on, bought a sledge hammer and a pick and started busting through the floor. The cement I had put in was a goddamn sight harder than the original. It took me forever. When I got through, I found the water level was halfway up the side of the safe. The dial was corroded, and when I finally got in it my coins were fine, but, of the hundred grand in notes, all that remained was a murky sludge.

Just as I was loading the coins into my vehicle, I was interrupted by a woman who'd driven up to make a long-standing appointment. She insisted on me telling her what was going on and why was it closed. In the end I told her I was working for the New Orleans police. I said that the owner had died in suspicious circumstances and I was looking for more bodies. She didn't hang around. It was a damned fool thing to do, I guess, but worth it for the look on her face – and I was out of there within minutes.

On reflection, getting the gold up was the easy part of the whole operation. At this time, with apartheid still in operation in South Africa, krugerrands were not negotiable in the USA. I had to sell them at a loss to some guy in Miami and he wired the money to Cristiano. All this meant that it was several days before I got back to West Africa. Once there, I lost no time in paying the fines due on the tankers and the back-wages, after which we were able to finalise the transfer of ownership. When I went to get the Belgian guy out of jail, I learned that the price of his freedom had gone up. But I kept my word. Always do. The sonofabitch was so grateful he would have flung his arms around me and kissed me on both cheeks but for his handcuffs.

Before the ink was dry on the registration documents, I had Darren out getting crew for the tankers while I went travelling down the coast, putting out word that I was looking for owners of fishing fleets who were ready to buy fuel at 20 per cent below world prices. They were soon falling over themselves to get in line and I was able to arrange deals all the way from Dakar, Senegal, to Accra, Ghana, by way of Bissau, Conakry, Freetown, Monrovia and Abidjan.

It wasn't long before we'd taken delivery of the ships and were able to start loading fuel straight from the refineries, just as Habib had promised. This was a damned sight easier than all those midnight rendezvous in the swamps. I was worried about how Lucky – or rather the gang that was now ripping off oil for me – would react, but for a while I heard nothing. While the tankers plied the coast, I was constantly fixing up the next contracts for the rest of my fleet. It went far better than I could've hoped. Chevron signed up seven of them on two year contracts, which was as good as having money in the bank. I got three hired by Mobil, McDermott still had three going, and six were on hire for OCI. Three more were kept working as chase boats for various seismic companies and one was plugging away for Texaco. I now had what all ship owners like to see, an empty dock – all except for my yacht, which was my new home in Warri. I had a new crew too. The original one, the South African and Kiwi guys who'd had it so good up in Cannes, had all taken one look at the place and quit.

When I was back in Warri, I used a ship's radio system we'd set up so that I could talk to Tony in Rio without all the hassles and insecurity of using the phone. It worked well – apart from him belly aching that I was always getting him out of bed at some ungodly hour.

The fact was, my day in Nigeria started at four o'clock in the morning. I could think clearly then. It was cool and the place was relatively quiet. I began by working out a plan for the day, decided who needed to do what, then put lists of individual tasks on my executives' desks. Around six, I'd go to the gym that I'd set up in the yard. After that, I'd grab a bite of breakfast with the guys as they came in.

Many of these were old buddies. As I came to need more help, I brought over a few more of the guys from Louisiana who had been involved in the marijuana business in the seventies, been to prison in the eighties and now needed work. Once you've been in jail, especially for drugs-related offences, no one will hire you, which is why so many go back to what they're familiar with. But these guys knew ships and I could trust them. I had no problems with them.

After breakfast I worked at my desk. By about nine, I was impatient to tell Tony what was on my mind. I'd look at my watch and figure, yeah, five o'clock in Rio, time the lazy bugger was up and at it. I never could stand people who slept late.

Things were going well. The business was ticking over like a well-oiled machine. Then I got a visit from an OCI guy. Not Fraser White, but one of his senior VPs. It was bad news, but not entirely unexpected. OCI had finally over-come the obstacles that had prevented them getting their fuel from legitimate sources. Whether bribery was involved or not I never found out, but it was apparent from the body language and the tone of the guy's voice that he was delighted to have the opportunity to break the news to me in person. I couldn't blame him. I'd been charging them over the odds and ripping them off for the hire of my ships for over a year. Now they could stick the knife in where it hurt. They were cutting five of my ships loose and planned to reduce the rates for the one they were keeping on. The choice was mine: take it or leave it.

I tried to call Fraser, but he was over in Houston and it was either, 'He's in a meeting right now' or 'Shall I get him to call you back?' Of course, they never did. I tried talking to the guys in authority, Nigerian officials who'd been behind the original impediments to OCI's progress, but they all came back with the same line. 'Sorry, but it's done; end of story – although … those monthly goodwill packages you've been sending? You won't stop them, will you?'

More bad news followed. I got it from the admiral, who told me there was no way my little tankers could continue to load from the refinery in Warri. There were riots on the streets over the fact there was no diesel at the pumps for the ordinary people, and they could plainly see these ships loading up with Nigerian product and shipping it out. I saw his point. I was taking out at least 20,000 tonnes a month. No wonder there was a shortage. I soon found out that the gang Lucky had put me in touch with was living up to its threats to divert the pipelines. I saw more than one news item about the crude refineries – lethally dangerous set-ups that the gang members had rigged up in remote locations. Spillages were constantly making the headlines. Hardly surprising – if you let a bunch of bandits loose in an oilfield, you're going to have trouble.

Uppermost on my mind, however, was the loss of my prime local source of fuel. For a while I saw my enterprise going the same way as Pescado de Brasil. I went back to the admiral and asked him straight, 'If I can't take my tankers into the refinery, where the hell do I go for fuel?'

I needn't have worried. I'd forgotten how dependent the admiral was on my pay-offs. He was hooked, he needed to feed his habit and, therefore, he had a plan. Looking at me like I was some dumb idiot, he said, 'Why, Port Harcourt and Lagos, of course. I also have an idea that will increase your sales. I will introduce you to a friend of mine, a high-ranking army officer. This man is a general. He will be your – what is the word, your conduit. This man is very powerful. He is in charge of the peacekeeping forces in Liberia.'

Liberia, I thought. This gets weirder and weirder. He went on to tell me about a body called ECOWAS, the Economic Community of West African States. I'd heard of it on the news, nothing more. Their Standing Mediation Committee had set up a Military Observer Group (ECOWAMOG) to help resolve an internal conflict which had broken out in Liberia the previous year. They had over 3,000 troops there and a whole fleet of vehicles which were using a lot of fuel. I'd be in a position to supply all they needed at international prices – so long as I greased the general's palm, naturally. According to the admiral, there was a shortage of fuel in many other countries along the West African coast. 'They are not all as lucky as Nigeria,' he said. 'Maybe we can help them out.'

I remember, after that conversation, going out to the gym and running on the treadmill for a while, mulling over what the admiral had said. It seemed I was suddenly being swept along on a tide of events over which I had no control – and was making decisions over which I had no choice. It was a situation I hadn't encountered since I left home and it made me nervous.

Meanwhile, thanks to OCI, I now had five vessels out of work. That was losing me fifteen grand a day, plus a million a month, minimum, in fuel sales. With that in mind, Liberia looked like a golden opportunity. After I'd showered off and dressed, I looked in the mirror. I still had a full head of hair, so maybe I was coping better than I thought.

I decided not to rush into anything just yet. I took a break, spending a month in Scotland with Linda and the baby, after which I headed down to Switzerland and Lichtenstein. In Vaduz I met with some lawyers Jack knew. These guys were brothers named Grünwald. It was an old, established family law firm. I explained that I needed a safety deposit box and a couple of accounts. Here, I introduced myself as William Hammond, using my UK passport. They were perfectly happy to handle my business. I put $1 million in cash that I'd picked up in Zurich in the box and had Christiano wire $4 million to be split between the two accounts. I explained that these funds were proceeds from my shipping company and African fuel sales that I was hiding from my soon-to-be ex-wife. Smiles all-round and everything was very amiable.

Banking was taking up more and more of my time just now, but that was good news. I was kept busy wiring funds to all the people who were effectively on the payroll – the guys who opened the doors for us. They had all set up secret bank accounts to receive their take from the deals.

While I was in Vaduz, the office in Rio contacted me to say that the Z Group CEO wanted to talk, that it was a matter of some urgency. That brought me out in a cold sweat. I'd been waiting for that business with the turbos to come home to roost, and it looked like it was finally happening. I braced myself for some sort of legal action. But when I called the guy, he complimented me on the way I'd handled the purchase. He said that he'd heard about the rapid growth of my business in Nigeria and had a proposal he'd like to discuss, in person, at their head office. I took a train to Monaco the very next day.

On the way down, I thought about what might lie in store. Maybe I was about to enter the big league. The Z Group was the third largest tanker owner in the world. I reflected on how rapidly things can turn around, thinking back to the time, not many months previously, when I'd stood on that loose container in an angry Arctic sea, freezing half to death and wondering whether my time was up.

The Z Group guy greeted me warmly. His people had heard I was handling large quantities of fuel and he wanted to know whether I had the capacity to load a big tanker. I asked him what kind of capacity he had in mind and tried to act nonchalant when he said they were thinking about a 90,000 metric tonne vessel – for a trial run. 'Sure,' I said, 'I can handle that.' Beyond that, he told me they were after crude oil. That's where the real money would be. If I could line up a supply of crude, they'd send down a VLCC (Very Large Crude Container) with a capacity of 2 million barrels.

This made sense to me. I'd been hearing rumours that the president of Nigeria would sanction such deals in return for around $5 a barrel up front and a further $5 after loading. We were talking personal bank accounts here, nothing to do with tax or the national interest. I'd also heard that the lawyer who fronted him – a guy called Judge Williams – wanted a million up front, just to put a proposal to lift crude forward, on a no return basis. That is, if the deal was not approved, tough shit, you lost your million bucks. It was surely worth the risk. If we ended with 2 million barrels at a cost of $20 million, we'd be selling at around $40 million in Europe. I left Monaco, having shaken hands on the proposal, and told the Z Group man that I would get on it as soon as I returned to Nigeria. But first, I needed to get home again. Linda had called to say she was expecting our second child.

It was some weeks later that I flew out to Lagos and then caught another flight to Warri. On that second leg, I happened to be seated next to a German woman. She told me she was a journalist and was on her way to report on pollution in the Niger Delta. We exchanged pleasantries, then she buried her head in a magazine. I looked out the window, watching the ground slide by. As we approached our destination, I saw great swathes of land that looked like those photos you used to see of the war zone in Vietnam after it had been napalmed. There were thousands of acres of blackened areas adjoining the rivers, where the landscape looked completely dead and stumps of what used to be trees, with rainbow colours lighting up on the surface of the water as it caught the sun's rays. I'd seen it before, but never quite on this scale.

The journalist leaned across me, letting her magazine slide to the floor. 'Look at that,' she said. 'Those oil companies. Do they have no conscience? No shame? They're destroying a landscape, and a way of life – all for the mighty dollar.' I didn't answer. What was going on down there was a crying shame. I could see that. But the fault? It was the fault of a lot of people: oil companies, corrupt politicians, bandits, even the villagers who waded in with their buckets and helped themselves from fractured pipelines. And yes, people like me were priming the pump. But she thought she had the answer, and I didn't think she would want to hear what I had to say. So I left her to her convictions, got off the plane and went back to my business.

14

Aberdeen and Lagos, March–May 1992

It's hard to be married to someone and not let them know what you're doing. I mean, everything you're doing, like when you take off to earn a living in the dog-eat-dog world of the self-made – although, as someone once said to me, we're all self-made, but only the successful will admit to it. Throughout my relationship with Linda, I'd never told her the full story of my involvement in the drug trafficking. There was no choice there. I was never going to. I'd sort of confessed to the dope runs in the Caribbean, but that was different. Hell, I was only in my teens when I got into that, and I think I pitched it in such a way that it seemed little more than a youthful indiscretion. It was sufficiently long ago that it was a closed book.

The problem was that she knew I was still involved with the friends I'd made then – Muscles, Doug Kane, Jack and the rest of them. But she knew nothing about the Alaska gig, and if she'd found out about that I'm pretty sure she would have shown me the door. The thing with Linda was, she came from a good family. Her folk were people of conscience, and she took after them. Also, she was aware. She was no bimbo; she read the papers and thought about what she read. She had a good grasp of what was going on in the world – although not in my world, and to me that meant that she didn't really have a grip on the realities I encountered day to day. Who does? Certainly not the average guy in the street, although in recent years it seems that people have become sufficiently sceptical to believe that, yeah, politicians are on the take or on the make, and nobody really knows where the dividing line is.

The point is, Linda had a good idea as to the state of affairs in Nigeria. Hell, she'd been places that most journalists hadn't. She'd been to Warri, up the Escravos River, and seen for herself how people lived and what was happening to the environment that had sustained them for centuries. So she'd been chewing my ear for some time about my dealings in that part of the continent. 'It's a dirty business,' she said, 'and you shouldn't be involved in it. You'll be tainted, whether you realise it or not.'

I didn't like hearing her say that. Who would? Especially when she started telling me the Z Group deal was a bad thing to be getting into. 'Just look around Warri,' she said. 'I'll never forgot what I saw there, and I really don't know how you can either. All those wretched people. The broken communities – and the filth. Get away from it, Rob.'

'Oil makes the world go round,' I said. 'I mean, if that's how you feel about it, what are you going to do? Stop driving your car, stop heating the house? The responsibility starts with the government of Nigeria, and in a democracy that goes back to the people, doesn't it? If I quit dealing there, if Chevron pulled out, you think those poor people are suddenly going to have the good life all of a sudden?'

I told her this was my chance of making some real money, and I wasn't about to let it go. I had a dream. A castle, with maybe a couple of thousand acres and a salmon river running through it, something that would set the family up for generations. Was that a bad thing to want? Plenty of respected people in Scotland had it – royalty, nobility, businessmen. Would she like to take a look through the history books and figure out how those guys had climbed to the top of the pile and accumulated their wealth? They didn't get rich by giving a shit about the fate of the common people. Her answer to that was, why not be happy with what we already have – a house and 10 acres? It's more than most people could ever aspire to.

But I wasn't going to be shifted. By good luck or good judgement, this opportunity had landed in my lap: the chance to make enough money in two or three shipments to set myself up for life and establish a legacy for our children.

Arguing – I hate it. Always have, and always will. I grew up with parents who argued – correction, they fought. I remember my mother going for my old man with a knife. So the idea of arguing with the person you're supposed to love, I didn't like that. In fact, with Linda, it rarely got to a full-blown row – I didn't let it – although, the way things were, we never really had time to hammer out our differences. Instead, we pushed them aside.

Work was top of the list for me, always, and once I was back in Nigeria I had plenty on my mind. There was always a new problem to deal with. The latest to come up, however, wasn't mine – or didn't seem to be anything to do with me, although that didn't stop me stepping in and helping to sort it out. There was, as usual, an incentive.

All the companies out there ran crew boats, fast boats that got people to and from the rigs and refineries, and so on, with minimum waste of time. And some of the boats were driven recklessly fast, like they owned the damned waterways. You just knew that one day something was going to happen. And so it did. A crew boat owned by C-Kor, one of the other supply vessel companies, went barrelling down the Escravos River, shot past a canoe and roared on towards the estuary. It never stopped to notice that the canoe had flipped and fourteen people had been flung into the water. The pilot had something else on his mind: getting the crew to work, then turning round and taking the other crew off, fast. Nothing else mattered. Except that every last one of those sorry bastards drowned in the oil-streaked waters, and when word got to the captain of the crew boat, it was, 'Canoe? I never saw any canoe.'

But the incident had been seen by plenty of people, and once word got out it was as if someone had put a spark to a powder keg. The day after the incident, a group of men from the drowned victims' villages, armed with axes, staves and machetes, descended on Chevron's base at Escravos where two of C-Kor's crew boats were tied up at the dock. The expat crew took one look at the advancing mob and ran for their lives, leaving the vessels to be destroyed. They were simply hacked to pieces.

Now the mob stormed Chevron's yard. The remaining staff had long since taken flight, apart from a couple of managers who had to seek refuge in the false ceiling of their office and pray that the mob didn't torch the place. Despite frantic calls to the navy and army, there was a substantial delay before they sent in helicopters to disperse the crowd.

This wasn't the end of the matter, however. Such was the outrage amongst the locals that, all along the river, villagers were stopping crew boats from travelling. It soon developed into a full-on blockade. The company, desperate to keep the operations moving, started flying crew to and fro at huge cost – and boy, were they squealing about it. When I got to hear about all this, it seemed to me there was one obvious solution. I hopped on a plane and flew up to Lagos. I needed to talk to a couple of people.

The transport situation around the capital was chaotic. Had been for years. The daily commute was a total nightmare. The nub of the problem was that Lagos is built on and around a number of islands. Every day, some 6 million people needed to cross from the mainland to the business and administrative centres on Lagos Island or the government buildings on Ikoyi. With the roads and bridges congested to the point where nothing was moving, the governor decided to look at alternative ways of getting people around. He set up the State Ferry Services Company and purchased a couple of catamarans from a shipyard in the Isle of Wight. They were a huge success, cutting people's travel time from several hours to a matter of minutes. Each cat carried 140 passengers, travelled at 30–35 knots and, because of their design and their shallow draught, left very little wake, meaning that they didn't trouble smaller, slower craft around them. Something like that, I figured, would be perfect for the Escravos River.

I went to the governor and, with the help of a sackful of cash, persuaded him to 'loan' the vessels to me. The price? One million naira, or approximately $100,000, per year – for each of the ferries. I would pay him cash, in advance. How he would account for the ferry service's sudden termination would be up to him, but the guy was a politician, he'd come up with something.

From there, I went to Chevron and met up with a senior figure in the firm. I explained that I had a solution to their problem, showed him pictures of the ferries and said I could have two such vessels in service within two weeks, for a daily rate of $2,000 each. Only one catch: I needed a firm two-year contract, otherwise I couldn't afford to do it for them. The guy almost bit my arm off. They were spending way more than that per day on the helicopters. 'Prepare the contract,' he said, 'and get those cats here as soon as you possibly can.'

From Chevron's offices I made my way back to the governor and told him to send the vessels to my yard in Warri. He was concerned that the sight of new green and white ferries would make it obvious what was going on. 'Don't worry,' I said. 'Won't take my guys any time at all to paint them orange. Just get them here as fast as you can, and there'll be 2 million naira waiting for you.'

So far so good. Now I needed to be sure that my newly acquired vessels could travel up and down river undisturbed by local activists. I went to meet Habib. He was the man who could fix this for me. We stuffed a duffle bag full of naira and started down the river, calling in at one village after another. Some of the chiefs we talked to were ones I'd already met on my goodwill tour with Lucky. They each struck a deal with us, and explained to their villagers that they had personally arranged for the new vessels to be brought in, and that the crew was under strict instructions to pay more attention to the regular river traffic.

Everybody was now back at work, and all interested parties had made money. It was the classic win–win situation – unless you were a commuter in Lagos.

While I was on this piece of business, I happened to be sitting on a traffic jam one day, in downtown Warri. I was half-watching the policeman on point duty, standing in a rickety, faded blue, wooden booth. I could just about make out the lettering on it, advertising a company I knew had gone under some time ago. Later that day, I called on a senior police officer I knew, and asked him what the situation was. As far as he remembered it was the mayor's project, I should talk to him. The mayor listened to my pitch. He shook his head. 'The company paid for them in perpetuity,' he said. 'We cannot replace them.' Of course, he was angling for a backhander.

I rephrased my opening pitch. 'Mister Mayor,' I began, 'can we put our boxes on the roundabouts where the old ones have fallen down – or are no longer there? For a fee, of course.'

'Why, yes, that would be fine,' he smiled.

'And when the others fall down as they get old, can I replace those?'

'Yes of course you can. For a fee.'

I went to the yard and got my carpenters to start building a new set of booths, painting them orange and sticking 'Coastal Shipping' on all four sides. A few days later, with the paint still drying, I sent out a couple of my guys in trucks with orders to destroy the old blue booths. They did one hell of a job. They mangled them, every last one. Only problem was, I should have given an order to make sure the booths were unoccupied. Nobody was seriously hurt, but several traffic cops had to jump to safety – and I found myself under arrest for attempted murder.

I fixed that with a couple of payments, of course – one to the mayor and one to the police. In return I got the green light to install my new booths and give the brand name the kind of exposure I wanted.

15

Monrovia, Liberia, June 1992

Now that I was involved in delivering oil to a bunch of West African countries, I knew things were going to get complicated. This was a turbulent area. That's why there was big money to be made. Try making a fortune in a nice settled democratic country. It's a long, slow process. I knew damned well there was a chaotic civil war going on in Liberia, but as to the details and the reasons behind it, no, I never really figured that out – although I had got to know a bit about the various groups involved; you needed to. You never knew when you might have to strike a deal with one or other of them.

First, there was the NPFL, or National Patriotic Front of Liberia. Their head honcho was Charles McArthur Ghankay Taylor. Nice fellow, later to be indicted on eleven separate crimes against humanity, including human sacrifice and cannibalism. He would be sentenced to fifty years in jail. But, at this time, he still claimed to be in charge of the country, although he was challenged on all sides by

ULIMO, the United Liberation Movement of Liberia, and the rival RUF, the Revolutionary United Front. Just to complicate things further, ULIMO was splitting into two factions along ethnic lines.

Trying to keep everyone apart was a peacekeeping force comprising mostly Nigerian troops. At the same time, Taylor's mob had started to launch attacks upon their neighbour, Sierra Leone. I hadn't yet worked out what that was about, but when it came to the politics of the area I wasn't the only outsider who tended to shrug, mentally – this was West Africa. Every time the smoke cleared, if you took a look around you spotted an opportunity. It was just a matter of staying alive long enough to grab it and get the hell out.

Given the circumstances, then, it was no surprise that logistics in Liberia were complicated, with transport constantly subject to interference. But as far as I was concerned, so far so good. I'd recently sent out the first three tanker loads of fuel for the peacekeeping forces. They'd arrived safely and the first two had successfully been unloaded and turned around.

Then I got news that, for some reason, the last ship was still dockside, waiting to discharge. Someone had shoved a machete in the works. Before I could find out who, or why, I got word that the general, the guy I'd been dealing with down there, wanted to speak to me in person. Yeah, I thought, the feeling's mutual. I flew to Monrovia, the capital. I was feeling pretty pissed off. I'd put a lot of effort into getting this deal up and running, and it promised to pay me a huge dividend, so I wasn't going to let things slide if I could help it. I had every incentive to see it through.

While I was in my hotel room, waiting to see the general, I caught up on the local news, and tried to make sense of it. It seemed the NPFL was still fighting troops from Sierra

Leone along Liberia's border. ECOMOG, the monitoring group, was trying to separate the two sides and create a buffer zone along the border. It had managed to open all roads into and out of Monrovia, which had, for a time, been blockaded. The latest reports were that Taylor had agreed to disarm his troops under the supervision of an expanded peacekeeping force. He would even confine his fighters to camp as part of an ongoing peace process.

So much for the reports. There was a lot of head shaking going on. Had he carried out his promise? It didn't look like it, and the way I saw it, why would he? And even if he did, was he in full control of all the different bands that made up his army? To call them irregulars would be to put it mildly. There had been authenticated stories of child soldiers loyal to Taylor committing horrible atrocities. Entire villages had been overrun and their inhabitants massacred after the women had all been raped by teenage boys, high on drugs.

Taylor, meanwhile, seemed to be stalling. He had made it clear he was unhappy about the fact that most of the peacekeepers were Nigerians who, he felt, were hostile to him. He still claimed he was willing to sign up to ECOMOG's plan, provided that its composition was changed. He wanted it to draft in troops from Senegal. Until that happened, he couldn't persuade his men to lay down their arms. I guess he – and they – feared they'd be massacred. So when ECOMOG sent 500 troops to disarm them by force, Taylor turned the tables and had his men capture them.

I sat there in my room, listening to a rain shower pounding down on the roof, wondering whether I'd made the best choice getting involved in such a chaotic and war-torn country. It seemed like anything could happen, any time. Just then, the front desk rang to tell me a driver had come for me. The guy took me to the ECOMOG headquarters to meet the general, but when he came to greet me, instead of inviting me into his office or some meeting room, he led me outside and into his personal jeep. I wasn't happy about this – at all. Where was he planning to take me?

He drove in silence, leaving the compound and making for the fringes of the town. Pretty soon we were heading out into the country. The rain, which had cleared by this time, had made the road muddy. There were occasional hollows full of water. The atmosphere was heavy, the sky mostly grey. I was feeling real edgy. After that sequence of arrests in Warri, I had an aversion to magical mystery tours, especially when they took me away from the comparative safety of the city.

We drove with our windows down, enjoying the brief coolness. We were out into the jungle proper by the time the general slowed down and pulled over. The clouds were already breaking up, and the vegetation that hemmed us in on both sides was steaming as the midday sun started to beat down. I was pretty nervous by now. What the hell was this all about? Soon as he switched off the engine you could hear that weird mixture of dense silence fragmented by the chatter of unseen animals and birds. It has a way of making you jumpy.

The general lit a cigarette, then turned to me and said, 'This third tanker of yours ...'

'The one that's tied up in the docks?' I said.

'Correct. That one. Is it possible – I mean, is there any reason why you cannot send it to Freetown and unload it there?'

'Any reason why I should?' I answered.

'Just let us say that it might be a way forward.'

'What exactly is the problem?' I asked.

He conceded that he feared his troops were about to lose control of Monrovia. If they did, they would have to retreat across the border into Sierra Leone. On the plus side, they could attack the capital more safely from there. On the other hand, they'd have no fuel. My first thought was, Jesus Christ, you're the fucking peacekeepers – but I didn't say that. Instead I reassured him. 'Yeah, we could do that,' I said. 'My crew don't really mind where they go – so long as they get paid at the end of the month.'

That's when he finally came to the real point, the point where I understood why he'd driven us all the way out into the jungle. He wanted total privacy, and he wanted a chunk of the money I would realise from the deal: $50 per tonne of fuel delivered, for himself. He wanted it as a separate pay- ment, a private deal to be kept a secret from his friend the admiral. Even as I deliberated, he was handing me the details of one of his numbered accounts in Switzerland. Accounts, plural. The guy had several, and he wasn't ashamed to let me know it. I think he was proud of the fact, like it gave him added status.

Personally, I had no problem with any of this. Corrupt or not, these were the good guys. That's what it said on the news, at least. They needed fuel, and I was able to provide it – and cream off a fat profit for myself. Did that make me one of the peacekeepers? Not exactly, but otherwise what was the problem? We shook hands on the deal. He leaned forward and reached for the ignition key. Not for the first time, I looked around at the jungle that enclosed us. There was plenty of cover and very little sign of civilisation. I didn't like it.

It turned out I was dead right to be edgy. Through the open side window, a sudden rustling sound caught my ear. Looking up, I saw the foliage part, and out stepped a tall, slim, black kid, 13 or 14 years of age, carrying an assault rifle. He was, maybe, 10 yards ahead of us. He was barefoot, but he was wearing a long red dress and had a string of beads around his neck, a long belt of ammo over his shoulder. As he turned, jerking the rifle in our direction, two things happened. First, the general reached to his side for the revolver he was carrying. Second, a bunch more kids, all of them armed, all wearing female clothing, some in high-heeled shoes, spilled out onto the road from both sides and surrounded the vehicle.

I glanced in the wing mirror and saw several more behind us. There must have been twenty of them, maybe thirty. I was about to wind up my window – until a fucking great machete landed – thunk! – beside my right elbow, embedding itself in the door frame. I could see black, dried blood caked along the blade. The kid holding it just stared at me, unblinking. He had a grubby bandage wrapped around his head, a glittery bangle of some kind on his slender wrist. I doubted he was 13 years old.

I glanced at the general. 'Let me pay them,' I said, offering up a silent prayer of thanks that I'd done what I always did in that part of the world, and come out with a wad of cash. It's the only way to travel. I could see the general taking a lungful of air, his brow furrowed and his eyes narrowing. 'This is nonsense,' he said. 'These people – '

He got no further. A big, lanky, raw-boned kid wearing a sort of lace chemise leaned inside the cab, his face inches from the general's. I glanced into his yellowed eyes. His pupils were dilated, so much so that it was like I was looking into two black holes. Whatever he'd taken, he'd taken plenty of it. He seemed to be staring unsteadily at a spot somewhere between the two of us, but his gun – that was steady, and pointed right at me. 'Money,' he said. 'We must have money.'

The general's face was contorted with shock and rage. 'What is the meaning of this? Do you know who you're talking to?' He put a hand on the gun and shoved it to one side. The kid pulled the trigger and a burst of automatic rifle fire blew out the back window of the jeep. My ears were ringing, and the smell of cordite burned my nostrils.

'You are using this road illegally. There is a fine to pay.' He held his hand out and repeated. 'The fine. Everybody must pay.'

The general still didn't get it. I had my wallet in my hand, but out of sight of the kid. I could see the general holding his own gun, which he carried on his hip. I was praying for him not to draw it from the holster. We'd both be dead before he had it halfway out. 'You do not set fines on this road,' he said. 'You are delinquents, and the law will bring you to justice.' He reached forward and fired up the engine. 'Whoever you are, you get out of our way this minute or I will run you down like dogs.'

I leaned towards him, and restrained his arm. For a moment I thought he was going to strike me. I gripped my lips tight like a ventriloquist and managed to get out, 'Look, let's pay them and get the hell outta here.'

'I cannot countenance this,' he began. 'It is extortion.'

'I can cope with that,' I said. 'I ain't proud.' I turned back to the boy who was leaning on my window, his arm stretched out and his hand groping along the dashboard. I could see what he wanted. 'Here,' I said, picking up my sunglasses. 'Raybans. Take 'em. Gotta look after your eyes, man. Very precious.'

He slipped them on, then crouched down to check in the wing mirror and smiled at his reflection. 'So who's the leader?' I asked. 'Who's your main man?'

He turned away, pointing his gun at a slightly built kid in a red mini-skirt and white blouse. Both were too big for him, and he was dwarfed by his rifle. 'Lemme talk to him,' I said. As I waited for the boy to amble over, I turned to the general who was eyeballing the kid at his window. 'These are killers we're dealing with,' I murmured through clenched teeth. 'Cold-blooded little fuckers. You know what they do.'

'That's because nobody stands up to them,' he replied. 'That is how they get away with it.'

I felt the barrel of a rifle tap my arm. The slightly built kid was there, with his hand out. I showed him my wallet, pulled out a bunch of $100 bills, turned the wallet inside out and showed him the inside. There was nothing left: just a photo of Linda. He took the money, made an attempt at counting it and said, 'This is good. You can go now.'

We drove away, fast. There were a couple of sharp cracks as one or two of the boys discharged their weapons into the sky. 'Just kids having fun,' I said, but even as I spoke the words I could feel my jaw quivering. I looked across at the general. He, too, was shaking, but that was with rage. 'C'mon, what did you think?' I asked. 'We were going to make them see reason? These kids are casual killers. They're high as kites.'

'That was the action of a weak man,' he replied. 'It will only make them more daring. They need to see that they cannot get away with this highway robbery, this banditry.' For a moment I considered asking him to pay his half of the money that had saved his life, but I let it go.

As we drove back to his town I convinced myself that the deal was off, the whole damned shebang. I'd blown it. The general clearly felt contempt for my actions. He maintained a moody silence, his eyes fixed on the road ahead. He was motionless at the wheel, except when he leant on the horn as an odd truck got in our way, or swerved around a puddle.

Maybe this is all for the best, I told myself. I was sure that the quicker I got the hell out of Liberia, the better I'd feel. However, it seemed I'd forgotten rule number one in West Africa. Always expect the unexpected. By the time we got back to headquarters, the general had calmed down. He told me to go ahead with everything as discussed. The deal was still on. Then he dismissed me, saying he had things to do. Yeah, I thought, like rounding up a few teenage soldier boys and dumping them in a mass grave. That might help keep the peace.

I didn't waste any time. I got down to the docks as fast as I could, hunted up the captain of my tanker and told him to take his load to Freetown. Next morning I was on a plane to Lagos. I was still pretty badly shaken up; I couldn't get the sight of those kids out of my mind, and every time I thought of the way the general tried to throw his weight around I started shuddering. Fuck, any one of them could have pulled the trigger, any time, and never thought a damned thing about it. On the way back to the office – wham! – my taxi ran headfirst into a light truck. I broke my nose on the back of the seat in front, and it felt like I'd cracked a couple of ribs where the belt caught me. My driver was injured too, but not badly. He was taken to the hospital. I got a cab to the airport and took the first flight home.

16

Lagos and Kinshasa, DCR, July–August 1992

I was with Linda for the birth of our second child, but knew I'd have to get back to the business, and fast.

I arrived in Lagos exhausted and grabbed three or four hours before I was awoken by a call from my operations manager, an English guy called Ian who I'd recently hired. He said there were problems at the refinery. I asked him what kind of problems. Big ones, sabotage, he said, and serious enough to bring production to a halt. He didn't know if it was about politics or if somebody was running an extortion racket. I immediately thought of Lucky. Now there was a guy with a grudge – and connections.

What all this meant was that I had no fuel to sell, either to the good guys or the bad. At the same time, half my vessels were now tied up in dock, rendered idle by a slowdown in the regular oilfield construction industry. There was nothing for them to do, and therefore no income. The difficulty I now had, just as I'd had in Brazil when the fishing thing imploded, was my network of contacts. The admiral, the police, the security people, they all still wanted their money: they had children to feed, bills to pay.

Not many hours later, Ian was back on the phone, expressing fears for the safety of property and personnel, particularly the expat element. Suddenly, it seemed, the city of Warri was in uproar. With the disruption at the refinery, the supply on the streets, which had been patchy at the best of times, had dried up. On the radio people were being interviewed. 'How is it,' they asked, 'that with so much oil in this country, we can't even fill our cars?' Pretty soon, unrest gave birth to full-blown riots. White faces would be an easy and obvious target for an angry mob. 'Right,' I thought, 'Welcome to Nigeria, Ian.'

'Hang tough,' I told him. 'And listen, if it gets real bad, we can evacuate you all on one of the ships.' That was the best I could do, encourage the guy. I now had to put all this to the back of my mind and sort out the Liberian problem. But events soon overtook me.

Later that day, I received a radio call from Friday, the Nigerian guy who ran the yard for me. I was in the office. He was beyond excited – he was in a panic. 'You have got to do something!' he shouted. 'They've taken all the foreigners.'

'How do you mean, taken? Who's taken them?'

'Taken hostage. They're demanding money.'

'You mean everybody, all the expats?'

'Yes. To a man. They came with guns and – '

'Who came with guns, Friday? The police?'

'No, it is your man, Lucky. He came with a gang, an armed gang.'

'Jesus,' I said. Ever since I started loading from the refinery I'd been buying less and less fuel from Lucky's contacts. He'd told me more than once that his 'father' was getting very unhappy about it. As Friday continued to fill me in on what was happening, I realised I hadn't a damned clue what to do. For the first time, I started to feel I really was in too deep. All the same, I could see this was down to me to fix. Friday was on the verge of losing it – not that I blamed him for that. 'So where are they now?' I asked him. 'The expats. What have these people done with them?'

'They drove them all outside, and …' He paused.

'Yes? And what?'

'They put them in a container.'

'Whadda you mean a container?'

'One of those 40ft containers. And they've – they've …' The guy was breaking up.

'Come on, Friday. Spill it, man. What have they done?'

'Oh man, they are pouring diesel into the container – all over everybody. Through the hole in the top. They want 100,000, cash – in dollars. If they don't get it they will throw in a match.'

'Oh, fuck me.'

'And if you don't agree, they say they will kill me too.'

I was thinking, fast. Trying to be logical, not make the wrong decision. These people's lives were in my hands. Even as I tried to think, I could hear the men screaming out orders in the background. 'Okay,' I said. 'First thing … Friday, you listening to me?'

'Yes.' He was almost whispering. 'Yes, I am listening.'

'First thing, you tell them I'm going to pay. That's number one.' I heard him sigh and mutter something – to himself or his captives – I couldn't tell. 'Okay? The money will be coming. Number two, there's a problem. I haven't got that much money right now, not in dollars. All I have is naira. Tell them they can have it in naira. It would take me twelve – no, better say eighteen hours to get dollars. Maybe longer.'

Friday was back on the phone in less than a minute. 'They accept your offer. There are two men in Victoria Island to collect the money from you. They are outside your compound now. You must give it to them immediately. One million naira. If you don't do this we will all die.' I knew now that they'd had this all planned. I tried to imagine myself in the shoes of those captives, my staff, people I knew well, people I'd shared food with.

Before I handed over the money, I called the head of the riot police and filled him in. 'You got to help me,' I said. 'There are a lot of lives at stake.'

'First you must pay the money,' he told me. 'You have to — '

'Yeah,' I said, 'I'm not that dumb. I've told them I'll pay. The money isn't the issue. It's my people.' The fact that I was willing to pay seemed to reassure him. I realised that in all likelihood he was getting a cut on the kidnappings. He told me he would establish a base across the road from the yard as soon as possible. This would never be allowed to happen again.

'But you must understand,' he said, 'it will not be possible to set up a new base on my budget.'

'Oh, for God's sake! What do you think I was, born yesterday? Just get it done and I'll pay what it takes.' I went to my strongbox and counted out the packs of 50 naira notes. Outside the main gate I found the two men. I got a good look at them as I handed over the ransom. I could've sworn they were the two minders Lucky kept at his bar, I was certain of it. Back inside, I picked up the phone and told Friday it was done. He told me the captives would be released as soon as the money was counted. Then the line went dead. I leaned back in my chair and closed my eyes. I needed breathing space, I needed time to make sense of all that had happened. Time to figure out a plan. Life was getting too damned hairy. First the hold-up, then the accident in the taxi, and now this.

Right at that moment, the last thing I needed was a call from Linda, but that's what I got. I could barely believe what she was telling me, her voice animated and brimming with affection. She'd decided that with two kids it was time, for better or worse, that we set up home together in Nigeria. I wanted to shout at her, 'No! It's fucking chaos over here!' But that would've required me to explain what was going on, and I wouldn't have known how to begin. Instead I heard myself say, 'Sure, sweetheart. If that's what you want. No problem.' The fact that she'd already booked a flight didn't fully register.

When I sat down and thought it through, I figured that having Linda out there with me might not be so difficult after all. Things had been changing in Nigeria. When I first started operating there, it was universally put down, within the oil industry, as a total shithole. Sure, oil was cheap and plentiful; sure, you could produce it for $2 a barrel rather than $10, but with all the hassles and uncertainties of the area, was it really worth it? The fact is, nobody wanted to work there. You only got sent out to Nigeria by one of the majors if you were on your last warning for some reason. Maybe you'd been screwing somebody else's wife, or maybe you'd fucked up at work but they hadn't got enough to get rid of you. A lot of guys would simply cash in their chips rather than go to Warri, for example, and the big corporations knew it. And, if I'm totally frank, you could say that that's how I managed to operate so successfully out there. There was little competition, and the oil majors didn't complain about dealing with me. It was almost like I was doing their dirty work for them, and that meant they could overlook the fact that they were dealing with a guy who was still in his mid-thirties, wore Hawaiian shirts and had a ponytail – and was probably evading taxes in the US.

But now things were changing. Maybe they'd been changing, subtly, for a while, and I hadn't noticed. Now it was staring me in the face. The first Gulf War came along, and for the first time in a decade or so supplies were being interrupted worldwide. The majors were starting to take West Africa seriously, and now, rather than sending out all their deviants and last-chancers, they were sending out top quality people – older people, who wore suits. In any meeting of oil people I was more conspicuous now, and so were my cowboy methods. I took the hint, and started hiring guys with grey heads, guys who looked the part and fitted in. I hired a tailor and paid a visit to the barber's, got rid of the ponytail.

Along with this shift in the kind of people who were coming to Nigeria, there was a general stiffening up of discipline, of standards. Health and safety people were coming out and bringing a more up-to-date notion of what constituted good working practice. Chevron, for example, had a guy inspecting the various boats working for them. When he ran the rule over mine he made it quite clear that he thought they were a pile of crap, and he was looking for any excuse to keep them away from his nice shiny installations. It didn't take him long to give the thumbs down to a whole bunch of them, seven in all. Of course, I wanted to argue with the guy, so he took me down to the dock to show me the problem. We went aboard the first one and he led me straight to the life jacket station. Everything was where it was supposed to be, in a safe place, in a box on deck – with a chain and padlock around it.

'What's the problem?' I asked.

He rapped the lock with the back of his hand. 'This isn't permissible,' he said, 'and you damned well know it. It contravenes every rule in the book.'

'But this is Nigeria,' I told him. 'I leave them unlocked and I guarantee you they'll be gone inside five minutes. If a thing ain't nailed to the deck some sonofabitch is gonna have it.'

He shook his head. 'It's simply against the law, Mister Stone.'

'Listen,' I said, 'soon as we get out to sea, we unlock them. What's the problem?' But he wasn't having it. I was in breach of basic safety regs with the life jackets and a dozen other things he was ranting on about. So now I had to make these changes for half my fleet or I'd lose the contracts. And until it was done and he approved it, they were off hire. End of story.

With this new influx of more regular oil company execs, I'd also had to rethink the accommodation for my expat staff. What I'd done up to now was rent various houses in and around Warri. It seemed secure enough, until one of the wives, who was heavily pregnant, was held up at gunpoint and brutally raped. There was an emergency meeting of staff and some family. I told everybody I would sort it out. I'd pay for more riot police and get the navy guards in. They weren't happy about that, at all. They made it plain they expected a compound, like Shell and other large multinationals provided for their staff, and they didn't come cheap.

It seemed we were all becoming image conscious too. Around this time, I took a look at my staff working in the yard. They were still coming to work wearing whatever cast-off clothes they could find, many of them emblazoned with the logos of my competitors. I went out and bought a whole bunch of coveralls, bright orange ones in various

sizes with 'Coastal Shipping' front and back. As soon as
I kitted the guys out the place looked … credible, was the
word Ian used.

The new look lasted 'til the first weekend – then it was
back to the rainbow assortment of cast-offs. I didn't get it.
I guessed the guys had sold their new coveralls. I planned
to tackle Friday about it but, as ever, I found a hundred
other things to occupy my time. Another week went by.
On the Sunday, I drove past a nearby church, a low building
built of corrugated iron. The sun was shining, and through
the windows I saw this kind of orange glow. For a moment
I thought the place was on fire. I pulled up, got out of my
car and peeked in through the doorway. There, in the con-
gregation, were a dozen or so of my employees, resplendent
in their brand new orange coveralls. Next day, I sent out
for another consignment and laid it on the line. There was
a dress code and we would adhere to it. The guys got the
message – they turned up to work in one set and saved the
best for Sundays.

Meanwhile, I'd found an office building in Lagos, on
Victoria Island. It was effectively a mansion, surrounded by
a high wall, plus a security fence topped with barbed wire.
It was a little fortress. I set up the lower floors as offices and
converted the upper part into living accommodation for
senior expat staff – Doug, for example – and a separate suite
for myself. When Linda and the children came out, that is
where we set up home. She loved the place as soon as she saw
it, and was delighted to find that we had a garden around it.
Once she felt settled, I started to scout around for contracts
for my idle ships, the ones that weren't up to the mark for the
oil majors. I figured I could also do with a few more bases.

My journey took in South Africa, Namibia, Angola,
Gabon and the Congo. I had decided already that it

wasn't good business to have all my eggs in one Nigerian basket. I could surely find buyers for my oil elsewhere, maybe among the many fishing fleets that worked the coastal waters. As ever, the journey threw up its own dose of excitement.

I was in the capital city of the Democratic Republic of Congo, Kinshasa. I needed to fly down to Pointe Noire on the coast of the other Congo (the Republic of). It was a small plane, maybe sixty passengers, and I was the only white guy on board. There was a bunch of high-ranking Congolese army officers sitting together in front of me. I had a simple modus operandi in Africa, one that had always worked for me: get in with the military. I tried to make polite conversation with these fellows but they weren't having it. They cold-shouldered me.

We'd been flying a half hour or so when the pilot told us we had engine problems and were going to make an emergency landing. We came down with a bump on a bush strip somewhere on the borders of northern Angola. After a while, a twin-engined six-seater showed up with a mechanic and some spares. The mechanic said it was going to take some time to fix our plane. I asked his pilot where he was heading. Pointe Noire, he told me. I offered to pay him cash to take me there, and he agreed. Then I figured here was a chance to cosy up to these stony-faced officers. I approached them, told them I'd hired the other plane, and asked them if they'd accept a ride.

None of them spoke. I was starting to figure I'd made a mistake all along: they simply didn't speak English. I was wrong. When I tried to repeat my offer, one of them looked at me like I was a piece of shit and said, 'If we want a ride on the plane, we take the plane. Now fly away, white man.'

After my trip along the coast, I got back to Lagos to find I had a message from Fraser White. He wanted to arrange a meeting with me. I had no idea what could be on his mind, and couldn't resist the invitation. A couple of days later, I was at Warri airport when he flew in. He arrived in a brand new Gulfstream IV-SP. He walked off the plane with his senior VP, a guy called Teddy, and greeted me with a wide grin. 'I'm telling you, Rob, the private jet is the only way to fly.'

We walked to the parking lot and got into my car. We sat in the traffic, making small talk. After we'd run out of subject matter, Teddy asked Fraser if he'd had time to think about his request for a vacation. 'What is this? I already gave you eight weeks last summer,' Fraser said.

Teddy sighed. 'Yeah, sure you did – but don't you remember, I had open heart surgery?'

Fraser thought for a moment, then said, 'Listen, Teddy, how you spend your free time's nothing to do with me.'

I took them to the *Caledonian*. Doug was waiting on board. While he poured us all drinks, I told Fraser and Teddy the story about how I had salvaged the yacht in Louisiana and restored her to her original condition. They couldn't believe the job I'd done. They loved it, especially the white patent leather ceilings and polished mahogany walls. Sitting down with our drinks, pleasantries over, Fraser got down to business. He didn't beat about the bush.

'Teddy, Doug,' he said, 'd'you guys mind stepping outside for a while? There's something I want to discuss privately with Rob.' I couldn't figure what could be on his mind. After that crack about Teddy's vacation it seemed he wasn't treating the guy with too much dignity. And Doug was my right-hand man. So what had he got lined up for me? He waited 'til the door had closed, then made his pitch. He said he knew I was a guy who would deliver, so he wanted me to be the sole supplier of vessels for his business – not only in Africa but in south-east Asia too. Only problem was, I had to update my fleet. His was a prestigious operation and he didn't want a bunch of rust buckets pootling around making him look cheap. I could see his point, but wondered where the hell that left me.

'Tell you what I got in mind,' he said. 'We order up some replacements. We'll send your old vessels to China, two or three years from now, when the new ones come. Let them earn some money over there 'til they sink.'

'Yeah but – new ones?' I asked him. 'Where from? With what?'

'South Korea. They're pretty damned accommodating.' I waited for him to expand on that. Fraser wasn't a guy you interrupted. 'You realise if OCI offers long-term contracts those guys will provide 110 per cent finance? How's that grab ya?'

While he spoke, I'd been doing the math in my head. Coastal Shipping could wind up being worth hundreds of millions. He knew that, of course. And he had the money side worked out. Maybe I'd wait a couple of years, then sell up and buy myself that estate in Scotland.

'OCI will want 50 per cent of your company,' Fraser said. 'As of now. We won't pay you, but we'll contract to buy up the other half in five years' time. Full market value.' I thought that was it, and I needed to chew it over. I was reeling. But there was more to come. 'You need to understand one thing, Rob. You're a smart operator but you got to clean up your act.'

'What exactly do you mean?' I said.

Fraser shook his head. 'You got to get out of that fuel business. Otherwise it's no deal.' I was thinking this was

pretty ripe coming from him, after all the time he'd paid
me to do the dirty work, but I let it pass. 'I can't have you
involved in anything remotely shady, y'understand? I'm
running a public company in the good ol' US of A and
there's no way I can afford to run foul of the FCTPA. You
got that?'

I told him I did. I knew about the Foreign Corrupt Trade
Practices Act. As he pitched in with the rest of the deal,
I was only half listening. The other part of my head was
dealing with problems I could already see on the horizon.
It would be one thing to stop the small scale fuel smuggling with my supply ships. I could do that easily enough.
It had run its course, anyway. As for the two small tankers,
I could put those on to another company, let Doug and
my guys run it, and take a cut of whatever fuel they carried, just like the general, the admiral and all the others had
done with me. All I had to do was be discreet. The main
issue was how to do the deal with Fraser and still do the Z
Group runs. Screw it, I thought. We'll cross that one when
we come to it.

I had to hand it to Fraser. He'd done his homework.
So far it all seemed too good to be true. There just had
to be a catch – and there was. 'I've been conducting background checks on you and your executives,' he said. My
heart skipped two beats. 'You know, you're the only one
who passed. Those other guys – I can't have them on my
payroll. No way.' He looked me right in the eye and added,
'So they're gone. Either that, or OCI walks away from this.'

My first thought was, Jesus, how do I handle this? Second
one was, shit, if he ever finds out the full story … I probably
thought, and thought hard, for a full sixty seconds, which
can seem a damned long time when some guy's sitting next
to you waiting for your decision on the opportunity of a

lifetime. Sixty seconds: that's how long it took me to make up my mind. It was time to cut with the past and press ahead with the future – my family's future. 'Okay,' I said, reaching out to shake his hand. 'We got us a deal.'

We called Teddy and Doug back in. I told Doug as much of the news as he needed to know. It struck me immediately that he didn't look too pleased at all.

17

Warri, Nigeria,
September 1992

Doubt, it's like a spot of rust on the underside of a ship – it starts out where you can't even see it with a scratch where you've nudged the concrete lip of the dock, or maybe run into a length of driftwood with a bolt through it. Once the raw metal is exposed, that's when the rust gets a hold and starts gnawing away. Pretty soon you have a hole, next thing you're sinking. Fast.

The following morning, when I climbed down the gangway from the *Caledonian*, I should've had a spring in my step. Everything was going my way. Just a few local difficulties to clear up; otherwise, the future was looking damned good. But the fact is, I was in a mood to match the weather, which was overcast and wet, with thunder rumbling in the distance. I hadn't slept well, and I knew why. It was Doug. As soon as Fraser and Teddy had left the previous night I knew something was eating the guy, and I couldn't put my finger on it.

It didn't take long to find out. Before I had a chance even to ask, he was off. Boy, was he off. He began with, did

I realise just how much I owed him? He didn't wait for an answer, just came out with this list of grievances from here to the middle of the next week. Number one, if it hadn't been for him convincing me to do the Alaskan trip I would not have done it – and number two, it was the money I'd earned from that which made everything in Nigeria possible. Number three, I didn't value him. Number four, if it wasn't for him I would have been wiped out financially after Ocean Harvest and Pescado de Brasil went tits up. He even seemed to think he deserved all the credit for coming over from Brazil, locating the yard, setting up the whole business and running things while I was away. In my version of events, I'd called him from New Orleans and told him to do all of those things. Sure, he did them, but only because he was doing what the boss said. But there you go: we remember what we want to remember.

I'm not often stuck for words, but I sat there with my mouth open. What was really eating him? And what the fuck had he and Teddy been discussing when they were asked to leave the room? Where was all this shit coming from? When I did reply, I gave him both barrels. 'Now listen to me, cocksucker. The reason the Brazilian thing went down was you and your fucking history. Not mine, yours. You had convictions against your name, not me. And yeah, sure the Alaska trip opened things up for us, but all you did was pass me a message from Jack. Who spent a solid fucking month in the jungle getting eaten up by mosquitoes? Who woke up and found scorpions and centipedes in his bed day after day? Who had the shits for three weeks and carried on working in the pissing rain? Me, buster. Did you captain a ship full of dope through the South China Seas? No. It was me. Did you stand to be fucking hanged if we were caught? No, that was my life on the line. And while I was dodging the Thai Navy, what were you doing? Sitting on your no-good ass in an air-conditioned office screwing those underage Brazilian whores you're so fond of – on my fucking desk, most likely. And have you heard me complain? I don't think you have. And why? Because, Doug, we are supposed to be a fucking team. Jesus Christ!'

I'd said my piece. I didn't want to hear what he had to say. Fuck him. I kicked the door open and stormed down below to my stateroom.

No wonder that, this morning, as I walked through the mud and the rain to my office, I was in a foul mood. As I reached the entrance, a navy guard was standing close by, his automatic rifle on his shoulder. Something about the way he saw me, then looked away, seemed odd. I approached the porch we had there, and there was that dumb old billy goat, soaking wet, lying right down in front of me. With his wet fur he smelled even worse than usual. It nauseated me. I'd told the guys to get rid of the stinking thing a hundred times. All I ever got was, 'Yes, boss, we will, boss. At the weekend boss.' But they never did.

The goat looked up at me and had a real sort of 'fuck you' air about him. I guess I just snapped. I grabbed the navy guy's rifle and emptied the clip point blank into it, gave the rifle back to the guard and walked over to my car. My driver, Solomon, was sitting there with his hand over his eyes. Whether he was laughing or not, I couldn't tell. 'Okay,' I said, 'let's go down town. I got some calls to make.' God, I wished I could make an international call without taking half a fucking day to do it. As we drove out, I noticed there wasn't the usual gaggle of workers pretending to be busy. And the ones who were present were avoiding eye contact with me. I guessed it kind of made sense. Maybe they were shocked by my action.

By the time I got to the exchange I'd calmed down. I didn't have that many calls to make but the lines were poor and I kept getting cut off, so it was the usual frustrating business. And then there was the traffic. It was getting on for three by the time we drove back into the yard. First thing I noticed was the riot police – or rather their absence. Normally, there would be several vehicles in their compound, and a handful of men lounging under the shade trees. There wasn't a soul – even though the sun was now out. I saw too that both the navy guards who were supposed to be on the main gate were missing. Probably something to do with me shooting the goat, I guessed. I made a note to go and apologise for that. I'd never done anything like that before in my life, and I knew it was wrong to take out my frustrations on a dumb beast, no matter what it smelled like.

The whole atmosphere around the place felt wrong. Normally the workers in the yard would try to look like they were hard at work, but they'd always stop and wave, or shout a greeting. This time they were all over the boat's hull, scraping, painting, moving scaffold poles, and every one of them had his back to me.

In the office I called for my PA. I needed her to send a telex. There was no answer. Doug, who I saw was sitting at my desk, told me the secretaries had gone home. 'What do you mean, gone home?' I asked. 'Why?'

Doug shrugged. 'No idea. They just got up and took off. Never said a word to me.'

I stood there, waiting for him to move out of my chair. I had questions for him, a whole list, but they would have to wait. I sat down, picked up the phone and called Lieutenant Ogabie. I'd been paying him money every month for over a year now and it was time for him to give me back more than a goddam handshake. I laid into him. Number one, why hadn't he returned my calls? Number two, why weren't my navy security guys on duty? Number three, what the fuck did he think I paid him for every month?

That's when I realised no one was on the other end of the line – and that I was sounding like Doug when he lost his cool with me. 'Did that cocksucker hang up on me?' I shouted. Even before I put the phone down I heard the noise from outside. Something was happening in the yard. Shouting and chanting. I went to the office window and peered through the latticed steel shutters. Doug came across and stood beside me. My entire shift, 700–800 big strong guys in their bright orange coveralls, had downed tools and were heading towards us, like a sea of molten lava. In the lead were four men carrying a wooden coffin, and all of them were chanting the words that were daubed on the side of it in red paint. 'ROB MUST DIE! ROB MUST DIE!'

I picked up the phone to call the commander. The line was dead. Shit. Now it all made sense. The navy guys – absent. The mobile police squadron – nowhere. My secretaries – gone home early, leaving Doug and me alone in the office. Maybe it explained, too, why the lieutenant hadn't been talking to me. This had nothing to do with the goat. This was something else. But what? I felt real fear now, deep down in my bowels.

I sat down in my swivel chair and tried to think. Doug was on his hands and knees, scrabbling round the floor for the clip he'd spilled as he tried to load a pistol. Emerging from under the desk, he waved the weapon at the window. 'We're gonna end up out there with blazing tyres round our neck, and you're sitting there like it's Sunday afternoon, you crazy sonofabitch.'

'So what's on your mind?' I said. 'You planning to take the mob on with your pistol?' Only years later would I realise he'd had the pistol in his lap when I entered the office – way before the riot started.

'You got any other ideas?'

'Relax, Doug. Just take a seat and watch the show.' I stood up, went across to the door and unlocked it. Then I paused with my hand on the knob, took a deep breath and said, 'I'm gonna educate you.'

If I'd learned one thing in West Africa it was that there are two ways to win people over. Fear, or humour. You terrify them, or you make them laugh. I had no guards and no way to contact the riot police, who would normally have come up and shot the bastards, to a man, without thinking twice. So it seemed to me that a situation like this – me against several hundred – required one top quality stand-up routine. Timing. It's all about timing. Ask any comedian.

I opened the door, walked down the flight of steel steps, and approached the men. Jonathan, a carpenter I'd fired only the previous day, was at the front of the pallbearers. Behind him was a chaos of machetes and clenched fists. Had to hand it to them: if they really were planning to kill me they were well prepared. I pointed at the coffin, and laughed out loud. 'What in the name of Jesus Christ do you call that thing?' No answer. Just a blank stare, and in the brief, shocked silence the distant sound of music from the radio, down in the welder's shop. 'Come on,' I said. 'You're gonna have to give me a clue here.' I stepped closer, looked at the rough matchboard structure, then laughed again. 'I mean, what the fuck is it?'

Jonathan frowned, and spat out his words in that very clear, deliberate way West Africans have. 'I will tell you what this is. This … is a coffin.' Then he leaned forward and eye-balled me. 'This … is your coffin.'

'That piece of shit?' I said. 'You call that a coffin?' I walked forward, reached out and touched it – first with my left hand, then my right, measuring the width. Then I walked along the side of it, checking the overall dimensions before pulling myself up to my full height and throwing my shoulders back. 'C'mon Jonathan. Take a good look at me. How you gonna fit me in there? Big motherfucka like me?' I grasped the lid and tugged at it. There was a wrenching sound as a lightweight hinge came loose, ripping a pair of thin screws from the flimsy timber.

I shook my head. 'Sorry. It won't do, man. It just won't do.' I tapped my chest with a forefinger. 'You're looking at a man of some standing around here. A man of substance. If I wanted a coffin, I'd build me a goddam coffin. Inch-thick hardwood, brass handles, satin lined. And I'd pay good money. Get a craftsman joiner on the job.' I looked the coffin over one more time. 'You seriously telling me you built this piece of shit?'

Jonathan gave a nervous look around before he answered. 'Yes. I built it.'

I threw back my head and laughed. 'No wonder I fired you, Jonathan – you are one useless fucking carpenter.' As the man next to him started to grin, I pulled a board loose and held it up for everyone to see. 'Hey, I hope he screws his wife better than he screwed this damned thing together.' They were loving it now. All except Jonathan, that is.

'Fellows,' I said, 'take a good look at his handiwork. This is why I kicked his ass out in the street. I mean, I could go into town right now and find a dozen men who could do a better job than this. And they'd have the sense to measure me up first, make sure it fitted. Jonathan, I'm telling you right now, there's no way you'd get me in your coffin

— not even if you chopped me in little bits.' I slapped him on the shoulder. Then I delivered my punch line.

'Fuck,' I said, 'I wouldn't be seen dead in that piece of shit.'

They liked the joke almost as much as I did. The guys at the front relayed it to the guys at the back, and within moments everybody was laughing. The coffin was on the ground, the mood had lifted, and you could feel the tension ebbing away from the situation. 'Tell you what,' I laughed. 'Why don't you bury that stinking goat in it?'

They really liked that. There was a shuffling of feet and a few murmured apologies. 'Sorry boss.'

'Won't happen again, cap'n.'

'Okay. Accepted. Listen, I got an idea. Why don't you all take the rest of the day off work. It's gone three. Nobody's done a damned thing anyway. C'mon, get a fire going with this so-called coffin. Get some beers out of the warehouse coolers. And somebody butcher the damned goat, eh? Have a barbeque!'

I stood there and watched them disperse, some through the yard and over to the warehouse, some clambering up the steps to the ship we had in dry dock, its black hull half smothered in bright orange paint, some to the shower stalls. Then I took a deep breath, pulled the front of my sweat-soaked shirt from my chest, and headed for the air-conditioned cool of the office.

Doug was at his seat. He still looked shaky. He had his gun on the desk in front of him. 'Shit,' he said. 'I told that wife of yours she'd married a crazy sonofabitch. Wasn't far wrong, was I?'

'Yeah, but you left out the good part, Doug. She married a *lucky* sonofabitch. That's the crucial difference. A lucky one.' I slumped in my swivel chair and put my feet on the desk. Then I looked at my watch. 'I'm going to head for Lagos.

Tomorrow I see the admiral. That lieutenant's gonna get his ass kicked for certain, allowing shit like this to happen.'

Doug frowned at me. 'You're going to Lagos? Now? And you think I'm holding the fort on my own? You really are out of your fucking mind.'

'Quit being such a pussy, Doug. I've given the guys the rest of the day off. Everything's back to normal. What's the problem?'

'You think this is normal, man, you've been here too long.'

'Yeah, whatever,' I said. 'You're not the first person to tell me that this week. Now get your pad out. We got plans to make.'

Doug sat there with a pen in his hand, waiting. He wasn't happy about this, but what was he going to do? I might have made him a millionaire but he was like everybody else, me included. So long as the money was coming in he wanted more. So he kept his mouth shut and started taking notes.

'Okay,' I said, 'I want you to take a speedboat and make a run to Escravos. Go see that new guy from the States, the guy at Chevron – Head of Safety or whatever the fuck they call him. That guy's a pain in the ass. Seven of our vessels still shut down, for Chrissake.'

Doug looked up from his pad. 'Because we had the life jackets locked up? He's only doing his job, man.'

'And what were we supposed to do, leave them hanging there with a big fucking sign on? *Steal me.* Jesus, this is Nigeria, not San-fucking-Ramon. You go straighten him out. Do whatever you need to, but get those ships back to work.' I banged the flat of my hand on the table. 'We're losing $21,000 a day. It's gonna take two or three years to get new ships here from Korea – and another year before OCI send their barges to China. There's a lot of money to be made in the meantime.'

I stood up and went to the window. The yard was all but deserted now – and the dead goat had disappeared, just a bloodstain showing where it had been lying. I turned around and looked at Doug. 'Well, you think you should be running the show, pal? Time to get off your ass and show me you're up to it. And I'll tell you something for nothing. This shit didn't just erupt out of thin air. It's been brewing up, and you should've spotted it.'

'That it?'

'No, that's not it. I want you to get the 1,500-tonner ready to go. The fishing guys in Dakar want another load of fuel. And when you talk to Darren, you can tell him this is his last chance. Guy got off to a good start here, but he's slipping. They're claiming we were 150 short the last trip and they've deducted fifty grand from the transfer.'

'He says you owe him because of the Alaskan run.'

'Darren? You could be right. I do owe him. But he owes me too.' That's the trouble with a kid like him, I thought. You make him rich and he gets sloppy, or greedy like Doug. 'Anyway, they're also saying the last load had kerosene in it. Tell him to test and meter the damned fuel this time. Check it for water and kerosene, or his ass is going stateside and he'll never work for me again, not here, and definitely not on another run if, God forbid, I ever decide to go up to Glacier Bay and salvage that container. This is Darren's last chance. We get a reputation for delivering shit fuel and we're through. Jesus, why do I have to ride your ass about every fucking thing?' I looked at my watch and headed towards the door. 'Okay, I'd better get out of here or I'll be travelling in the dark.'

I never even said goodbye to him, just walked out of the office, crossed the yard and got in the car. Solomon was half asleep in the driver's seat. I told him I was ready for home and we set off for Lagos. I had a lot on my mind, but a part of me was switching off, thinking about the kind of stuff any family man thinks about at the end of the working day: seeing my kids, eating a meal with my wife. I wonder now what I would've done right then if I'd known what awaited me at the house: arrested in my own home, in front of my wife, and flung in jail. Would I have gone into hiding? Flown them home? Who knows? As it was, I hardly had time to think. If my life over the past few months had been a roller coaster ride, this was the moment when the train I was riding jumped the rails, broke through the barriers and plummeted towards the ground.

18

Lagos, Nigeria, September 1992

How I lost consciousness I don't know. Maybe it was exhaustion, maybe one of the guards whacked me as they shoved me through the door. Whatever it was, I woke up lying on a concrete floor with my tongue stuck to the roof of my mouth and my head pounding. It was pitch dark, and I couldn't see a damned thing, but I was sure some hours had passed. As soon as I tried to move I felt the gun in my underpants, jabbing into my groin. Why hadn't they searched me? Why? To this day I shudder every time I ask that question.

I levered myself up onto my hands and knees and crawled across a rough concrete floor to the edge of what I guessed was a prison cell. The walls seemed to be made of concrete blocks. I felt around and figured it measured about 8ft by 8ft. Along the way I knocked over a bucket – empty, thank Christ.

I stood up. Jesus, my ribs hurt, and as I raised a hand I realised my left shoulder had taken a battering. I managed to reach up with my right and touch the ceiling, then staggered back to the wall, worked my way along in the dark and found a door. Steel. I banged my fist on it. It made no sound. At about head height there was a sort of opening with metal bars across it. There were other cells out there, I guessed – there must have been. As I stood there I could hear faint echoes of people snoring, farting, coughing and sobbing.

This was my first time in a Nigerian prison cell. I'd been arrested many times over the past few years, and I'd got used to it. Invariably they took you into someone's office and you negotiated the price of your release. It was all very gentlemanly. This was different. It reminded me of my first experience as a young diver in the Mississippi River, unable to see a thing, totally at the mercy of the elements and the topside crew. Except that now, instead of a tobacco-chewing redneck supervisor, I had the Nigerian police pulling the strings, and they were working to the orders of an American puppeteer.

My guts were about to explode. I unfastened my trousers, squatted down and took a dump. There was nothing to wipe myself with. I moved the foul smelling bucket carefully to a corner; I could do without tripping over that. The stench soon filled the entire cell. I pulled my trousers up with my left hand. In my right I held the gun. It occurred to me that in other circumstances I really would have considered doing myself harm – not to end it all but to get myself out of this place to a hospital. But I had a family now, and even as I thought of them I couldn't help wondering whether they'd be better off without me.

I shoved the piece back down my pants. I thought of putting the gun in the bucket, and my mind rolled forward to the moment when it would be found, as it must. The smart-ass in me knew exactly what I'd say. 'Hey, I don't remember eating that.' I heard my laughter echo out into the passage-way. A voice called out, 'Who is that?' I didn't answer at first, then I called out, 'Can I get a drink in here?' Nothing.

I wondered how Linda would be coping. Had she remembered to tell Blessing to contact Judge Williams? I'd told her often enough that arrests down here were part and parcel of everyday life, and if it happened she shouldn't worry. But, of course, she would. I just hoped she wasn't fretting too much.

I sat down, my back against the wall, and went over the events that had led up to this. I remembered that I'd seen Barry and Doug out there being interviewed. Had they been arrested too? I shouted out their names, but the only response I got was catcalls and fragments of whispered conversation between other inmates. Doug's presence I could understand. He'd most likely been hauled in, same as me, but Barry? What the fuck was he doing in Nigeria? Was he negotiating some kind of deal with them? And how the hell had the US government agencies got involved? And the Drug Enforcement Agency? What could they have on me? They didn't know about the Alaska trip. How could they? No one had been arrested with any of the pot at any stage – not during the trip, nor the distribution. Nobody had been picked up exporting their money either – I would have heard about that right away.

My mind was still going round and round with various scenarios when I heard boots marching towards the cell. I got to my feet and shuffled around to the wall opposite the door. Through the vent I saw flashlight beams. The door opened, and I raised my good arm to shield my eyes from the light. Someone grabbed it, twisted it behind my back and slipped the handcuffs on. Real slick.

They dragged me out into a passageway. I heard other prisoners yelling, it sounded like encouragement. I stumbled up the stairs between two guards, one gripping each arm. I was back in the main building and my eyes were pierced by the bright lights. We stopped outside a plain brown door, number 203, and they shoved me inside. A voice said, 'Wait in here.'

I was alone in a small interview room. I sat straddling a chair, my arms cuffed behind my back, and looked around. There was a single framed photograph on the wall opposite me, the President of Nigeria. I'd met him once, president and chairman of the Armed Forces Ruling Council, Ibrahim Babangida. The people called him 'Baba'. He was a good man as far as dictators go. In the glass that covered his picture I could see my own reflection. I looked like some wasted investment banker emerging from a week-long orgy of drugs and booze. I looked around for water but all I saw was a plastic coffee cup with cigarette ash in it.

I must have been sitting there for half an hour when the doors opened. Two guards walked in and told me to follow them along the corridor. They took me to a door marked 'Deputy Inspector General'. I entered the room. Seated at his desk was the guy who'd thrown my ten grand onto the floor. He looked up at me and gave a sort of condescending smile. Yeah, I thought, you'd look like a piece of shit too if you spent the night down there, most likely smell like one too.

There was no preamble, he just said what he had to say as one of the guards unlocked my cuffs. 'Mister Stone, we are releasing you. There are, however, conditions. You will be allowed to go to your offices, but you will remain there until further notice. You will recall all of your ships to port immediately.'

'What about my passport?' I asked, rubbing my wrists where the cuffs had bitten into them, the feeling gradually returning to my hands in a surge of pins and needles.

'You will not receive your passport back at this moment.'

'What the hell is this all about?' I began. Now that I was out of the cell, I suddenly found myself enraged at the way I'd been treated. The deputy inspector general brought his hand down on the table with a bang.

'Silence!' he shouted. Then he leaned forward and looked me right in the eye. 'If I had my way, Mister Stone, you would rot in a cell for the rest of your miserable life – or be executed. It is against all my principles that I am allowing you to leave this building.' He pressed a button on his desk and the two guards came in. 'Take this man back to his office,' he said, then dismissed me with a flick of his hand, like he was batting away a fly.

As the heavies escorted me to the door, I stopped and turned back. I was about to ask where my ten grand was, but I checked myself. What the hell, I was out of there. The sooner I got to the judge, the sooner I would sort this out.

They dropped me off at the gates of the house. Security opened up, no problem, but I could sense a change in their attitude. Linda burst into tears when I appeared. She came towards me, concern on her face, her arms ready to embrace me. I didn't even hug her, I knew I stank. I told her I'd be back in five and hurried on up to our room. In the bedroom I took out the pistol, threw off my clothes and went into the bathroom. I was still showering when she came up to tell that me Judge Williams had just arrived and was sitting downstairs with Doug. I got out and started drying myself. 'When did Doug get back?' I asked her.

'Last night. I was so worried, Rob. Why were you kept overnight and he wasn't?'

That's what I would like to know too, I thought, but right now I didn't want to speak or think about it. 'Let me deal with our visitors,' I said. 'Then I'll fill you in.' As she left the room to go deal with the kids the usual question was there in my mind: how much should I tell her?

The Judge shook me by the hand and brought me up to speed. It seemed he had worked his magic. None of the other expats were under investigation and he would soon have the ships back at work. I turned to Doug, who'd been standing there saying nothing. 'What about Barry?' I asked. 'What the hell was he doing down at police HQ? And you, for that matter?'

Doug took a deep breath. 'Soon as you left they came and arrested me,' he said. 'Brought me here and shoved me in a room with him. It – uh, it looks like he's been talking,' he said.

'Talking?'

'Yeah, as in ratting you out, the sonofabitch. They asked me to corroborate his statement. Said Barry and I could send you down and take over the company.'

'Jesus,' I said. I didn't say that I'd feared as much. I sat down. 'So what's he told them?'

'That he's got proof you were involved in drug smuggling. Told them that he personally had prepared the *Adnil*.'

'Prepared?' I said. 'Didn't think to tell them that he sent it out to pick up a boatload of hash? And then set fire to the fucking engine room?'

Doug shook his head. 'No. His story is he prepared the *Adnil* for hash smuggling operations – for you. And he knows you were using the *Rig Mover* for pot smuggling in the South China Seas.'

'That's total bullshit,' I said, mainly for Judge Williams' benefit.

'Seems the US authorities were pissed off when they drew a blank in Brazil.'

'You mean when they destroyed my fishing business?'

Doug shrugged. '*We* know there were no drugs, but *they* think it's the only way you could've built up the business so fast. They think they just didn't catch you. And here you come to Nigeria, and within three years you have twenty-three supply vessels, coupla tankers, almost 1,000 employees, and you're turning over tens of millions – while the whole industry is in a slump.'

'So you can't fucking win, right?'

'Looks that way, Rob. Listen, they're obsessed with the idea that there's a massive cocaine and money-laundering scheme going on. They're determined to take you down.'

'But that's stateside,' I said. 'How did the Nigerians get involved?'

'Simple. The US authorities put the squeeze on them. All they have to do is arrest you, then they start extradition proceedings.' He paused, then said, 'Seems Barry used to burn ships for insurance money.'

'You're kidding.'

'No. Worked for some guy in Sharjah. Did a string of jobs. Lloyds started digging around, put a case together, targeted him and arrested him in the USA.'

'Now I get it,' I said. It was all starting to make sense.

'Yeah, he didn't wanna get extradited to the UK so he cut a deal.'

'What kinda deal?'

'Well, immunity of course – in exchange for which he incriminates you. So he comes to Nigeria, tells the police here the same story. Says the *Rig Mover* and the *Adnil* were mixed up in it.'

'The scheming little shit. He's trying to take me down, and the entire fucking business with me.' Even as I spoke I got the impression that Doug was enjoying this. Couldn't figure why, but that's the way it felt.

He carried on. 'But to give the Nigerian police their due, they demanded actual evidence of a drug smuggle – and proof that you'd taken the proceeds to buy the ships.' Doug shrugged. 'Of course, the fucker couldn't give it.'

'Well, you know what I always said, Doug. The federal government is a business. When they spend millions of dollars investigating you, sooner or later they're going to want a return on their investment.' Then I looked right at him. 'And you?' I said. 'What did you say to the police to get yourself released?'

'Me?' He sensed the menace in my voice. 'Ah come on, Rob. You know me better than that. I told 'em he was talking out of his kazoo. You could see their attitude change, big time. Attitude to Barry, I mean.'

'Yeah, it would. So what did they do with him?'

Doug laughed. 'Beat the shit out of him, dumped him on a plane and sent him back to the States.' As Doug spoke, I was thinking it all over. Maybe this wasn't as serious as I first thought. In all that Barry was supposed to have told them, the word 'Alaska' hadn't been mentioned once. He knew squat about it. Doug knew the basics, like what boat I used. He was the one who managed the handover back to the Norwegians when the *Deep Marianas* landed back in Rio. And of course, he knew where some of the money went. But not much else. The boats had a history of the aborted runs – but they couldn't prove shit with that, and in any case they weren't legally under my control at the time. The more I thought about it, the more I figured maybe this would be okay after all. Costly, sure, but okay.

I turned to Judge Williams. 'So, what do you advise? What do I do next?'

'In my opinion, the best thing would be for you, and Doug here, and your family, to leave the country.'

'Yeah, but the cops still have our passports – and they've told us we can't leave.'

'Do not worry,' he said. 'Leave it to me.'

Just as I was seeing the Judge out, I heard the phone ring in the hallway. I closed the door and picked up. 'Hello?' It was Jack. He sounded breathless.

'Listen, man. They know everything, fucking everything. Somebody's talked.'

I said, 'Relax. There's nothing to know. Barry went to the cops and told them a cock and bull story and it backfired on him. That's all there is to it. He got beaten half to death and sent back stateside – and you know what, it's what he deserves. It's what any fucker deserves who rats on me.' I paused, waiting for a response. At this stage Jack was on my list of suspects – he had to be – and there was a meaning in what I was saying. But Jack didn't seem to get it.

'No, I'm telling you,' he insisted. 'The feds know about everything. Everything we – listen, we gotta meet up, man.'

I was sweating now. There was every chance the phone was tapped and Jack was wired up. 'Listen,' I said, 'I don't know what you're talking about. And as for meeting up, I sure as hell ain't coming over to the States. I'm way too busy here.'

'Well I wouldn't be here if you did, man. I'm getting the fuck out, day after tomorrow.'

'To Europe?'

'Sure.'

'So you know what to do, don't you? Soon as you get over just check the want ads.' I hung up fast. I didn't hear his reply. Then I told Doug what Jack had said.

'That proves it,' he said. 'He's your other rat. Most likely working with Barry. We should set up a meeting.'

'I'm working on that.'

Doug nodded, then said, 'Yeah, and wipe the bastard out.'
I looked at Doug. His response had surprised me – especially the speed with which he had arrived there.

'Maybe,' I said, 'but first I need to know what exactly he disclosed. Like, how much.'

After Doug went to his room, I filled Linda in as well as I dared. I gave her the usual smokescreen – a shakedown over fuel, bribes and so on – then I called Tony in Rio. It was three in the morning his time. I told him to get hold of the captain on the 6,000-tonner and divert her to Montevideo. 'Find a buyer over there,' I told him. 'It shouldn't be a problem.' The fact was, after the run-in with the Nigerian authorities, I no longer trusted ECOMOG to pay for the loads. Why should they?

Next morning the Judge came back with good news. He'd fixed it for both Doug and me to get out. I thanked him, then asked the obvious next question. 'How much?'

He pursed his lips. 'This is an expensive business. I had to go to the very top.'

'And?' I said.

'One million dollars. You must pay it all before they will let you go. You are going to Scotland, I presume? And Mr Kane to Brazil?'

I nodded, then said, 'But there's no way I'm paying it all up front, no way. I'll pay half to get us out. Soon as my family and I are home – and soon as Doug gets to Rio – that's when you get the other half.'

'I will ask,' the Judge said. 'It may be they will accept if you agree to pay the other half to me in person, in London.'

'That'll be fine. So what about my ships? When can we free them?'

'I have set the wheels in motion. I should have clearance for them to carry on working within a few days.'

As soon as he'd gone I called Cristiano, our banker in Rio, and got him to send half a million to me in Lagos next day and another half million to Aberdeen. He told me the best way to shift that amount of cash was with chartered jets. There was no real customs search on them. Of course it bumped up the price, but what else was I to do? 'Okay, if we're chartering,' I told him, 'send the million to Lagos and have the jet refuelled and standing by ready to fly me and my family to Aberdeen.' That was me done. I put the phone down, went to find Linda and told her to pack. While she was shoving things from the bedside table into her case, she picked up my Hans Hass book. 'Never did read that,' she said.

'Take it,' I said. 'And listen, you take good care of it. It means a lot to me.'

That night I had a meeting with my expat staff. I told them I'd been hit with a shakedown. They knew how things worked. I told them it was more heavy than usual and I'd be leaving the country for a time. Meanwhile they should continue trading as normal. There were bound to be rumours, but they should ignore them. They took it in their stride. As the six of them sat there looking at me, I think I expected some sort of empathy. I was the one in the shit, after all. But what I saw was something else. Call it the dawning realisation that this could be a big break for them. With Doug and me out of the way, how much could they skim off before the whole house of cards came crashing down?

I left the meeting feeling punch drunk. I was staggering from crisis to crisis, barely able to maintain a grip on things. It seemed like a rerun of the Pescado de Brasil fiasco. But at least, if it all went belly up, I had that five million tucked away in Lichtenstein. I'd get by.

The money from Cristiano arrived the next day. I sent a car and escorts to pick up two of the bagmen; the other two remained on board with the balance. They were all former cops, Brazilians. We'd used them several times. I checked the contents of the briefcase and called the Judge over to the office. He assured me he'd negotiated the 50/50 payment plan, and I handed the case over. He was back a couple of hours later with our passports. 'I depart for London tomorrow,' he said. 'When can I expect the balance to be paid?'

'I'm flying to Aberdeen,' I said. 'From there I'll come down to London. Give me a day.'

His eyes were smiling as he said, 'Wonderful. Why don't we meet at the Dorchester? They serve an excellent lunch there.'

'Sure,' I said. 'Look forward to it.'

Linda was packed. Doug hugged me as he left to catch his flight to Rio. I told him I'd contact him as soon as I got home. Then Linda and the kids and I got in the other car and made our way to the airport.

As our plane took off, my little boy gripped my hand. I smiled at him, then looked out the window at the land rapidly falling away beneath us. I looked at the vast sweep of blackened mangrove swamp, the rainbow patterns where the oil had spilled out onto the rivers, blighting so many lives, and I guess a part of me was relieved to be out of there. But deep down I was in despair about the fix I'd got into – and grieving for all the dreams that seemed to be breaking into pieces.

19

Aberdeen and London,
October 1992

It was around mid-afternoon when we flew into Aberdeen. From there we drove up to the house. While Linda fed the kids, I got on the phone and booked a seat on the overnight sleeper to London. Flying down with a case full of money was out of the question. Way too risky with all the security checks. Linda didn't understand why I was in such a hurry. Didn't I want to catch up on some sleep? I could hardly tell her I was delivering half a million in cash to a senior member of the Nigerian judiciary. In her world, that sort of thing happened in movies. I told her it was a condition of my release from police custody that I report to Scotland Yard in person, and I'd be back the day after tomorrow. Then I called the Judge to confirm our appointment. I wanted this thing done, and done fast. There were other things piling up in my mind.

I arrived at Kings Cross Station around eight the following morning and took a taxi to the Cadogan Hotel on Sloane Street. Not fancy, but a great location. The fact is,

I was known there. I always used the place when I was in London. Even now, months after my last visit, one or two of the staff met me with a smile and addressed me by name. The way I was feeling, a friendly greeting seemed to mean a lot.

I arrived at the Dorchester at noon, as agreed. I was imagining we'd have a glass of mineral water, I'd hand over the money and then maybe we'd get a spot of lunch. This was business and I wanted to keep it that way. Not so, Judge Williams. I found him in full Nigerian dress, already sitting at a table. In front of him was a bottle of champagne in an ice bucket. It was open, and his glass was full. We shook hands and I sat down, putting the briefcase under the table, but nearer him than me. The waiter drained what was left from the bottle into my glass. A couple of mouthfuls at most. I noticed it was Cristal we were drinking. Fancy stuff, at a very fancy price. The Judge leaned forward, grasped the briefcase and pulled it closer to him. 'For me?' He didn't utter the words out loud, just shaped his mouth around them. When I nodded, he smiled and raised his glass. 'Here's to the success of your departure from Nigeria,' he said.

As the Judge sat back, put on his glasses and surveyed the menu, I realised that the sonofabitch was celebrating. He'd just taken possession of half a million bucks and it was clear it was heading for one of his accounts in Europe. Now I saw it. He'd paid the police. They hadn't set the price of my freedom at a million bucks. Or, if they had, he'd talked it down – supposedly on my behalf. Now he was pocketing half a million of my money, the grasping piece of shit.

After he'd ordered, he sat back in his chair and looked around at the opulent surroundings, the pillars, the heavy drapes, potted palms. 'I like England,' he said. 'I like it very much. You know, I came here as a naïve young man, to study law at Oxford. I had such a lot to learn. I was an idealist back then. Later, I came to London.' He chuckled and sipped the last of his champagne. 'In London I continued my education. It is a very worldly place. It made me a very worldly man.' I didn't answer. He'd said all that needed saying.

The waiter brought us another bottle of Cristal, then the food started to arrive. Lobsters, oysters, prawns … a bowl of caviar. I love seafood, and I'd hardly eaten a bite since flying out from Lagos, but on this occasion I barely touched what was in front of me. My mind was elsewhere. I was thinking about Muscles, about Doug. Jack too. Besides, the Judge was eating enough for two men, and trying to tell me about all the women he'd known in his London days. I switched off. It was only when I heard him say something about 'and it may be that it cannot be fully loaded' that I realised he was talking business again, talking about my tanker, the big one.

'I beg your pardon?' I said.

'You must understand that there will be difficulties in the light of your arrest and the accusations made against you.'

'Even if the accusations are unfounded?'

The Judge dabbed at his lips with a napkin. 'They have a saying here, don't they? There is no smoke without fire. But I will do my best.' I waited for the rider, because I knew it was coming. 'Of course,' he added, 'there will be a significant cost factor.'

'Yeah,' I heard myself say, 'I already figured that.' The table was littered with the debris of demolished shellfish. It reminded me briefly of my days longline fishing and the parties we would have after we'd landed a catch. I wondered whether this was the beginning of the end of the good times. Not for the Judge. I watched him push away his plate and order coffee and cognac. He offered to get some for me, but I declined. I was trying to unscramble my mind.

Ten minutes later, he was checking his watch. He reached for the briefcase and stood up. Said he had an appointment. He picked up the bill, frowned and patted his pockets, where his wallet might have been, then shrugged and dropped the slip of paper onto the table. Numb with anger, I watched him walk away. I grabbed one of the white linen napkins and wiped my hands. Without thinking I shoved it in my pocket on my way to pay the bill. Then I walked out onto Park Lane, turned towards Hyde Park Corner and took the first left. I needed to make some calls, and for that I needed the usual pile of coins.

I found a bank right around the corner on Curzon Street, with a payphone nearby. First call was to Tony. I asked him what news he had, and what he told me almost floored me. Doug had been arrested when he landed in Rio, right off the plane. He didn't yet know what for. He was still in police hands. Tony had called our Brazilian lawyers immediately and was waiting to hear what they could do. As for the tanker, he told me that was on its way to Montevideo, and should arrive in a couple of weeks. He had retained an agent who was looking for someone to buy its cargo of fuel. So that part, at least, was working out. I told Tony where I was staying, and to keep me up to date.

The second call was to Jack's house in Aspen. His wife said he'd left the day before to go sailing. I hung up – you don't sail in the Colorado Rockies. It sounded to me like he was already on his way to Europe. As I stood in the booth, thinking it through, the phone started ringing. I hesitated, then picked it up. Nothing, just a dead line. I didn't like that; it was not a good sign. I took out the napkin and wiped the phone, nice and careful.

I made my way to another phone box and called Eric, my first mate on the Alaska trip. His wife answered and said he was out; she didn't know when he would return. I hung up. Almost immediately it rang back. I picked it up and, once again, no one was there. I replaced the receiver, wiped down all the surfaces of the phone and the door, and left the box fast. So Eric's phone was tapped as well as Jack's.

I took a cab back to the hotel. One of the benefits of staying at the Cadogan was that they had a storage facility. I could leave documents, suits, shirts, extra shoes and gym gear in there. I slipped a UK passport and various other bits of ID in the name of Anthony Adams into my pocket. Then I picked up a small travel case, where I put my Robert Stone passport and ID in the lining before packing a few things and heading for Victoria Station. There, I bought a ticket for Paris, via Dover and Calais. An hour later, as my train slipped out of the station, I realised I'd forgotten to call Linda. She was expecting me home – possibly that night, certainly the next day. At that moment, I had no way of knowing what lay ahead, let alone that it would be three full years before I set foot on British soil once more.

20

France, Switzerland, Spain, Brazil and Uruguay, November–December 1992

I arrived in Paris that evening as Anthony Adams and put up in a hotel barely five minutes' walk from the Gare du Nord. First thing next morning, I picked up a copy of the *Herald-Tribune* and scanned the want ads. There was nothing for me. I found a phone booth, called their office and placed a coded ad for Jack to meet me in Zurich. I checked out of the hotel and took a cab to the Gare de Lyon where I put a suitcase with a change of clothes in a left-luggage locker. Then I scanned the timetable and booked myself on a mid-morning train to Geneva.

It was getting dark when I arrived, and snow was falling. Normally I would've been excited. I love the snow, love skiing, but right now the wintry landscape seemed to reflect the dark mood that was enveloping me. From Geneva I took another train to Montreux, about an hour away. I had two safety deposit boxes there, one containing only cash and the other containing further sets of ID. I put my Stone papers and the Anthony Adams IDs in the cash-only box;

from the other I took out a British passport and driver's licence, both in the name of William Hammond.

All of my passports were in the names of real, living people and all were legitimate – until I started using them, that was. Bill Hammond, for example, was an actual UK citizen from Barnet, in north London. I'd got his passport, as I got all of them, from a guy who lived down in Malaga. He had a beautiful little scam going. Every so often he'd visit London and scout around for a subject about the same age as the client he had in mind. The guy had to have no criminal record and he must never have possessed a passport. That kind of narrowed the field down, as most people travel abroad these days, so he ended up homing in on down-and-out types, losers. Once he found a suitable target he would make the guy's day by giving him £5,000 for his birth certificate and any other ID. Their part of the deal was, they would never apply for a passport. My part was that I would only ever use these passports outside the UK, and after a maximum of two years I'd destroy them. My fee to the guy in Malaga? £10,000. Like I said, it was a nice little scam. Neat.

From Montreux I called Tony again. He had news. On the face of it, the reason Doug had been arrested was the Drug Enforcement Agency in the States putting the squeeze on the Brazilians. He was in a jail in Rio. There was, however, a further complication: the Brazilian police now wanted to charge him as well. When they arrested him they searched his place and found a stack of photographs, the ones he liked to produce for me every time he wanted to boost his dumb ego: good-looking young hookers he'd been screwing. The charge in Brazil was conspiracy to traffic young women.

When Tony went to see Doug he was screaming for me to come over and get him out. He would not have been having a fun time in that jailhouse. I told Tony to tell him I'd come as soon as I could, and be patient. Meanwhile, our lawyers could do nothing. As to the tanker, Tony reckoned it would be arriving in Montevideo shortly. Also, the news from Nigeria wasn't good. The expats in Warri were sweating, wanting advance payments to be wired to their banks. Either we produced, or they'd all quit.

I talked that through with Cristiano, got him to send some money, and then took it easy for twenty-four hours before heading for Zurich. With time on my hands, I called Linda and reassured her I was dealing with tax affairs. She had been worried half to death. She smelled trouble and told me so. I promised to keep her up to date. I spent half of that first day in Zurich watching the rendezvous point. Three or four times I saw Jack appear, wait around a few minutes, then split. He knew the score, and I knew he would be cool about it – I had to be 100 per cent satisfied that he wasn't being followed. It was in both of our interests, and that's the way he would've played it.

When we finally met up, we walked around the city for a couple hours. He told me his legal team had advised him that there were sealed indictments on me, him, Dominic and around forty other people involved with the Alaskan smuggle and distribution.

Sealed indictments aren't used that often. They're used when the authorities want to round up a bunch of suspects all at once. What they do is, they go to a grand jury and present the evidence they have. The magistrate decides whether there's enough evidence to press charges and may, if it seems useful, allow the indictments to be sealed while the authorities track down the suspects and swoop. Once the magistrate's clerk has sealed the indictment, its very existence remains secret until a warrant is to be issued

– so not even the guys they're after get wind of it. So if they were sealed, how the fuck did Jack know about them? That was mistake number one.

According to Jack, the problem was Eric's wife's brother. He had found out that Eric had money in the safe, helped himself to 2 million and then turned the guy in to the cops. Jimmy, who was a very long-term friend of mine and had been one of my crew members on the *Deep Marianas*, was also arrested, along with another of the crew, Tommy. It seemed that Tommy had then rolled on Jack and me, thereby also implicating Doug – even though Doug had nothing to do with it. This all seemed plausible, until Jack said something else that made me doubt every word he'd said.

Mistake number two: Jack told me the feds had come to him and offered a deal. He could stay out of jail and keep his house and his money; all he had to do was turn everyone else in – especially me. He said he'd gone to his wife and told her about it. She reminded him that most of us now had young families. If he ratted on us she would leave him, period. That, he told me, is when he decided to skip the country and head to Europe.

I had a different interpretation. The way I figured it, Jack had tried to cut the deal and told on everyone. His wife wouldn't accept the deal, so he ran instead – because he had to. The fact was, the feds now knew everything, had everyone indicted and had started making the arrests, but with me having paid my way out of Nigeria and Jack getting to Europe, there were two big fish who'd slipped the net.

Being on the run is no cakewalk, and Jack had the usual practical problems. He wanted to know whether I could get him a couple of passports under assumed names. Sure, I told him, I can do that. I told him to get photographs, then named my price. The passports would cost him fifty grand

apiece – half up front and half on delivery. He squealed
some, then agreed. He had no choice. He told me that
while he was waiting he was going to live on his yacht in
Mallorca. We agreed to meet up there in four weeks' time.

I was in such a state by now that I seriously thought of
going down there and wiping him out. It was only when I
phoned Linda next day and tried to bullshit her about what
I was up to that I found myself thinking, what's happening
to me? I always thought of myself as some kind of pirate, a
freebooter, a guy who played fast and loose with the law –
but a guy who was, deep down, straight, loyal and decent.
And now I was thinking of blowing away a former partner.
What was I turning into, a fucking killer? Is that what was
happening? But then I thought it over some more. The law
was gunning for me. Maybe that automatically redefined
me as a criminal. It wasn't a feeling I liked, at all.

After I got Jack's photos, I left by train for Spain, but
I didn't go direct. First I got a ticket to Geneva. As soon as
I arrived there I bought another ticket, this time for Paris.
Then I went to the left-luggage locker and traded clothes.
I put William Hammond away and pulled out Bobby
Greenwood, my only US passport. I'd never used it before
so it was totally clean. The kid had died at birth back in the
1950s. I filed for copies of his birth certificate and I was
able to use this to get the passport. They didn't check birth
certificates against death records.

I called Linda again to make sure she was okay. I told her
I was heading to Amsterdam. I was pretty sure my phone
was tapped, and as soon as I rang off I bought a ticket to
Marseilles instead. Once there I bought another ticket to
Barcelona and crossed the border without a hitch. Finally,
I took a local train to Malaga. Doing it in stages that way
made it less likely anybody could trace my movements.

I surprised my passport dealer as he was heading to his corner café for an early morning espresso. Walked out of a side street, grabbed his arm and frightened the living shit out of him. After he'd calmed down, he told me he thought something had gone wrong and I was there to wipe him out. Not for the first time, I found myself wondering why people were frightened of me. I apologised, bought the guy breakfast, and explained that I hadn't dared call him as there was too much heat right now. I told him I was going to need several passports as soon as he could get them. I gave him two photos of myself and two of Jack and explained there would be more needed when I returned in about a month's time.

With that in place, I took a train to Madrid and boarded a plane to Buenos Aires. After spending the night there, I flew on to Montevideo. I thought things were going to calm down now. I called Tony to find out whether the tanker had shown up. It had. I was all set to ask the next question – do we have a buyer lined up? – when he socked me right where it hurt. 'It was seized on arrival,' he said.

'You what?'

'They think we're using it for smuggling.'

'Smuggling what, for fuck's sake?'

I heard him take a breath. 'Cocaine,' he said.

'Cocaine? Why the fuck would anybody smuggle cocaine into South America? It's a cottage fucking industry down there. Man, this is crazy.' I banged my fist against the side of the phone booth. 'Jesus Christ.'

'They got a theory,' he said.

'Go on. This I gotta hear.'

'They think you diluted it in the fuel.'

'You are fucking pissing me, man. That is totally insane.' Something in Tony's tone told me he hadn't finished. 'Okay,' I said, 'let's have the rest of it.'

'The crew are all under arrest until the results come back from the lab.'

'Which they could fix any way they want to, right?'

How I was going to straighten out this sorry mess I couldn't imagine, but Doug I could help. He was still in jail, seriously pissed off. He thought I was neglecting him. I couldn't fix it from Montevideo, so I flew up to São Paulo and called on Cristiano. He'd heard what had happened to Doug and presumed I would be staying the hell out of Brazil.

We soon worked out a deal that would get Doug out. With the help of a friendly cop we obtained a forged release certificate for him. That was stage one. Next up, we arranged for a car to take him to the airport where he would get a ticket and boarding pass for Paris. Just in case the airport was being watched, we had a contact of Cristiano's who worked there. He would crash the airport's computers for the crucial ten minutes while he boarded. That way, his passport details wouldn't go through the system. So that was the plan, all set up. Now I had to get the details to Doug himself. He had to receive those in person, and the only person he would take it from – the only person right now that he trusted – was me.

Cristiano's lawyers made arrangements for me to be allowed access. I would go as Doug's US lawyer. Seeing him shook me; the guy was filthy, unshaven and had lost weight. I got the impression he wasn't fully concentrating on what I was saying. Christ knows what they'd been doing to him in there, but I didn't have time to find out. The point of the visit was to get the plan across to him and make sure he remembered it. After that it was down to him.

His first response was that I was bullshitting him. He figured it was all a set-up, and the minute he walked out the prison gates he'd be blown away by me, Cristiano's hit men or the cops. He was so jumpy I almost thought he was going to turn me in to the prison guards, earn himself a few bonus points and maybe a pack of cigarettes. That's when I lost it. 'You're an ungrateful fuck,' I told him. 'Listen, you got two choices. When the release paper comes you take it and go home, or you stay in this shithole and use it to wipe your sorry ass. After which they fucking extradite you to the good old US of A. Your pick, my friend.'

In the end he saw the light. 'Okay' he said, 'okay. I'll do what you say.' I told him he was booked on a flight to Paris in a few days' time. Soon as he got there he was to go to the Hotel Angleterre, right by the Champs Elysées. It all seemed simple enough. In the end, it took far longer than we expected to get him out – months – but at least we were able to get food and money to him inside.

From the prison, I went to see Cristiano to authorise the payment to the cop. Then I took off for the airport and boarded my own flight to the French capital. Once there, I went to the Gare de Lyon and got my suitcase out. I took out the passport of Anthony Adams and went into a toilet where I destroyed all the Bobby Greenwood ID. That was one guy who no longer existed. I burned the photo page and tore the rest into pieces before flushing everything down.

By the time I boarded the train for a repeat of that fractured journey down to the south of Spain, my head was pounding. Linda was starting to ask more questions every time I called her; my money was running out fast. I was still trying to work out who had flipped and here I was once more tracing patterns across Europe. As the train sped through the night, I realised that a profound change was overcoming me. I was turning into a fugitive.

21

Spain, France and Switzerland, January– October 1993

It was mid-afternoon when I arrived in Palma de Mallorca and took a cab out to the marina. Jack had told me to meet him at a bar down by the water. The sun was out and it soothed my aching head. I was carrying a light case with the bare minimum of clothing, plus a bum bag with ID and cash. We strolled along the jetty to his yacht, *Zephyrus II*, a beautiful aluminium-hulled yacht which had won a Whitbread Round the World Race some years previously. It had come into Jack's hands after an accident, when it was crushed between two freighters in the Panama Canal. Maybe Jack had got the idea from me and my *Caledonian* project, but he bought it as an insurance write-off, took it to the Dutch shipyard where it had originally been constructed and had them do the conversion from sleek, spartan racing vessel to the beautiful luxury yacht that was his current home.

Jack suggested we should get away from Mallorca. It was too crowded for his liking right now, and we were both edgy. We set sail the next day for Ibiza, anchored there overnight, then went on to its smaller, sister island, Formentera, dropping the hook off the Playa de Ses Illetes. It was a beautiful spot, with white sand stretching out to a blue, blue sea. We spent a couple days there, going ashore to the beach during the day and visiting the fish restaurants and bars in the evening. Although it was wintertime, down here it seemed like perpetual summer. We walked along beaches dotted with people playing volleyball. Some were even swimming in the flat, calm water. Music played outside the cafés and everywhere you looked there were beautiful girls from northern Europe. For those two days it felt like we were on vacation – and I realised I'd almost forgotten what that was like over the past few months.

Being relaxed, being at ease, and despite the doubts that crowded my mind, I was able to enjoy Jack's company. As one of my oldest friends, he'd shared some good times with me, exciting times. Could he have ratted on me to the feds? I found it hard to believe. All he wanted to talk about right then was how he feared losing his family, his home, his money, his freedom and his precious yacht – everything, in fact. He did seem genuinely scared, same as I was. We were certainly on the same wavelength there, and unless he had acquired some fantastic acting skills, he surely couldn't have been faking the concern he expressed. And yet this was the guy who, only a few weeks ago, I'd seriously thought about killing. I handed over his passports and he gave me the hundred grand. I had no problem taking the money from him. Somehow, whether directly or indirectly, he had played a part in all this shit, so why shouldn't he make this worth my while?

We headed back to Palma after a couple of days. We both had things to do. Jack was going to head over to the Alps, the French side, Chamonix most likely. He'd rent a house there and keep his head down. We agreed to meet up in a month's time.

I took the ferry to Barcelona and the train back to Paris. I felt rested. Having had time to think, I'd decided I needed to do just what Jack was doing: find a hideaway and disappear for a while – a year, maybe two. There was no way I could return to the UK, and I was missing Linda and the babies real bad. The more I thought about where I could go, the more I kept coming back to the Alps. I couldn't go to Switzerland. You try buying or renting a property over there and they hit you with some pretty thorough background checks. Chamonix was out of the question with Jack being there, but I liked the idea of being in the Haute-Savoie. It wasn't far from Geneva, where I had money, and there were good train services if I needed to travel.

In Paris, I got busy. There was no point in delaying; I bought a black Range Rover using the cash I'd got from Jack, and headed out of the city, driving east until nightfall when I stopped at a hotel somewhere in Alsace, near the German border. Next day, I headed down to the Alps and put up in a *pension* in Annecy. I spent most of the next two weeks looking around for a place. I wanted it to be fairly remote, but at the same time I'd need shops, maybe even schools. I wanted a place where they got a lot of visitors passing through, a place where my presence wouldn't attract any curiosity.

After a couple weeks, I settled on the village of Megève, almost under the shadow of Mont Blanc. It was a year-round resort, originally founded by the Rothschild family as a sort of rival to St Moritz. Linda and I had skied there a number of times before we had the children – she would enjoy it. I could take the kids skating and skiing when they got a little older, maybe teach my son how to play ice hockey. I was planning long term, that's how dumb I was.

I now looked around for a house. I soon found an *agence immobilière* that had a chalet available. I took a look, decided I liked it, and paid a year's rent upfront, in cash. They nearly kissed me. From the moment I stepped through the door of the place I felt some of my strength and vitality returning. After almost a year of being on the run and living in hotels, I had a base once more. No reception clerk watching my movements, no fear of the police calling in to check the register. Even so, I kept up my habit of making any calls from payphones a good hour away by car. I was damned if I was going to give myself away.

To call Linda, I drove all the way to Albertville, along the road to Grenoble. I told her she needed to go to a payphone in a village about thirty minutes away from where we lived. I chose that one for the simple reason that I'd used it so often I'd memorised the number. She wasn't at all happy about turning out with the kids for an hour's round trip in the middle of winter, and kicked up a fuss. One needed feeding, the other needed a nap, and why did I need to be so furtive all the time?

I was too uptight to explain a damned thing at that moment. 'Just shut the fuck up,' I shouted down the phone, 'and be in that phone booth an hour from now, you got that?' I could hear one of the kids wailing in the background. I shut my eyes and slammed the receiver down. This was the way it had to be. If I let down my guard I could be traced, and that would be it, game over.

I got back in the car, drove for an hour and called her back. When she answered, her voice was hoarse with crying, her every sentence broken by sobs and shushes as she tried to comfort the baby. I waited 'til she'd calmed down, and apologised. 'Listen,' I said. 'I'm in a jam. I can't explain it on the phone, but the tax authorities are after me and I can't come back to the UK. I got to stay abroad.'

'I get that bit,' she said. 'I'm not stupid, you know. I just don't understand why you need me to be rushing around in the middle of nowhere.'

'Because they'll be tapping our phone,' I said.

'But you're not a criminal,' she said. 'Are you?'

'Course I'm not, honey. But these people are getting heavy. There's a lot of money at stake. Look, the bottom line is, you're going to have to come out here to see me. You and the babies.'

I then had to explain that I couldn't have her buying tickets using her credit cards. She had to pay cash. She had more questions; she always did. She knew I was bullshitting. 'Listen,' I said, 'the longer we talk, the greater the risk. Just do as I ask, get yourself out here with the kids and I'll explain everything.' Then I told her that even buying tickets was dangerous. Maybe she should get her father on the case. Get him to buy them. Say they were a birthday present or something. 'Look, just get yourself out to Geneva and I'll meet you there. Then I can explain everything.'

I'd said all I needed to say. I told her I'd call back in a couple days on the same number, same time, and she could give me the flight details. I told her that if for any reason things went wrong, or if she suspected that the police had become aware, she wasn't to tell me; instead, she would slip the code word 'Hans Hass' into whatever she was telling me. We fixed a time for our next call, then I hung up.

I now needed to call Tony and find out what was happening in Rio. I soon wished I hadn't. Just about all my ships were now off hire, the oil companies were months behind with their payments, and Fraser White had telexed to say his deal was off. In Nigeria, Z Group was calling every day asking where the hell I was and all the expats had quit. The only good news was that Doug had finally left prison and made his way to Paris as arranged.

Right now I needed cash. There was plenty of that in the Coastal Shipping accounts, but even there I had a problem. Only Robert Stone could draw on that account, and he was effectively dead and buried. Maybe I should've seen that coming, but the fact remains that I didn't. It's one thing to kill yourself off, another to bring yourself back to life when you feel like it.

This was turning into a long day, and I had plenty more work to do. Determined to be disciplined about leaving as few traces as possible, I got in the Range Rover once more and drove for an hour. I pulled up at a payphone outside a service station and called my bankers in Vaduz. The receptionist answered. I asked for Harry Grünwald – either him or his brother. 'Yes, sir, and may I ask who is calling?'

I opened my mouth to answer her and froze. Fuck. Who was I? Which ID was I using and which name had I used for the bank account? I hung up, caught my breath, closed my eyes and forced myself to concentrate. I actually said the words out loud. '*Concentrate, you dumb fuck.*' It took a full minute, but I figured it out. William Hammond. That's who I was when I opened the account.

I called back, apologised for being disconnected, and the woman put me through to Harry. I started to explain that I had a cash flow problem and needed to release some funds. I didn't get very far before he interrupted me. 'I'm very sorry, Mister Hammond.' The tone of his voice gave it away: there was a problem. I remember standing there looking out the window of the little booth wondering what he was going to hit me with. 'I'm sorry, sir, but the United

States government has asked us to put a freeze on all of those accounts.'

'What do you mean, *those* accounts? What accounts you talking about?'

'We refer to accounts in the name of your associate, Jack McBain.'

'And what the hell's that got to do with me?'

'As I said, you are an associate of his, and as such we fear that you may be implicated in the same offences of which he is suspected.'

'And what are they?'

'Drug trafficking, Mister Hammond. At least, that is what the United States government tells us.'

'So what you're telling me is that my account is frozen too?'

'Yes. Precisely so.'

'Let me put you right, buster. You're telling me I'm an associate of this guy? You've been misinformed. We're friends, that's all. I've never done business with him. No reason to. And let me ask you, have the US government told you to freeze my accounts? Is that what you're saying?'

'No, sir. But we're taking what we consider necessary precautions.'

'I get it. Guilt by association. Well, let me tell you, you've no right to keep hold of my money. But I'm a reasonable man, Mr Grünwald. I'll get you your assurances that I am not a business associate of Mr McBain. Meanwhile, I'd like to have access to the contents of my safe deposit box.' This was the last shot in my locker, and it misfired. The sonsabitches told me they 'didn't think that would be prudent'.

I resisted the temptation to kick the phone booth to pieces. Instead, I drove to Albertville, parked at the station and took an overnight train to Paris.

I arrived early next morning and spent half the day trying to locate Doug. When I finally caught up with him, he greeted me like I was the US cavalry riding to the rescue. He looked better than last time I'd seen him, but his face was creased with worry and his skin was pale and blotched. He'd left Rio with hardly any cash, and what I had given him was all gone; in France he had no means of getting any more.

We found a restaurant, ordered a meal and a carafe of wine, and I asked him how his getaway had gone. 'Oh man,' he said, 'that was one monumental screw up. I'm waiting, like months. I dunno. They treated me better after you visited but, Jesus, I thought I was there 'til I dropped. Then one day – boom! They take me out of my cell and down the corridor, right? They're setting me free. So where's my release paper? I ask them. Oh, don't worry – it's at the main gate. We get out into the compound and the wind's blowing like fuck. We march to the main gate and just as they open up there's this guy running up with a piece of paper in his hand. There you are, says the head guard. There's your release. The guy who's waving it doesn't have a fucking clue what he's supposed to be doing. He tries to hand it to some guy on the gate and lets go of it. Next thing it's blowing down the road, half a dozen guards are running in and out of the traffic chasing it down and I'm standing there in handcuffs.'

'But they got it, right?'

'Did they hell. It was some street kid. Thought somebody had dropped a hundred dollar bill or something and dives for it, right in front of a bus. The driver slams the brakes on, the kid ducks out the way, and there's my freedom pass under the front wheels. Fucking guard had to crawl underneath and rescue it.' Doug looked at me and raised his glass. 'Well, man, here's to liberty. And remind me if I ever get locked up again to make damned sure it ain't in fucking Brazil.' Then he turned and said, 'So tell me about that sonofabitch Jack. You fixed him?'

I shook my head. 'Listen,' I said, 'I been down to see him. He's cool.'

'Cool? Whaddayou mean cool? The guy's fucking ratted us out. You shoulda wasted him.'

'No,' I said. 'I don't think he talked. I can't prove it, but it's a gut feeling. What can I say?'

'I still say you shoulda whacked him.'

I persuaded Doug to drop it for now. We'd get back to it in a few weeks, arrange a meeting for all three of us and iron things out. Meanwhile, I told him, he needed to get a haircut and start eating properly. 'You look like shit, and I need some new passport photos of you.' He didn't like that – thought it might compromise him somehow. 'So how else you gonna get a passport?' I asked him.

'Okay,' he said. 'Okay. I'll do it.'

After I parted company with Doug, I called Linda. She was there right on time, sounding a lot happier. She said her dad had bought all the tickets in his name. He liked a bit of cloak-and-dagger stuff. He'd worked in the Special Operations Executive during the war, and once told me that returning to normal life had been a disappointment to him. I got the flight details off Linda, told her to expect a car to meet her, and left her to get on with packing.

22

Haute-Savoie and Paris, France, and Ibiza, Spain, November 1993–March 1994

Excited as I was about Linda and the kids coming over, I was edgy as hell. So edgy that I decided to send a limo taxi to meet them. Nothing conspicuous, just a van with seats. I hired a driver in St Gervais and gave him the flight number, her name and a description. I told him to bring them to a hotel in the centre of town. Even then, I was wary about greeting them in the open. Instead, I found a spot from which I could observe the entrance. My fear was that some sort of surveillance operation would be set up, with my family as the bait.

When I saw Linda and the kids get out of the van it was all I could do to stop myself running over and grabbing them. Jesus, I'd missed them so bad. Instead I left them waiting in the hotel lobby a full half hour before walking over. We hugged and kissed each other, then I picked up the single bag they'd travelled with and walked them to my car. All the way I was looking around, half expecting to see somebody jump out with a warrant in their hand. But nothing happened. We piled into the Range Rover and headed out of town, around the mountain to our new home.

Linda loved the chalet as soon as she walked in the door, said it was the perfect holiday home. That's when I told her it was permanent, that I couldn't go home and neither could she. She hit the frigging roof. 'What do you mean, we can't go home? Tell me what you've been up to. And no lies this time!'

There were times – and this was one of them – when I would've given anything to unload on her, to tell her the whole damned story. But I didn't dare. In part it was out of loyalty to my friends, in part a fear that she would reject me out of hand – either for all that I'd done or for the fact that I'd kept the truth from her. But it was her approval I needed, so I couldn't risk opening up, not fully.

In the end, I explained about people getting arrested. I put it all down to tax evasion charges, and she bought it. 'So the fact is,' I said, 'I need to fight this thing, and I can only do that here.'

'You mean in exile?' she said.

'You got it.' I thought I'd smoothed things over, but I hadn't. Telling her that I was now Anthony Adams and she had to call me Tony, and that I was going to get fake passports for her and the kids – that just fired her up all over again.

Linda wasn't naïve as such – she'd travelled, and she'd lived. But in my world she was a total innocent, and here I was trying to give her a crash course in living as a fugitive. She questioned everything, and I didn't help by losing my cool. Bit by bit, however, she accepted that she had to do as I said, even down to using the payphone to call her dad. In the end, I guess I had done one thing right. Finding this place in the mountains, with winter sports on tap, that was a good move. That part she liked.

The snow came early and the ski runs opened for business in the last week of November. I taught her to ski again, even gave lessons to my little boy, coming up to 3 now. Suddenly it felt like family life, which was a novelty to me. Then Christmas approached, and Linda naturally wanted to be home, or to bring her family out to France. She was homesick, and the worse it got the more she blamed me. We had a stand-up row about it, which ended with her screaming, 'Just pay the bloody taxes! Then we can go home.' I wished I could explain, but I didn't dare.

We got through Christmas in one piece, but by now I was getting nervous about Doug. What was he up to? I went up to see him in Paris. He'd met a Dutch girl and moved into her apartment. She was out when I showed up. Doug and I went into the city and reviewed our situation. Of all the guys involved in the Alaska job, only three were still at large. That was myself, Jack and Dominic Stopani, who was still back in Houston. I guess there was Muscles too, but he'd had nothing to do with Alaska. He was still on the run from charges arising from his smuggling activities in the 1970s.

Everyone else was now in jail, and we could hear the bastards singing from 3,000 miles away. From what we'd found out, there were up to 100 indictments against us. As Doug said, if I were caught, and the charges were proven, the American justice system would hand out prison sentences of several hundred years apiece. 'So what the fuck do I do?' I asked him.

'You wanna know?'

'I'm asking you, aren't I?'

'Okay. Here's what I think. We get Cristiano over and you sign the company over to him. I spoke to him and he has the paperwork already prepared.'

'You serious?'

'Listen, man. Your fucking assets are frozen, you're on the run and your business is gonna fold if we don't act. You sign it over to him, then you go into hiding – I mean serious hiding. Like ditch the family, dye your hair, the whole nine yards. Carlos will make sure your wife gets a regular income, and you'll get everything the company makes, less a commission for me and Cristiano.'

'Jesus. You make it sound easy. Ditch everybody and disappear, leaving you in charge. That's all, huh?'

'Rob, man, I've given it a lot of thought.'

As we spoke, it occurred to me that Doug might be looking for an opportunity to have Cristiano meet up with me, except that he'd send over a team of hit men instead. I needed time to think. 'Okay,' I said. 'I'll meet Cristiano, but gimme a few weeks. Let's say April.'

After seeing Doug I went down to Ibiza to check on Muscles. I told him to watch out for Doug as I no longer trusted the guy. Muscles laughed. 'I've known Kane almost as long as you have,' he said. 'There's no way he'd roll. Maybe you're getting paranoid. Maybe that's the problem.'

'Sure,' I said, 'I could be paranoid, but that doesn't mean the fuckers aren't trying to kill me.' The more I thought about it, the more I wondered whether Muscles had it right. The doubts were in my head all the time. Maybe they were starting to affect my judgement. That's what worried me now: was I seeing things the way they really were?

I returned to France and went to Chamonix. I wanted to talk to Jack. He wasn't troubled by doubts. He was planning more pot runs, but I half expected that. He'd been in touch with an old friend of ours who was now in Amsterdam. He could get containers through Dutch customs, and wanted to tap into our contacts to import huge loads of marijuana. 'Jack,' I said, 'we're already in the shit.'

Jack's response was typical of the guy. 'My point entirely, man. We're fucked as we are. Why not make some more money before the ship goes down?'

I could see his logic. I told him that if it wasn't for my family I'd be with him. Or maybe Doug and Jack were right. Maybe I should abandon Linda and the kids. What use would I be to them if I rotted in prison for the rest of my life? At least if I was free I could send them money.

I was in a bad place now, fearful for my freedom and my life, and uncertain about the wisdom of the decisions I was making. From Jack's place I headed to Montreux, where I still had some money in a safe deposit box. I took out fifty grand and wondered how long that would last. There was only a hundred left. After that I was broke, unless I could get access to my bank accounts. I needed a plan, and I needed it soon.

Back in Megève I went into retreat. Apart from Linda and the kids I didn't speak to another human being. In the daytime we skied. At night we sat by the fire, my baby daughter in my arms, sleeping peacefully as I watched the flames licking around the hearth. I weighed up all the possibilities. I reflected on my life so far. I thought about Linda and the children and what I wanted for them. It took me a couple of months of figuring, but in the end I saw it quite clearly, what I needed to do.

I told Linda I had a meeting with a lawyer in Paris. I took the train north. As soon as I got there I started making phone calls, lots of them. It took me a while, but I tracked down my lawyer friend, Charlie, in New York, a guy who had been like a father to me over the years. I told him the entire story – the Alaska gig, the frigging lot. If I was going to find the best lawyer available – and that's what I needed – I was going to have to be 100 per cent honest about everything, starting with him. He said he knew someone who might help, a guy called Christopher Forbes. We'd met, briefly, way back in my Bahamas days. He was now a very high-powered lawyer working for Jackson & Schneider in Washington DC. In Charlie's words, if anyone could save my skin, it was him. He would call Chris and set us up.

I gave him a couple of days, then made the call. I told Chris what I'd done and asked what I could do about it. He didn't beat about the bush. He asked me straight, 'Do you have money, serious money? Because this is going to be costly.' I told him I did. He told me he'd like a few days to think things over.

As soon as I put the phone down on Forbes I contacted a guy who used to work for me in Honduras. Barney was many things, but above all he was a man of action, a former soldier and now a mercenary. He would do anything he thought he could get away with if money was involved. He knew no fear. I asked him if he wanted to make fifty grand and he jumped at it. We set a date to meet up in Zurich.

I was focused now, knew exactly what I had to do. I felt good again, confident. I went to an arms dealer I knew and picked up a couple of .22 calibre pistols, fitted with silencers. That was me finished in Paris. I got the train south and relaxed. I'd broken the logjam.

Back in Megève the next day, I told Linda I had good news for her. Things were on the move, I said. I'd hired a hotshot lawyer who was going to get these revenue bastards off my back. She could go to Aberdeen with the kids, take a month off and catch up with things back home. She screamed with joy and started packing.

A few days later, first thing in the morning, I had her and the kids taken by taxi to Geneva airport. She was so happy to be leaving she hardly looked back. My little boy did, though. I stood there in the doorway of the chalet that had been our home for the past few months and watched them drive away. Dawn was breaking. The last thing I saw was his smiling face pressed against the window and his little thumb sticking up to wish me luck. Somehow, I managed to hold back the tears 'til they were out of sight.

We'd had fresh snow overnight. When the sun came up the scenery was heartbreakingly beautiful. I went into the garage and got my skis. As I rode the ski lift there were a thousand things on my mind. But up there in the mountains, I knew the fog would clear. My most enduring memory of that day is standing on a bank of fresh powder, looking around at a horizon of nothing but snow-covered peaks. There wasn't another soul in sight, not even the trace of where another skier might have been. It was pristine, it was still, it was silent – until I shouted, 'I'm free. I'm alive!' and the sound of my own voice came back to me off the neighbouring slopes. I think they call that 'living in the moment'.

Then I sped down the mountain. Linda and the kids were gone and I needed to get busy.

23

Haute-Savoie, Switzerland and Vaduz, Lichtenstein, March 1994

Back at the house, I dismantled the guns and covered the parts with bubble wrap, then wound duct tape around each package. Next job was to go the garage and start on the Range Rover. I took the inside door panels off and taped the packages to the frame. It wasn't exactly foolproof, but the likelihood of me having to undergo a rigorous search on the Swiss border was pretty remote. With my skis on the roof and a pile of down jackets, salopettes and so on hurled in the back, I'd be one of thousands on their way to enjoy the deep, clean snow that had accumulated over the winter.

Next morning, I drove to Zurich to meet up with Barney in his hotel, as arranged. When I checked in, the girl at the desk greeted me with a smile and addressed me in German. '*Alles Gute zum Geburtstag, Herr Hammond.*' I looked at her. I didn't understand. 'Happy birthday,' she said. It still didn't register. She took another look at my passport, frowned and said, 'But it's your birthday today, isn't it?'

I had to take the passport off her before I got it. This was Bill Hammond's birthday. 'Oh yeah,' I laughed. 'Thanks.' She was only young, so I said, 'The closer you get to 40, the less notice you take.'

I called Barney from the house phone in the lobby and arranged to meet up with him in the bar in half an hour. I then walked to the elevator with my bag, cussing quietly under my breath. Christ, I thought, it's basic errors like that gaffe at the desk that get a guy busted.

I got to my room and unpacked, then went down to meet Barney. He still didn't know what I had in mind, only that there was a good payday in prospect. We had a beer together, then went for a walk along the banks of the Linmat River towards the old town. As we leaned into the wind that was whipping up from the lake, I told him about the plan I'd come up with. I didn't tell him where we were going, nor who our targets were; I just gave him the outline – and what his role was to be. If he didn't like it, I would give him his expenses and he could walk away. This guy I trusted. There were no worries about security. He listened to what I had to say, checked his stride for a moment, then walked on, head down. 'Yeah,' he said, 'let's go do it!'

The following morning, we met in the hotel garage. We were both dressed in suits. Two guys going to do a bit of business with their bankers, very Swiss. We got into the truck and headed south. It was maybe 100km to Vaduz, and we made it in a shade over an hour.

Our first move was to take a look at the Grünwald brothers' homes. They lived very close to each other. I drove slowly and we made notes – like the type of house, what kind of stuff they had in the yard. At one of them we could see a woman in the kitchen, make out what she was wearing and the colour of her hair. Once we'd got that done we headed to town and pulled up at the guys' office, right across the street from their bank.

It was only 8.30 a.m. when we went through the big wooden door and into the foyer. The front desk was empty: the receptionist hadn't shown up yet, but Harry Grünwald was there. As soon as we walked into the foyer he appeared at the doorway to his office. We walked towards him. He tried to back away and close the door. I stuck a foot in the way. 'We've come to talk,' I said. Inside the office, Barney got hold of the door. Harry was trying to close it.

'You can't come in,' he said. 'Not without an appointment.'

Barney pulled his piece out, stuck it against the guy's head and said, 'Yeah, well we're in already, and we're making an appointment — now.' Harry let go of the door and Barney pointed to a chair, gave Harry a shove and said, 'Sit the fuck down.'

'Where's your brother?' I asked.

'He is *nicht* — he is not here.' He looked at his watch. 'He will arrive in some minutes.'

'Fine,' I said. 'We'll wait.'

Harry didn't seem to be listening. He couldn't take his eyes off Barney. Finally he turned to me and stammered, 'He is a killer, isn't he?' I nodded. If the guy was that scared we had the job half-done already. Just then, I heard the front door open. Barney shifted position so that he was behind the office door as Heinz Grünwald walked into reception. I showed Harry the gun I had in my attaché case. 'Call him in,' I said. 'And no funny stuff.' He looked at the gun and nodded.

Heinz entered the office. He looked shocked to see me, then he turned and saw Barney close the door behind him and point the pistol at him. Barney jerked the gun towards the empty chair next to Harry. Heinz got the message and sat down. It takes a very brave man not to be shitting himself in that situation, and neither Heinz nor his brother were strong on courage. 'What is it you want?' Heinz asked, his voice quavering.

I handed him a piece of paper. It was a deposit slip for an account in Vienna. 'It's very simple,' I said. 'I want you to give instructions to have the money wired out of my account with you and into this one.'

Heinz looked at the slip and passed it across to his brother. They both frowned and shook their heads, like some fucking comedy double-act. 'It cannot be done,' Harry said. 'Every account we manage has been frozen.'

'Well,' I said, 'you're just gonna have to unfreeze them, right?' Even as I spoke, I knew I was pissing in the wind.

'The United States government is going to examine all of the accounts,' Heinz said. 'Until they are done we cannot act. It's not just the law, the accounts themselves are no longer under our control. They are frozen by the government.'

I weighed up the possibilities – that he might be bluffing, or that he might be talking the straight truth. On balance, it seemed the US government might have done just what he was talking about – and for me and Barney the clock was ticking. Any minute now and the receptionist would show up, and that was a complication we could do without.

'Okay,' I said, 'that may be the case with the accounts, but I bet you didn't tell them about my safety deposit box, huh?' I could tell by the way they looked at each other that I was right. 'Guess you keep that secret for you and yours, huh?' The answer was written on their faces. 'Okay,' I said, 'this is what we'll do. Barney will escort you – you, Heinz – to the bank. You will open my safe deposit box. If you attempt to give any alarm signal he will shoot you in the head. We have men outside your home – the nice new chalet with the red roof and the yellow swing in the garden? The blonde wife at home with the green blouse on? Don't worry, pal, we've got it all covered, every last detail. Any fuck-ups, they kill your wife, then your children.' I turned and looked at Harry. 'And I will kill your brother. You got that?' He didn't answer as such, just kind of whimpered. 'So, you get the contents of my box and you bring everything back here. You both do what we say, and your families will be safe. You too.'

The fact is, at this point I didn't really care what happened once we got away. As far as the brothers were concerned I was William Hammond – and I knew that Hammond was going to be dead and forgotten within a few short hours.

I think Barney and Heinz were half an hour at the bank. It was the longest thirty minutes of my life. Of course, the brothers had no way of knowing we hadn't got any men outside their houses; neither did they know that we wouldn't have killed them. Barney was an enforcer, a tough guy, not a hired assassin. Thinking back, I reckon all they had to do was scream for the cops and everything would have been over. However, when it came right down to it, these were bankers we were dealing with, not action heroes. Barney finally came back with Heinz and the contents of the box. 'You emptied it?' I asked.

'Sure,' Barney said. '100 packs of $100 bills, 10,000 per pack. Total $1 million – just like you said.'

I turned to the brothers, still sitting in their chairs. 'Okay,' I said, 'we're leaving. Got that? We are leaving. You can report this incident to the police if you wish – but you're going to wait two full days. Any sooner, you and your families will die. Maybe next week, maybe in a year's time.

That's the way we do things. We can wait. Oh yeah, we can wait. The police won't protect you forever.' They nodded agreement and we walked out, just as the receptionist came through the front door.

Once out of town we headed for the Austrian border. I was sweating at the wheel, wondering whether the brothers had called the cops. Every instinct told me to put my foot down, but somehow I managed to stay within the speed limits. Barney occupied himself with breaking the guns apart for later disposal.

As soon as the border police saw the colour of our passports they nodded us through. Same again as we entered Switzerland, just a couple of guards beside a patrol car waving us on. I drove towards Zurich and dropped Barney at the airport, paid him his fifty grand and thanked him from the bottom of my heart. He seemed embarrassed. To him it was a job – and a well-paid one. To me it was new territory, gangster shit. There was no way I could've pulled that off alone, no way at all. As I made my way back to Montreux, I stopped along the road three or four times at rest stops, throwing the pieces of the guns into rubbish bins.

As I entered the town I felt the first faint glow of satisfaction. It had all gone to plan – like a Swiss watch, you might say. High on the feeling, I stopped to buy gas. I stood there at the pump until the vehicle was full, went to the shop and paid up, then drove off, an idiot grin on my face. I'd gone less than 100 yards when the Range Rover started bucking and farting, then shuddered to a halt. I smelled my fingers, then whacked the flat of my hand against the steering wheel. Diesel. I'd pumped her full of fucking diesel. Not a smart move when you've just done a stick-up on two Swiss bankers and walked away with a million bucks in cash …

I locked the truck and walked back to the gas station. From the way they reacted I could tell I wasn't the first customer within living memory to get it wrong. The guy even yawned as he called the tow truck. While he was on the phone I checked the racks for anything I might need.

The rescue guys arrived quickly. They said the car would be fixed by noon the next day. They gave me a ride to town and dropped me at a small hotel. I checked in with the brand new toothbrush I'd bought in the gas station and a million in cash. It seemed the perfect metaphor for the state of my life right now.

Next morning, after the truck was returned, I drove to Montreux and deposited the majority of the money in a bank I was using there. Against my better judgement, I hung onto the William Hammond passport. The way I figured it, I was damned if I was going to leave $4 million in the Vaduz accounts when it was legitimately mine. I'd come and get it – someday.

I chose to drive down the southern side of Lake Geneva to Martigny, and crossed the border just before Vallorcine. As I pulled up to the post, I picked the oldest border patrol guy on duty. I figured they wouldn't be so gung-ho when there was no chance of promotion.

I got through, no problem, and was approaching Chamonix when I sped round a corner and smack into a police roadblock. I nearly crapped in my pants as I slammed on the brakes. It was way too late to turn around without drawing attention to myself. The game was surely up. They were stopping every vehicle and looking inside, then waving them on. When I pulled up to them they looked at me, saw my skiing things and asked for my licence. They checked the details, then told me to pull over to the side. Fuck. Fuck. FUCK. For a brief moment, I wished I still had the guns. I tried to think what Barney would have done in the circumstances.

'Would you please step out of the car?' the cop said. Perfect English. I did as he said. Then he asked me, 'Have you been drinking?' The question took me aback. It was two o'clock in the afternoon.

'Of course not,' I answered.

He looked at me and said, slowly, 'Have you taken any alcohol?'

'No,' I said. 'What do you think I am?' He ignored the question, and told me I was required to take a breath test. I felt myself starting to relax. This was routine, surely. Nothing to worry about here. Then I remembered how recently I'd got rid of the pieces, and started to tremble. Jesus, that was a close shave.

The test ran negative. Better than negative, a big round o per cent. The cop smiled, and I was on my way. He even wished me '*bon voyage*'. Mercifully, he didn't seem to notice that I tried to start off in third gear, stalling it, nor the uncontrollable shaking of my hands as I corrected the error and made my way back onto the highway.

24

Haute-Savoie, April 1994

Back at the house, I made the call I knew I had to make. It took me a while. It was about summoning up the courage, the determination, to tackle this problem at its very root. The fact is, I wished I could just shut my eyes, go to bed and wake up to find it had all been dealt with. After an hour or two of prowling around the house, muttering to myself and fantasising about all kinds of scenarios in which my enemies woke up dead, or suddenly decided they had better things to do than pursue me, I picked up the phone, sat on the sofa and called Chris. I had a photo of Linda and the kids on the coffee table in front of me. I'd taken it when we were out skating. The news wasn't good. Chris confirmed that international warrants had been issued for my arrest.

'Okay,' I said, 'so what does that mean in practice?'

'It means I must advise that you have to turn yourself in, I'm afraid.'

I didn't answer at first. My mind was seething. All my life since I'd left home, whatever else had happened to me I'd managed to remain free. How could any sane human being expect me to surrender that freedom willingly? 'And if I don't do that?' I asked him.

'If you don't, then you and I must part company – because I would be accused of aiding and abetting a fugitive. And then, when you're rounded up – and they all are, Rob, in the end – you won't have me fighting your corner.'

'And there's no way round that. That what you're saying?'

'Correct. I'm duty bound to tell the feds that I've been in contact with you. On the other hand, you've been extremely careful, haven't you? You've never told me where you are – apart from somewhere in, or near, Switzerland – nor even what name you're using.'

'So tell me what you advise.'

'To turn yourself in, as soon as possible.'

'Yeah, but who to? I can't just walk into the nearest police station.'

'That's the crucial point. You need to hand yourself in to the Swiss authorities. Turn yourself in, in Switzerland. The feds will want to extradite you, but we can fight that, buy ourselves time to negotiate the best deal for you. You have to trust me. I'll be working on that the minute you tell me you're going to surrender.'

I thought for a few seconds. I looked at the photo of my family, all smiling at the camera, eyes narrowed against the dazzling sunlight on snow. 'Get working on it, Chris. I'll go in, but give me a bit of breathing space, will you? Something like a couple of weeks. I got to tie up a few loose ends.'

I remember sitting there and hearing him say goodbye. Some time later I became aware of the phone whistling at me. I'd been in a daze, too stunned to think about ringing off. The fact is, I still didn't know – didn't really, truly, know what the hell I was going to do. Part of me was ready to pack a bag, grab the remainder of my fast-diminishing funds, and split. I could go to South America and go to ground, disappear, but then I started to imagine what that version of freedom would be like. I would have no contact with my wife and children, ever. How much pain would that cause them? But the alternative – to surrender my freedom and go to jail – I started shaking every time I thought about it.

I left the house, got in the Range Rover and drove 10 miles down the road. There was a callbox that I'd not used before, beside a bus stop. I put in a call to Doug in Paris. He said he was real glad to hear from me. He told me Cristiano was ready with all the papers. We could make the transfer any time. Everybody was relieved to be back at work and happy to continue, so long as the two of us – Doug and I – were not involved. He told me that the oil companies would be happy to continue trading once we were out of the picture.

Then we got on to talking about Jack. Doug asked me if I would bring him along when I came to Paris to sign the papers. 'But not to my apartment,' he said. 'We can meet in a public pace, like a park. It'd be safer that way.'

I didn't answer. What did he think, that I'd just stepped off a fucking banana boat? I was convinced he was setting us up for a hit. 'Okay, sure,' I said. 'I'll be there Thursday.'

I took a risk then, and used the same phone booth to call Rio. I wasn't prepared for the news from there. Tony had been arrested, poor sonofabitch. Turned out he had an old unrelated warrant in America, which was why he was in Brazil. The feds had arrested him as part of the investigation into me and Doug. Once they'd fingerprinted him, it was only a matter of time before they found out who he was.

I drove home, slowly. I didn't realise how slowly until some guy passed me with his horn blaring, giving me the finger. The picture was taking shape in my head. I was starting to see that the enemy held all the aces. I also saw, quite plainly, that Doug, the guy I thought was my closest friend, was the traitor I'd been looking for. And that he was, quite possibly, looking for a way to have me wiped out. As to the chances of me retrieving any of my assets or business, they were remote. No, more than remote, they were zero. And if I wanted to stay on the run, I would have to – absolutely have to – abandon my family. That was the sticking point. Everything that happened from here on hinged on that.

I knew her phone was tapped, so even though I'd thought through what I was about to do, and reconciled myself to the consequences, I still found my hand shaking when I dialled Linda's number in Aberdeen. 'How's it going?' she asked. She sounded pretty upbeat.

'Yeah,' I said, 'not bad. Nothing you need to worry about.'

'Any chance of you getting home, or are you still a tax exile?' The gap between us, between my mood and hers, my true circumstances and her idea of what was going on, was too painful to consider.

'No, I'm afraid not, honey. Listen, I need you to come out with the kids. Got some things we need to go over together. How soon can you make it?' She told me she'd got a place in the London Marathon, but once that was over ... We agreed on 24 April. It was a date that was to be imprinted on my mind for a long, long time. 'Sure,' I said. That gave me – and whoever was listening in on the call – three weeks to get our shit together.

I knew precisely what I had to. I knew, too, that I had plenty of time. I remember looking out of the window after I'd said goodbye to Linda. There was more fresh snow on the mountains – just a light fall this time – and the sun was out. It was another dazzling alpine morning. I went out to the garage and loaded my skis on the roof rack of the car.

That was the pattern for the next couple of weeks. More or less every day I went out skiing and snowshoeing. The mornings were cold, sunny and frosty, the mountains so fucking beautiful that I almost wept every time I looked at them. Some days, I got so wrapped up in the pleasure of the moment that I just stood still looking at the sun. My face was burned almost black except for my goggle marks. Since the time I had cut my hair short, I'd noticed it was growing back with a lot more grey in it. I'd stopped shaving and was now sporting a beard that was three parts white.

I took some pleasure in my solitude. I've always taken solace in food, and I visited the market once a week for fruit and vegetables, bought some nice cuts from the butcher on the way home and had some lovely red wines. I went to the garden centre one time to buy some new season's geraniums to put in the windows, to make the house look occupied and give people the idea that I would be return-ing. My evenings were spent going through every scrap of paperwork in the entire place and burning it, then stirring through the ashes to make sure there were no clues left. I double-checked the notepads by the phone, the bedside, the noticeboards in the kitchen, totally purging the house of any name or phone number. Hairdresser, florist, doctor and dentist, Linda's own relatives: I destroyed every trace of the life we'd had, just in case it might somehow lead some-where I didn't want it to go.

It was the last day. A blanket of fog had descended over the place. I got in the car and drove up the mountain. I was determined to ski one more time, so I went to the highest piste in the region on the off-chance that I could climb above it all. I arrived at an empty car park and took the first chairlift. The fog was icy cold and condensed out on my beard and eyebrows, making me shiver, then it froze.

From the drop-off I skied slowly across to the terminal of the second chairlift and hopped on that. Visibility was barely 50m.

When I got through the fog, it was like somebody had switched on the floodlights. The sun was brilliant, the virgin snow glittering. As I rose further, I was looking down on a level blanket of cloud that stretched from one horizon to the next, with scattered mountain peaks breaking through like ships on a flat, calm sea. The lift dropped me at the summit of Cote Deux Mille. There wasn't another soul in sight.

Everything was buried in fresh powder. I skied down, off-piste, trying to delay the moment when I re-entered the fog, finally making my way to the foot of the lift. Then I hitched a ride to the top again, and repeated three, four, five times, before looking at my watch and seeing it was now time to go. Time to head for Geneva and face the music.

Before the final descent, the fog had lifted. I took off my sunglasses and looked slowly around me, taking in the full panorama, mouthing a description of what I saw. I knew I needed to carry this with me for as long as it took to regain the precious freedom that I'd grabbed twenty or so years before, and which I'd always – always – taken for granted. Then I put the shades back on, stabbed my poles into the soft snow and shoved myself forward to begin my final descent.

I reached the car park and sat on the tailgate of my truck, taking my boots off and having one final sweep over the peaks. God, I loved the mountains. Then I turned my back on it all, climbed in and headed down the road to the highway to Geneva.

Arriving at the airport, I drove into an open parking lot. I left the car and walked across to the terminal building. I timed it to perfection, arriving just as the automatic doors slid open to allow the first passengers out of the customs area. A gaggle of business people and tourists came through, and there was Linda, pushing the baby in a stroller while my little boy held onto her free hand. Blinking back tears, I squeezed them each in turn, big hearty bear hugs. I remember Linda laughing and shrugging me off. 'Plenty of time for that when we get home,' she said.

I picked up their suitcases and we headed for the Range Rover. All this time I was bracing myself, expecting to be collared, but nothing happened. It wasn't until I got out my keys and opened the tailgate that I heard the shouts. 'Freeze! All of you! Put your hands above your head and do not move.'

Linda looked at me. She didn't speak. The baby was asleep. My son looked at me with a puzzled expression on his face, his mouth agape. Armed police seemed to be swooping in from every side. A helicopter was overhead. Jesus, was I that important? Linda shouted my name as the cops grabbed her and the children. I knew I had no choice but to stand and watch. When they took her to one car and the babies to another I thought my heart would burst. The last thing I heard, as I was bundled into the back of a car with my hands cuffed behind me, was her screaming and my son's plaintive yells – 'Mummy! Mummy! Mummy!' It was years before I could get that sound out of my head.

25

Champ-Dollon Prison, London Heathrow, Washington DC, Sacramento, April– November 1994

It's not a good feeling, being arrested. The freedom that was yours all your life, up to the very moment they grab you, is gone; the future that used to belong to you is in someone else's hands; a hundred regrets cascade through your mind. And along with all these feelings comes shame, humiliation, frustration and, in my case, a stabbing pain in my shoulder as they grabbed my arms, twisted them behind me and forced me into the wagon. Throw in the sight of your wife and kids being bundled into two separate police cars heading in a different direction and it's all your worst fears realised at once. I was desperate to know what was going to happen to them. Frantic. What had I got them into, for Chrissake?

But right now, I had one cop holding me in my seat while his buddy read me my rights, addressing me by my real name. 'Stone?' I said. 'Hey, that's not me. My name's Anthony Adams. I can show you my driver's licence. The guy you're talking about – he hired me to pick up his

family. That's all I know. You've got the wrong man, guys.'
It didn't wash. They didn't even bother to argue with me.
They knew damned well who I was. They knew everything
about me, including my false IDs, every one of them.

In the end, I shrugged my shoulders and asked them
about Linda and the kids. What were they doing with her?
They had one answer, and they repeated it every time
I asked the question over the next few days. She was in
custody and the kids were being looked after. I had nothing
to worry about. I wondered whether any of them had kids,
that they could say a dumb-ass thing like that.

They took me to some kind of local jail. I spent the rest
of the day and the following night in a cell, alone. I barely
slept, and when they took me to court next morning I felt
like shit. But my mind was clear. Cold and clear. I listened
to what they said and I got it in one, what they were doing
with me. I wasn't sure it was good news. They were charging
me under Swiss law with all the offences the US authorities had accused me of. I thought they would just hold me
for the US warrants. These charges would add up to a life
sentence in a Swiss jail, whatever that added up to, before
they turned me over to the US authorities to do time there.
What the fuck had Chris got me into?

The court proceedings were conducted swiftly and effi-
ciently – just as you'd expect. As soon as they were through,
I was back in a van and on my way to the outskirts of
Geneva, to a prison called Champ-Dollon, where I would
await trial.

They put me in isolation, and I have to say that suited
me, because if there was one thing I needed right then it
was time to unscramble my mind and think. The last thing
I wanted was to share a cell with a bunch of wheezing,
farting, chain-smoking criminals. I was allowed out to an

exercise yard once a day, for sixty minutes, walking around a stonewalled enclosure on my own, with guards on all four corners watching down on me. My meals were brought to the cell. I was not allowed to send a message to anybody. No phone calls, nothing. When I tried to talk to the guards who came to the door and opened the grille every now and then, they ignored me. I was still there, and I was alive. That was all they wanted to know. They made a note of the fact and disappeared. I divided each day into chunks of time and made myself – forced myself – to do stretches, push-ups, that kind of thing. I'd met enough ex-cons to know what imprisonment could do to a guy, mentally and physically.

It was over a week later that I was visited by a Swiss lawyer, appointed by the court. He told me they'd held Linda for a week in the same prison I was in. The children had been taken into care. I wanted to know when I could see them. Surely that would be permitted? The guy explained that it was too late. My family had gone. Linda had been reunited with them at the airport and been deported immediately to the UK. 'Deported?' I said.

'Yes,' they replied. She would not be allowed to re-enter the country for five years, maybe ten. So they were safely home. I nursed the fact in my mind, and tried to draw comfort from it. It just made me feel lonelier. I told the guy I already had a lawyer in Washington DC and needed to talk with him. His answer was that I wouldn't be allowed to contact anybody at this stage, not even Linda. He would speak with Chris himself.

After that meeting, I expected something to happen. I expected some kind of contact from Chris. A call from Linda. But I was to learn that in prison you had no say over your life. Every decision was made for you, and whatever unfolded did so at a pace dictated by the people who held the keys. They pretty much told you when to eat, when to sleep, when to wash and when to shit. As for meeting your hotshot lawyer, they were in no hurry to fix that. It most likely meant trouble to them.

I stayed in isolation for a full month, after which I was put in with what they called 'general population'. I moved into a cell with five others, on a floor that held 200. Most of them were low-level troublemakers from Eastern Europe or Africa. I retreated into my head. The less I revealed about myself, the better. That's the way I figured it.

After a few days, during meal times, I started to see that there was another group of prisoners around the place, white collar criminals of American or Italian origin, along with one or two Sicilian Mafioso types. They seemed to hang out together, and they dined together, in a separate room. They looked kind of aloof, detached.

Finally I got word that I was allowed a phone call with Chris. It took place in the company of two prison guards, the Swiss lawyer and two cops, and it was recorded. I remember looking around and thinking, they aren't taking any chances here. We kept it short and sweet. Chris told me the authorities had cleared it for him to come and see me, which he would do shortly. After I put the phone down I asked my guards if I could now call my wife. The answer was still no.

Chris showed up just a couple of days later. We had the luxury of meeting in private, in some kind of interview room. As far as we knew, our conversation was unrecorded, and we talked freely. 'The good news,' he said, 'is that just as I thought they might, the Swiss authorities have levelled the same charges at you as the feds.'

'You fucking knew that?' I asked. 'How in all that's sane can that come as good news?'

'Because you have the option of pleading guilty. That's a big break.'

'Really?' What was he? Drunk? 'And what'll that do for me?'

'Plead guilty and you'll most likely get five years, maximum. Of which you'll serve two and a half if you stay out of trouble.' He was wearing a big smile.

'Whereas in the USA?' I asked.

Chris shrugged his shoulders. 'You know what they're like in the US. They give out years the way you give your kids candy. They just sentence you for each offence, twenty, forty, sixty, eighty, add them up and lock the door.'

'Okay, you're convincing me,' I said.

'There's another advantage to pleading guilty,' he added. He was wearing a big smile that was quite infectious.

'Yeah?' I said, smiling now myself.

'You can't be tried for the same offences twice.'

'So that's it,' I said. 'Beauty! I plead guilty and do my time in Switzerland.'

Chris surprised me by shaking his head. 'Well, that's not what I'm recommending. What we do is' – it was the first time he'd used that word, 'we', and it made me feel a lot better – 'we threaten the feds with the guilty plea. That'll really piss them off. It'll make them amenable to doing a deal.'

'Better than the five year deal?' I asked.

'I'm hoping so. But you have to trust me.'

What else could I do? I was in his hands, and he knew it. 'Go ahead,' I told him. 'You do your part and I'll do mine. Now you've got to promise me one more thing. Call Linda, tell her I'm okay – and talk some sense into these heartless bastards. I need to talk to her.' He promised to do that, and took off.

I felt better after meeting Chris. He'd eased my worst fears – that I'd rot in jail 'til I died. Maybe it was my more upbeat mood that persuaded one of the white-collar guys to come speak to me. I'd hardly spoken to anybody for weeks, but pretty soon they were inviting me to eat with them. Not only did they have a separate room, but they had their own food, ordered from a nearby restaurant and brought up by the guards. I guess money must have changed hands. The guys seemed to like having me on board and told me which guard could arrange for me to be moved from my cramped six-bed cell to a single down their end of the landing.

Among the members of my new dining club were Fabio Fabrizzi, an Italian thug who had posed as a hotshot businessman and bought MGM Studios with a rubber cheque, and Paolo Grosso, one of the highest profile fraudsters of the twentieth century. He had built up a huge fortune through his private asset management business. Grosso's downfall came when one of his clients – a member of a very powerful Mexican family – disagreed with the way he was investing their money, and told him so. In response, he told them exactly what he thought, which was, 'Hey, you buncha fucking wetbacks, how dare you question my methods?'

They pulled out all the stops and had him locked up. And while he was locked up they sued him in New York for the return of their \$120 million. Being in jail in Geneva he couldn't make the trial, so the judge decided in favour of the Mexicans by default. I could see it from their angle, but I reserved judgement on the guy, Grosso. He seemed okay to me. Besides, he gave me some very useful advice which would later save me many years in prison. He explained about the prisoner transfer treaty system, whereby prisoners get sent back to their home country to serve their sentences. 'It affords each country's taxpayers the dubious privilege of looking after their own, rather than another country's criminals,' he explained. I got Chris on the case straight away. Far better for me to serve time in Canada than in the US, surely?

My new buddies were good to me. They showed me how to make a 'stinger'. You wrapped the bare wires of a flex cord around two soup spoons separated by a piece of wood, plugged it in and dropped it in a bucket of water. The water boiled in minutes. Dangerous as hell, but it worked – and it allowed me to make coffee any time of day. It was nearly the death of me too. The final of the World Cup was on, Brazil v. Italy. I wasn't that interested and decided to make myself a cappuccino. What the difference was between water and milk, I don't know, but something caused a huge back-surge in the line, blowing out all the power, including the high-voltage transformer coming into the prison. It happened slap-bang in the midst of the penalty shootout. I melted away 'til the heat died down, then joined with everyone else, belly aching about the dumb fucking electric system.

Hanging out with Grosso and his buddies was no more than an hour's brightness in a very long day, the rest of which I spent in my cell, alone. When you're in prison, the smallest break in routine becomes something you look forward to with huge anticipation. I was now able to call my lawyers once a week, but of course that didn't always bring good news. I hadn't been in Champ-Dollon very long when I heard that the Swiss authorities had found safety deposit boxes containing various of my fake passports and $930,000 in cash, the remainder of the million I'd taken from the Grünwald brothers. Not that they knew where it had come from – yet. It seemed that Barney and I had done a job of frightening the bankers. They'd kept their mouths shut tight.

Chris, of course, was in like Flynn, obtaining permission for me to use some of the money to pay his mounting bills. Later, he got the authorities to let me use money from my Coastal accounts to help Linda out.

When Chris finally reported to me on what he'd arranged, I realised that the money had been well spent. He'd cooked up a deal with the various government attorneys in California, Colorado and Louisiana. In return for my full co-operation in testifying to my illegal activities and surren-dering all my assets worldwide, they would drop all charges against me. I would then plead guilty to the single charge of smuggling goods into the United States. This was a Class D felony, for which there was a maximum sentence of five years, to be served within the United States penal system.

As I pondered the prospect of doing time in a federal pen, I heard from Chris what had happened to some of my buddies.

Dominic Stopani had been caught earlier in the year. He'd agreed to tell the authorities everything he knew and forfeit all the assets he had. In exchange, they'd reduced his sentences from a possible 120 years to twenty. Eric and Jimmy had, likewise, told everything and got away with ten years each. Brett Eastwood had been caught in Spain and was to serve five years there on gun charges before being extradited to the US for sentencing for whatever they cared to throw at him. Jack had been caught and was negotiating for thirteen. The only guy still at large was Douglas Kane – and it seemed nobody was interested in him for some reason. So my five-year sentence – albeit with the surrender of $40 million worth of assets – seemed a pretty attractive proposition. I agreed.

To wrap up the deal, Chris came over with the assistant attorney for California and representatives of the FBI, DEA and US Customs and Border Patrol. I told them my story and signed a deal agreeing to my extradition to the US of A.

Champ-Dollon was no summer camp, but the moment the US marshals came for me I realised I'd had it pretty damned good over the previous eight months. Grosso had warned me about what I might face. He wasn't exaggerating.

There were two of them, typical of the breed, as I would later find out. Big guys, but gone to fat with bellies hanging over their belts, shirt buttons about to blow off at any moment, khaki trousers straining to hold their fat asses in, and jowls hanging over their tight shirt collars. The fact that they were bringing in a fugitive from the American justice system seemed to make them feel good about themselves, like they were heroes from a western, bringing in some renegade Indian. They'd sent word that I didn't need to pack. I would wear the jumpsuit they brought with them and would be allowed no personal possessions for the journey.

At three in the morning they came for me and brought me down to a kind of changing room. They told me to strip – everything off – then they searched me, every fucking orifice. I put on the orange jumpsuit. Immediately one of the guys threaded a waist chain through the belt loops. I held out my hands for the cold steel cuffs. They came attached to a black metal box which restricted the movements of my wrists. After that, the leg shackles, one around each ankle like I was going on a chain gang. I could now take a 12in step. Final thing, they rigged up a chain from the ankles and linked it to my waist chain. That was me, parcelled up and good to go. Twenty-four hours to Sacramento, and if I needed a leak, I would have company.

Once the US authorities have you in their hands, you realise the full significance of your situation. You're their prisoner and you have no freedom whatsoever. They possess you, and if you don't feel pretty damned humble already, you ain't trying hard enough. It is total humiliation.

We were booked on a commercial aircraft with regular passengers. The marshals waited until everyone had boarded before leading me onto the plane. We walked through first class – where I had regularly travelled in the good times – and shuffled through business. People stared at me. We had a row of seats in economy. I sat between the marshals, still fully chained up. I wondered where the fuck they thought I was going to run to.

At Heathrow, the marshals took off the ankle chains. They put a jacket over my hands so that other passengers wouldn't see the cuffs around my wrists. They let me go through security first, saying they would follow. They got their cheap laugh when I set off the metal detectors and had the guards reaching for their guns, shouting at me to raise my hands. All the way to Washington they wouldn't take the handcuffs off – not to let me eat, nor even to go to the toilet. When the food came, they wouldn't risk a plastic knife and fork – here, have a spoon. I chose not to eat.

In DC the system got its wires crossed. We were going through immigration when they ran my passport through and up it came – wanted! Now I had the marshals arguing with the INS about who got to keep me. It was eight hours before they stopped arguing and the Department of Justice made its mind up. We boarded a flight to Sacramento.

When we landed there, they stopped the plane on the runway. The marshals chained my legs back up before the stewardess opened the door. It's not easy walking down those stairways with your legs in irons. I took a look around at the night sky and wondered when I'd see that again.

I didn't wonder for long. A size 48 boot propelled me into the windowless vehicle which was to take me to the county jail. Here, my chains were taken off and immediately replaced by a set of the California prison system's very own 'jewellery'.

I sat in a holding cell for a few more hours, then started the registration process. There were very few words involved. Name? Hair colour? Eyes? Tattoos? I shook my head. 'I don't have any.' That surprised them. Later I learned that just about everybody in the US prison population is covered with them.

I'd been a captive long enough now that I thought I knew what it was like. Fact was, I had no idea. Once I was handed over to the guards, I started to learn what it was to be a piece of shit. That's how they treat you.

I was pushed through a steel gate and along a corridor. I hesitated, and was hit in the back. 'Move, cocksucker!' I walked and looked up at the rows of cell doors. Guards in the galleries above were shouting at me, 'Eyes to the floor, asshole!' Another blow to the lower back from the guard behind.

'Stand right there, you shit-licking sonofabitch. You will not move until we fucking say so. You will not speak. Now strip. Naked, you miserable fucker. Let's see what you got, white boy.'

Someone was opening a sliding door. I was shoved into a tiled room, and the door shut behind me. They sprayed me with delouser, then put me under a shower and told me to wash. My eyes stung; the bitter-tasting soap got in my mouth. I was standing with my hands against a wall, dripping wet. 'Spread 'em, you fuck.' One rubber-gloved hand had grabbed my right butt cheek and a finger was in my asshole, probing around. 'How d'you like it, pretty boy?' I heard a distant wolf whistle.

We were on the move again, along another corridor. I had a rag of a towel around my waist, but was otherwise naked. We passed through one barred door after another, each one slamming behind me, and at every pause the jingling of keys, the scratch of pen on clipboard. We got to a place where they gave me clothes to wear – shirt, T-shirt, trousers, underpants, socks and plimsolls. No belt, no laces.

We passed through more doors until they pushed me into an unlit cell. I could make out a cement platform, a plastic mattress, a stainless-steel toilet and a sink. No blankets and no pillow. The door was slammed shut. I was still handcuffed, my hands behind my back. They instructed me to back up to the door and stick my arms through the opening through which my meals would be delivered. I did as they said, and felt them unlock my hands. The hatch was shut and bolted.

What the fuck had I done to myself? I walked three steps forward and lowered myself onto the mattress, face down to stifle the sound of my sobs.

26

The Federal Prison System, Con Air, December 1994

I was woken up by the sound of the hatch being opened. They threw in a paper bag and slammed it shut. I got off the mattress, picked up the bag and looked inside. There was a carton of juice, a boiled egg, a cheese sandwich and an apple. I had no watch and no idea of the time, but assumed this was breakfast.

I hadn't eaten since leaving Champ-Dollon, so I downed the contents of the package fast, sat for a few minutes, and then began a workout routine. I'd started it in Switzerland to stop myself going nuts and I'd developed half a dozen variations, anything to break up the monotony. Today, a set consisted of 100 push-ups on my fingertips, 100 stomach crunches, fifty side bends each way, 100 toe touches and 100 jumping jacks. I did fifteen sets of each, and between each one I ran on the spot. I guess it took me about three and a half hours. I was drenched with sweat and so was the floor.

They came by with another paper bag – lunch. But first they wanted all the rubbish from the first meal. I gave them the paper bag. The guard looked inside where I'd put the crushed juice carton. 'What you do with the apple, asshole?'

'I ate it.'

'Where's the fucking core?'

'Ate that too. It's nutritious.'

'Don't get clever, fuckwit. Hands behind your back and through the hatch. Now!' They put the cuffs on, then came in and began to search the cell. 'What the fuck you do? Piss on the fucking floor, you asshole?'

'Just sweat, man. I've been exercising.' They hoped I'd been lying about the core, but they found nothing. Looking at me like I was something from another planet, they grunted and left.

Later that day I was given permission to use the phone. I called Chris, collect. He told me he'd hired a local attorney to assist with the day-to-day stuff. Her name was Caroline Ferguson and she'd been trying to see me, without success. He also told me that my father had called and hoped to come see me. I thought that was strange. It would be only our second meeting in twenty-six years. He had left when I was 11. Next time I saw him after that was shortly after my son was born. Linda talked me into it. 'How would you feel if you hadn't seen your son for that long?' I guessed she'd called him and let him know where I was.

The other news from Chris was that I was due in Federal Court the next day for my arraignment. That's a process that involves two separate procedures. The first is the initial arraignment, and has to take place within forty-eight hours of an individual's arrest. This is where the defendant is formally told what the charges against him are and of his right to retain counsel. The presiding judge also decides whether you can be bailed, and for how much.

I was taken early the next morning to a shower room where I had to strip and wash. Then I was given new coveralls to wear. Once I'd got them on I was handcuffed, brought out through the various locked doors again, and taken into a hall where a dozen or so other inmates were lined up against a wall. The guards came out and handcuffed us individually, then hooked us all together and marched us out to a bus. We sat on a bench where our leg chains were padlocked to bolts on the floor. When we arrived at the court, we went through the reverse process and were marched to the courtroom.

One by one, we stood up as the judge called out our names and the crimes of which we were accused. The other guys had a mixture of felonies: auto theft, larceny, arson, violation of parole, possession of narcotics. The judge read them out and described the potential sentences they each carried. It didn't take much time at all. There was a bit of sniffling, a few whispered expletives, but otherwise, none of us said anything.

When it came to me, I realised the judge knew nothing of my plea bargain arrangement. He had several sheets of paper on which was written my list of indictments. He asked me to stand up and he read the charges out, one by one. Nobody in the room had any idea how long it was going to take. If they had, the judge might have adjourned for refreshments.

It started out with: 'Robert Stone did unlawfully, wilfully and knowingly combine, conspire, confederate and agree together and with each other, and with others known and unknown to the grand jury, to commit certain offences under Title 18, United States Code, Sections 1956 and 1957 ...' He went through pages and pages of legal jargon, listing such crimes as 'attempting to transport, transmit and transfer a monetary instrument and funds from a place in the United States to and through a place outside the United States with the intent to promote the carrying on of specified unlawful activity ...'

The other guys in there with me, the petty felons, stood with their mouths hanging open. For all the sense it made to them, the judge's words might have been in Navajo. In places, it had me baffled too. Then it came to things we could all understand – 'conspiracy to import, possess and distribute marijuana, minimum twenty years ... importing, distributing, possessing marijuana, minimum twenty years' – and I could feel their eyes on me. By the time he'd added 'racketeering, minimum twenty years', and 'trying to conceal from the tax authorities certain financial transactions, twenty years', plus a few more charges under the Continuing Criminal Enterprise statutes – minimum twenty years – the guys were nudging each other and sort of whistling their appreciation. They were in the presence of a player, a player who stood to rack up well over 100 years of time – the classic 'pine box' sentence, meaning that you only get out of jail feet first. Such men are respected and feared in the joint, partly because of the stature of their crimes, but also because they have nothing to lose. They could kill a fellow prisoner – and what? Add another life sentence to the others? Why would that worry them? You didn't mess with these people.

The judge continued, adding gun charges and a whole bunch of others. I stood there for three full hours listening to my rap sheet and the judge's repeated interjections, most of which consisted of the words 'minimum twenty years' or 'twenty years to life'. The information was teeming through my consciousness like I had my head out of a train window travelling at the speed of sound. I could see everyone in the court room staring at me. I stayed standing upright, arms out, chin up – 'Yeah, fuck you all'.

Finally, I heard the judge say, 'Last but not least,' and then read out some other charge. Then it was, 'The prisoner may sit down.' My ass had no sooner hit the wooden bench than he was saying, 'Sorry, stand up. There's one more thing to add here. In light of the serious nature of your charges and your international fugitive status over a period of years and the fact that, upon your arrest in Switzerland, you were using a false identity, it's inconceivable that I should consider bail of any amount, as I find you are a flight risk and a danger to the community.'

The judge left the room and we were escorted out, chained up and returned to the county jail. I went to my holding cell where I would be kept in isolation for a couple more weeks before being let out into the general population.

By now, of course, everyone else in the place was aware of the charges against me. When I went out for our daily hour of recreation and association, knots of fellow prisoners would disperse as I approached. People walking in my direction would swerve to one side and give me room. The one thing everybody wanted to do during this precious hour was use the phone. There was always a bunch of guys standing in line, but whenever I needed to make a call, no worries, they just melted away. Even guys in mid-call would wind it up and disappear.

When I called Chris for an update he told me that the assistant US attorney from Sacramento was in deep shit for giving me such a lenient deal. I started laughing, then all but choked as he said, 'So now the New Orleans attorney is pressing for no deal – at all.' I could feel the fear work its way from my stomach right down to my asshole. 'Jesus,' I said. 'You're telling me I'm going to rot in this dump and be carried out in a fucking box, or what?'

'Relax,' he said. 'So long as you co-operate fully, they can't back out. Trust me. It'll be fine.'

After I hung up I tried to dial Linda's number. The line went dead. I tried again. Same result. Then some guy who was waiting asked me if I was dialling abroad. I nodded. 'No international calls,' he said. 'None.' I wondered how I could get around that. There were a lot of foreign guys in the joint. There had to be a way.

In prison you have to adapt. There are a lot of things you simply have to get used to, because they ain't gonna change. I could cope with most of them. The thing that bugged me most was coffee. There was none – and I was a guy who'd had several cups a day since I left home twenty years previously. I got headaches until my body got used to the idea that caffeine was off the menu. Food worried me too. There was very little of it – maybe 1,500 calories per day. If you were a guy who sat at a desk all day, it'd maybe stop you gaining weight, but I was doing my three and a half hour aerobic routine a couple of times a day, seven days a week. When I tried to store away a little food to bulk it up, of course the guards searched my room and threw it out – not allowed.

My father showed up and did what he'd been doing since I was running round in short pants. He fucked me up. I got the call in my cell: 'Stone, visitor.' I walked up to the visiting room and saw him through the glass. First thing he did was whip out a camera and take a flash photo of me. 'Jesus!' I said. 'They allow you a camera?'

He shrugged. 'I was taking photos as I came in and they didn't say anything at security.' We talked a while and it got a bit emotional. Seeing him face to face, all that shit from my childhood came right back to me. The drunken fights, the disappearances, the neglect. But at least he'd come to see me. Then we were told time was up. I could see his flash going off as he left the room. It made me smile.

A week later, I was rousted up in the middle of the night and thrown in the hole. Next morning I was chained up – legs and waist. They made me put my hands out in front with the palms facing out away from each other, then put on the handcuffs, which were then tightened by a black box that stiffened the chains and put the wrists in a 90° bind that cut off the circulation. My shoulders felt like they were going pop out of their sockets. The handcuffs were connected with chains to a waist chain, which in turn was connected by another chain to the shackles which went around the ankles. I could barely move once the process was complete. A couple of US marshals escorted me to a waiting truck. I could see more armed marshals all over the garage. Nobody said a word. I had no idea what was going on.

They drove me to the airport, where yet more armed marshals spilled out of the vans and went to the perimeter fence, weapons to their shoulders. I was shuffled towards a waiting aircraft, my leg chain clinking and rattling. Still not a goddam word of explanation. The marshal at the foot of the steps stood in front of me. 'Name?'

'Stone, Robert,' I replied. He found my name on his list and ticked me off, then the other guys helped me up the stairs. With the chain, it was one foot up, next foot up alongside, shuffle forward and repeat. It took forever.

Inside the plane, I saw rows of fellow convicts in seats, all chained to the floor. They took me to a seat and strapped me in, shackled my leg-iron to a bolt in the floor – 'Welcome aboard Con Air'. The doors closed and we taxied down the runway and took off. Later, I would take a number of these flights and the pattern was always the same. A magical fucking mystery tour. Nobody ever knew where we were going until we got there.

On this occasion, we were in the air for an hour, maybe a little more. We came down in Los Angeles. People were taken off and new ones brought on board. After that it was Phoenix, Arizona. The first clue I had was when they came and unlocked my chains. This was my stop and, as I stepped outside, it was the same weird security blitz, like war was about to break out – marshals fanning out as if they were expecting ground troops to encircle them. I spent the night in a holding cell. In the morning, with the same security shit all over again, they put me on another flight.

I was getting my first taste of 'diesel therapy'. It's what they do to prisoners who are considered troublemakers. It consists of being put on buses or airplanes and being transported from prison to prison for days, even weeks at a time, constantly handcuffed and shackled. You have no contact with the rest of the world. Your family can't find you, your lawyers can't find you and, therefore, can't file court papers on time. You just disappear into a black hole dug and run by the United States marshals.

I spent a week travelling before ending up in El Reno Federal Correctional Institution. A three-storey cell block built in the early 1900s, it was designed to hurt you. It still had most of its original features, like striped mattresses and barred doors, and cells for two. Everyone was in transit. You stayed in the cell until you were escorted to the 'chow hall'. Lining up outside gave you your one bit of fresh air for the day. Even though it was winter and freezing cold, just to feel the sun on my face for the first time in eight months was glorious.

We entered the chow hall in a line and approached the most amazing buffet. Every kind of grub was piled high on tables: meat, bread, potatoes, fruit and drumsticks, followed by more meat. It was like being offshore on the oil rigs. While I stood there and looked at it all, trying to make up my mind what to have first, everybody around me shovelled piles of grub onto their platters and ran to the tables. Screw that, I thought. What are we, animals? I took a deep breath and prepared to enjoy my first proper meal since I'd left Switzerland.

I loaded up, sauntered across to the table and sat down. All around me, guys were shovelling food down their throats like there was no tomorrow. I took a bite out of a bratwurst. I'd had worse in my time. As I chewed, a whistle blew. The guy next to me was on his feet, ramming another fistful of meat into his mouth. All around me they were doing the same. The guards were whamming their sticks on the table and shouting at us to get the fuck out and let the next lot in. I decided I was going to stay. Fuck this, I thought, I got to eat. They grabbed me and threw me out of my chair. Even as I hit the deck, the next guy was in it, shoving a lump of pig meat into his mouth.

Turns out, we were only allowed five minutes to get our food, sit down and eat it. As they hustled me to the door I put a couple of pork chops in my pockets and an apple in my crotch. Back at the cell block, everyone was searched and I lost the lot. You live and learn – next time, I was first through that door and eating like any other pig at the trough. I figured out a way to beat the searches, making little tears in my jacket where they wouldn't look, and finishing off my meal in the cell.

The following day, I asked for permission to call my lawyer. I needed to find out what the hell all this was about. Why was I being dragged around the country in chains? Permission was granted. Chris was pissed off, big time. 'What the hell do you think you're playing at?' he asked.

'Why would you plan an escape – and why make it so damned obvious?'

'What?' I shouted. 'What are you talking about? What escape?'

'The prison authorities tell me they have evidence that you're going to attempt an escape. Your father seems to be helping you. He sent you pictures of – of the roads around the prison, the parking lot, the entrance, the exits, the halls – every damned thing. What the hell else would they think?'

Oh, Jesus. 'The fucking idiot,' was all I could say. Then I explained how dad had shown up with his camera, that, to him, the visit to the jail was like any other vacation and he was doing what he always did on a trip, taking photos.

'So where are you now?' Chris asked. He seemed a little calmer.

'Some place called El Reno,' I said.

'Nevada?'

'No, Oklahoma. Check it out. Listen, man, you got to straighten this out. I have no intention of busting out. I'm not that fucking crazy, not yet at least.'

They kept me down there another week, then shipped me out on Con Air once more. This time they took me off at New Orleans. It was New Year's Eve. As I shuffled down the steps, I couldn't help remembering the last time I'd landed there. Private jet, stretch limo and away to the yacht for fresh lobster and caviar. It wasn't the way it used to be. 'Happy Fucking New Year, Rob.'

27

Orleans Parish Prison, New Orleans, January–March 1995

When I was a kid, I hated being dragged out of bed in the mornings. I remember one time fantasising that if I wiped out my folks and got put away, at least I'd be able to sleep. Nothing else to do, right? Wrong. In my new home at Orleans Parish Prison I was awake most of the night, listening to the 'choir'. I mean 'the brothers', the black guys who sang religious songs all night long, trying to save their immortal souls with their fucked-up harmonising. 'I'm going down … down to the river, down to the river. I'm going down to the river, going down to the river, I'm going down, down to the river … and get down on my knees and pray.' Every muscle in my body was aching to tell them, 'And when you get to the river I hope you drown, motherfuckers! Give us all a break.' But, of course, I wanted to get out of there alive, so I kept my little white mouth shut.

Early in the morning, the guards came to get me. Handcuffed and chained, I was brought around the corner to the US attorney's office, just a few minutes away, at 650

Poydras Street, Suite 1600. I was led to a door marked 'Boardroom' and taken inside. As they took the cuffs off, Chris came up to me and introduced the government team. It was like meeting the entire bench at a pro football game. There were a couple of FBI guys, a team from the DEA, another from the Bureau of Alcohol, Tobacco, Firearms and Explosives and, of course, Customs and the IRS. Add the assistant US attorneys from New Orleans, Sacramento and Denver, and you've got the picture. The heavy artillery. Lined up in front of them on the table, a stack of box files, papers and correspondence.

I took my seat, and Al Summers, assistant US attorney from New Orleans, addressed the meeting, although it wasn't an address at all, it was a rant. The guy was pissed off, seriously pissed off, that a lowlife like me had been offered a five-year deal when I ought rightly to be inside for the rest of my natural life. He looked me right in the eye as he laid it on the line: one slip-up, one fact coming to light that I'd deliberately hidden, one asset not declared and the whole deal would be off. Boy, had he built up a head of steam. Thank Christ for Chris, who got to his feet, calmed him down and suggested that nothing would be gained by arguing.

So, that was the opening barrage. It was time to get stuck into the documents relating to all of the many companies, bank accounts and properties that were mine or partly mine, or in some way connected with me.

We spent the next three days going through everything, piece by piece. All I had to do was confirm ownership or a close connection and, where I had the legal right to do so on the strength of my own signature, sign it over to the government. First my ships, then my bank accounts and then my various properties. There were two homes in New

Orleans, another on Hawaii, plus the apartment in Rio. There were office buildings, the shipyard and a garbage dump – which was a serious money-maker, with trucks coming in all day dumping trash at $250 a load.

There was also a trailer park out by the airport. Just a small place, with ten trailers, most of them rented out to strippers who were known to pay their rent in favours. I'd delegated the job of collecting to Doug's younger brother, and as I signed it over to the federal government I felt for the kid. This was going to break his heart. There was also some development land up in Colorado, about 100 acres just outside Aspen.

It was painful, of course it was. This was the product of my life's work. Sure, I'd broken the law, but almost all of these things I'd paid for legitimately. Every time I put my pen to the paper I reminded myself that this asset, and this, and this, was buying me a few more years of freedom. I was trading it in and getting my life back, piece by piece. I was literally buying time. The one asset I was allowed to keep was my home in Scotland. That, I could prove, was bought before any of the offences in the original indictment had taken place.

We'd reached the fourth morning. I was in the groove. The faces were familiar, the procedure had become routine. And they had coffee. The previous day they'd ordered in food and I got a soft-shell crab Po-Boy. I was thinking I should slow down this process as much as I could, as I was getting used to nicer surroundings and decent food. Each morning when Chris came to greet me he had a smile on his face. I liked the guy and he seemed to be pulling it off, as promised. But this day, he had a face like thunder. 'Sit down,' he said. 'You got a serious problem.'

'What's the matter, pal? What is it?'

He pulled out a fat folder and laid it on the table in front of me. 'Why didn't you tell me about Michel LeBlanc?'

'LeBlanc?' I said. 'What's he got to do with this? Guy's been dead seven, eight years.'

'Yes, and it seems you killed him.' He had a real grave look on his face. It seemed to say, we're through.

'Get the fuck outta here, Chris.'

He shrugged. 'Well, they have an eyewitness who will testify.'

'No they don't. They can't have. LeBlanc was killed in Guadalajara, Mexico. I wasn't even in the same city. I was in Manzanillo.' I wanted to laugh. This was totally insane.

Chris checked his watch. 'Go ahead,' he said. 'Convince me. But make it good, and make it snappy.' We had about five minutes before the heavy artillery rolled in through the doors.

'Oh shit, Chris, this goes way, way back. Early 1970s I was working for Michel, right? Diving. Then in … eighty-three, I guess, I salvaged some Spanish treasure off the coast of eastern Florida. He heard about it and I went into partnership with him. We were gonna salvage a ship in Mexico, *The Golden Gate*. But you know about that. I told you already. It was supposed to have a pile of gold bullion on board?' Chris nodded. He'd enjoyed the story the first time I told it to him. 'I had the cash and Michel had a permit – from the Mexican government. We found the wreck, spent a ton of money, but couldn't get to it. It was buried in sand, 20 or 30ft of it. So we took a break. Meanwhile, Michel's old lady decided to get us all thrown out by the navy and take it over for herself. I was in Dallas. She had them seize my equipment and throw my divers in jail. I flew back down and got the guys out, but that was it. The authorities wouldn't release my gear. Said we'd got the gold and hidden it in the equipment or some such bullshit. I spent a couple weeks down there trying to release my things, but they weren't listening. I was in Manzanillo making a last-ditch attempt with the navy when Michel was murdered, shot six times in the chest, in Guadalajara. Nothing to do with me, at all. No way.'

'So where's the story coming from?' Chris turned towards the door. The feds were trooping into court. Things were about to kick off again.

'I got one guy I can think of. One of the divers, guy called Billy Bob Baines. When I sprang him from the joint in Mexico he offered to carry out a hit on him – '

'On LeBlanc?'

'Yeah, Michel. He told me he'd kill him for twenty grand. I just told him to fuck off. And that was that. Maybe he's trying to work something with these guys, Christ knows.'

Chris thought for a moment, then said, 'Listen, Rob, I can only work with you if I know – absolutely know – that you're being 100 per cent straight with me. You understand? You lie to me and we both go down. You go to jail for the rest of your life, and me – I'm out of a job.'

'Chris,' I said, 'I am willing to swear on – on my children's *lives* that I'm telling the truth on this. Will that do you?'

The feds spent the rest of the day trying to trip me up, but in the end they had to admit defeat. They didn't have a witness and I didn't move one inch from my original statement on the subject. They were just trying to get me to admit to a murder they'd never cleared up, to tidy up their paperwork.

This part of the process was now over. I spent the next couple of months in diesel therapy again, travelling Con Air around the country, in chains, shuffling from one lock-up to another before ending back up in Sacramento. When I finally got to call Chris, he told me I was going up for sentencing within the week.

Linda flew over for the hearing. I hadn't seen her in almost a year. She showed up at the jailhouse the night before my sentencing. I was taken to the visitors' hall. It was a circular room with stairs climbing up both the walls. When I walked in I had no idea where to go, it was the first time I'd been in the place. A voice over the loudspeakers boomed out, 'Up here, asshole.' I looked up and saw the panes of glass surrounding the room. I climbed up the stairs, and there she was, looking like a million dollars on the other side of the glass.

As soon as she saw me she cracked up, put her hand to her face and started sobbing. I picked up the phone, thinking to comfort her. 'My God,' I heard her say, 'you're so thin!' There was too much to say, way too much. There was the case, the kids, my health, her welfare, and there was me and her. When the voice cut in with 'Time up, asshole!' I looked at the big clock on the wall. Linda had made a 7,000-mile round trip for a fifteen minute talk, through bulletproof glass, on a greasy phone that stank of the previous caller's foul breath.

I saw her again in court the next day. I was in chains and she was on the bench seats. I stood up as the judge read out the single charge they had agreed upon, then asked if Chris had anything to say before he cast sentence. Chris was superb – he made an impassioned plea for leniency, cited my willingness to co-operate and evaluated the property I'd surrendered at $40 million. Surely I'd paid my dues?

After Chris had spoken, the assistant US attorney for the Eastern District of California confirmed that I had adhered to all the conditions and had been very co-operative. The judge then asked me to stand. This was it – now I would find out what that $40 million had bought me. As he read out the sentence, I genuinely struggled to believe what I was hearing – thirty months, less the ten months I'd already done. In addition, I was eligible, under the Prisoner Transfer Treaty, for a move to Canada – and the US authorities would do all they could to expedite the process. He then fined me an additional $100,000. I'd no idea where that came from, but when he put on another 50 bucks for some kind of paperwork I nearly burst out laughing. It was the Nigerian judge all over again. 'Thanks for the forty million, pal – and here's the secretary's bill.'

The last business of the day constituted another triumph for Chris. He'd asked that I be sent to a prison near the Canadian border, and we'd got it – Raybrook FCI, in upper New York State. As soon as the hammer came down, I shuffled and clanked my way across the room to thank the judge, then approached the desk where the assistant US attorney sat. The guards leapt forward, hands on their gun butts. They figured I was going to assault him. Fact was, I was planning to kiss the guy for sticking to his word.

28

Lewisburg Penitentiary, April–May 1995

From the court, they took me to the county jail again. The only difference this time was they put me in the hole. Not a hole like in Nigeria – that was a hole in the ground. Here it was just another term for a no-frills room – no view, no mirror, no toilet seat, no blanket and no pillow. And no pencils or writing paper; no contact with anyone – and no big deal either.

Right now, my mind was teeming with the events of the day. I hardly slept, and when they came for me at four in the morning, it was 'sure, guys, let's do it!' We went through the same old tight-ass security routine – way over the top – and I was taken to the airport and put on the plane. It was the usual Con Air scheduling, north to Seattle, then all the way back to El Reno.

I spent a few days there. I even got to go outside once a day. It was so damned cold that I pretty much had the place to myself. There was a track I could walk around, and coupled with the use of some weights, it had a lot going for it. It was a little bit like being free.

Once more, they grabbed me in the night. It was never their policy to let you know what was going on. This time we flew to Atlanta to pick up some female cons, things were looking up. The guards kept shouting at us to shut the fuck up. It made no difference. Some of these guys hadn't seen a woman, other than through a sheet of bulletproof glass, in years.

I got lucky. Out of the whole bunch there was one worth looking at, a hot little Hispanic girl, and they strapped her into the seat right in front of me. I leaned forward and started flirting with her in my street Spanish. There was another guy sitting beside me who tried to butt in, but she turned and gave him two handcuffed fingers, then started talking to me, fluently, in her mother tongue. I couldn't understand most of it, but since when did that matter? Her facial expressions said it all. Not that it went far before the marshal yanked me back in my seat and tried to put an end to it. She kept turning around, winking and licking her lips. Best flight I'd had in years.

My neighbour was telling me his life story and how his partner had dumped on him and left him to take the rap. I just stared at the ugly fuck, long and hard, 'til he shut up. Then I turned my attention back to the little *chica* in the seat ahead, and that whiled away the time pretty damned well until we landed in Philadelphia.

Twenty of us were taken off and herded onto a bus. It was just like a yellow school bus, apart from the fact it had armed guards, was painted blue and had steel mesh on the windows. Nobody knew where the hell we were going, but, as the high walls and gates of Lewisburg Penitentiary came into view through the grey morning light, a lot of the guys started bitching and groaning, 'Oh man, not this fucking shithole'.

Inside, we were stripped and searched, given an outfit of prison clothing and taken to the administration centre, where we were questioned. They wanted to know about our affiliations. What gang are you in? Bikers? The mob? Aryan Brotherhood? I told them I wasn't in a gang, and asked why the hell I'd ended up in Lewisburg. It was a dumb question, and it got the expected answer: ''Cos you broke the fucking law, asshole'.

'But the sentencing judge said I was going to Raybrook, New York State,' I said.

'Oh, so sorry pal. Did your travel agent book you in another resort? Well, tough shit. Take him to his cell.' I wondered what kind of joint this was going to be.

I didn't have long to wait. The next morning I was taken down to the cafeteria for breakfast. It was a big open hall with 200–300 men already in there eating. There were guards on duty, on high gangplanks, looking down on us with shotguns cradled lazily in their arms. I got some food from the counter and looked around for a place to sit. I walked past the tables full of blacks, past the Spanish, then I spotted a table of white guys, which turned out to be the Aryan Brotherhood. Someone caught my eye and nodded at a seat beside him. I said thanks, sat down and started eating.

There were a couple of empty spaces opposite me and a mean-looking bastard hunched over his tin plate. A guy walked up with his tray and, without asking, scraped one of the empty chairs back. I recognised him from the plane, the guy with the hard-luck story. The first guy half-turned towards him and said, 'That seat's taken.' Right, I thought, we don't want this whining sonofabitch.

The other fellow stood his ground. 'Sure it is,' he said. 'I just took it.'

It happened fast. Real fast. All I saw was a flash of shiny metal as a hand whipped across the other fellow's throat – and then there was blood everywhere: the plate, the table, the T-shirt of the guy opposite, and as the victim slumped into his food, face first, there was a dark pool on the floor spreading towards us. Plastic chairs were scraping as everyone backed off, and the riot squad was running towards us, knocking over tables, shouting and beating people out of the way with their guns.

In real life, everybody would have been stunned into inaction. There would have been gasps of horror and people rushing in to assist the victim. Not in this joint. This was a break in routine, a momentary lapse in the state of order. As we responded to the guards' shouts to get the fuck on the floor, there was a mad scramble – not so much for the floor as for the grub. Bacon, bread rolls and handfuls of scrambled eggs disappeared as it was shoved into mouths. I got my share as I dropped to my knees.

One by one, we were handcuffed and returned to our cells, where I listened as the rumpus died down and the speculation began. Who was that guy? What did he do? Then sporadic laughter as the tension eased. That night I sat on my bed turning things over in my head, trying to erase the image of that guy's life seeping away, trying to figure out just how the hell I ended up in a place like this.

Next morning, I was brought down for questioning. 'Okay, Stone, let's have it. What happened?'

'Sorry,' I said. 'I've no idea.'

'Come on, cocksucker. What did you see?'

I shook my head. 'Nothing.'

'Bullshit. You were sitting at the fucking table. You must have seen it.'

'Nah. Busy eating.'

'You got blood all over your fucking shirt. Don't tell us you didn't see anything'

I made a show of looking down. 'Blood? I thought it was ketchup.'

They didn't push it. They knew they were wasting their time. 'Funny, ain't it?' one of them said. 'All the blindest deafest cunts in the whole joint, all sitting at the same table. Take him back to his cell.'

I found out later that the Aryan Brotherhood make up less than 0.1 per cent of the prison population, but is responsible for up to 20 per cent of murders in the federal prison system.

After the murder I'd witnessed, the place was put on lockdown for a week and we were back on brown bags shoved through the hatch. In times like that, you learn to shut down your antennae. You train yourself to stop hearing the shouts and whispers. You ignore the insults of the guards and hide inside your head. You tell yourself you will get through it. And I exercised, like crazy.

When they came for me, it almost took me by surprise. I hardly had time to catch my breath before I was on the road in a bus, heading north. No word of where we were going, but I had an idea – and I was right. Raybrook. Thank Christ!

29

Raybrook Federal Correctional Institution, June–December 1995

It seemed like I'd taken another step towards home. Raybrook is barely 60 miles from the Canadian border, close by Lake Placid where the 1980 Winter Olympics were held. It's sited on what was the Olympic village, where the athletes were housed. Now it was surrounded by high fences – two of them, both topped with razor wire.

We were shepherded off the bus and put through the familiar process. We stripped and we were searched, questioned and issued with a new set of clothing – a kind of brown canvas suit of trousers and jacket – then taken to our cells. There were no singles here, and for the first time I had a regular cellmate. Previously, I'd only had company for a few days at a time, unless I count New Orleans, but that was an experience I'd rather forget – thirty of us in a dormitory.

I got lucky. My new 'celly' was a guy called Chopper. He'd been the top man in a motorcycle gang in Philadelphia. He was doing a fifteen-year stretch for running a crystal meth ring. Whether it was mutual respect or just the way our personalities meshed, I don't know, but we got along fine from the start.

I had no idea how long I was going to stay in Raybrook. Of course, I was hoping that Chris would fix a move across the border to Canada under the Prison Transfer Treaty, but if I'd learned one thing in prison it was that you take each day as it comes. Nothing you say or do will change the authorities' minds or speed up the process. What you have to do is adapt, then you'll most likely survive.

I slipped easily enough into the routine. We were woken at six for the count, the daily round when the guards checked that nobody had gone missing or died. The count served another purpose, of course, and that was to keep a record of where everybody was at specified times. That way, if an incident took place – a stabbing, a murder, a suicide – they could start piecing together a picture and rule out certain suspects.

Being an experienced con by now, I made a point of getting to know a couple of guys who worked in the prison kitchens. For a small sum of money they would smuggle out food. There was a limit to your spending power, though. We were only allowed so much in cash from our accounts, so we would trade instead – maybe chocolate or cigarettes. Among the most valuable items were sneakers. Someone could get stabbed for a brand new pair of Nikes.

To cook my food, I needed a couple more items. I got one of my kitchen contacts to steal an element from a dishwasher, then I ripped off a length of flex from a TV in the library. Wire up the element, immerse it in a pot of water, and there you go – the kitchen is up and running. Coffee? Pasta? Coming right up.

The point of cooking for myself wasn't simply to make life more tolerable; it was to stop myself degenerating

– physically, mentally and spiritually. A lot of prisoners looked pretty good when they came in, but over the months you could see them become pale, flabby and listless. They'd given up. They looked more and more like the grey slop they were eating, day after day.

So I now had a routine that enabled me to feel more like a human being. Wake up, make coffee, wait for the 'count' and then head to the track and outdoor weights area before returning to the block to call my lawyers. The icing on the cake was that I could now call home. International calls were still forbidden, but, as with a lot of prison rules, there was a way round it. When a prisoner made a call out, the guards could listen in and record it. But if it was to your lawyer you had the right to privacy.

The guards were only permitted to listen in for the first minute, to establish it was a bona fide legal consultation, then, by law, they had to hang up and stop recording. So, once that time was up, or as soon as I'd said what had to be said, the law office would put me through to Chris's PA, who would call Linda on another line and link me up. Hearing her voice, listening to her news, unloading on her, catching up on the children's progress – it all helped maintain my sanity and keep my spirits up. It reminded me of what I was aiming at, too – to get out of the joint and home to my loved ones.

So, with the day all mapped out, and another set of workouts built into the afternoon, I wasn't doing badly. After a while I started boxing lessons. I met a guy called Pete, a Lebanese gangster who had once been a Golden Gloves champion in the US Navy. He taught me how to hit the heavy bag and work on the speed bag. I was working out for seven to eight hours per day, seven days a week, and it wasn't long before I was bench pressing 150 kilos for fun.

I had a 54in chest and a 32in waist, and I'd never been fitter in my entire life, not even when I was a hungry kid diving for lobster in the Caribbean.

On top of my routines, I had a job. I had to, everybody did. Some worked in the laundry, or the cafeteria or the library – eight-hour days, just like in the outside world. Some freelanced on top of their day job, taking in laundry for guys who could pay, or cleaning their cells. And, just as you get crooks in the outside world, so you do in prison. I mean crooks within the system. There were guys who stole food and sold it.

As a white guy, and obviously well-to-do, I tended to stick with my own kind. The fact is, the vast majority of the prison population was black, so the only guys that I would speak with as a rule were mob guys from New York or Boston. I had a good friend in New Orleans whose uncle was the effective 'godfather' of the southern states. Once I let that be known, they accepted me.

That led me to one of the best jobs around, sweeping the sidewalks outside between nine and ten at night. It wasn't everyone's idea of fun, but it suited me. I got to be outside for an hour, on my own, with no interruptions. No arguments, no music from the cell next door, no banging of doors and rattling of keys – a sound I came to detest from the bottom of my guts. The job itself was a piece of cake. There were other guys doing the same round six times a day, so the sidewalks were always spotless. If you spotted a leaf you pounced on it. There was also the view, over the fence to the Adirondack Mountains. Seeing them in the moonlight, or through a veil of falling snow – sure, it almost broke my heart, but that was the price of a moment's beauty. There were people in Raybrook who were seriously pissed off that I got the job only a few weeks after I arrived, people who'd been waiting years for a soft option. But in the joint, if you weren't connected you didn't have a chance.

Being in a maximum security joint has its advantages over other jails. They're more concerned with keeping you in than giving you a hard time about petty rules. They let you get away with the odd indiscretion. When we arrived, we were issued with three sets of underwear, three pairs of socks, one pair of trainers and so on. Because I was working out so much I'd go through all three sets in a single day. Piece by piece, I collected ten complete outfits and had a guy come and pick up my laundry every night. Next day he'd return it, all freshly washed, ironed and folded. I'd spotted early on that some of the top cons always looked smarter than the rest of us. I soon discovered that they'd had their uniforms tailored. I found out who was doing it for them, slipped him some money and got a waist tuck in my jackets, had the trousers fitted to my new slimline waist, and had a general overhaul of my shirts so that the front fitted close and the cuffs sat neatly on my wrists. Self-respect: sure there was a price, but it was worth paying.

I took good care of my diet. Most days I cooked pasta. I started making tomato sauces and decided to grow a basil plant to season them. Whenever there was a search I just hid the pot behind my pillow. Then some guy got stabbed, and it turned out I'd walked through the blood, leaving a trail of footprints right to my cell door. The guards swooped and there was a big search – my bed stripped, closet tipped out, pillow slit open. They found my plant and destroyed it.

All this time, of course, I was waiting for news on the transfer, but I was an old hand now. I didn't get too hung up on it. I knew that these things would happen when they were ready to happen. Gnawing away at it wasn't going to help any.

I was aware that, in Canada, I'd most likely qualify for early release, and that I'd have to show them I had a place to live. The only contacts I had over the border were my mother and father. Maybe they'd welcome the chance to do something for their only son. But when I tackled my father, his new wife put her foot down. She didn't want some gangster coming to stay.

Then I called my mother and explained that I could get out twelve months early if she'd take me in. I would build a house on 5 of the acres I'd bought her and Linda and the kids could come over. When my sentence was finished, I'd sell the new build, which would give me some cash to start my life over. She said it wasn't an option – selling 5 of the 55 acres would be detrimental to the value of the property, and besides, another couple of years in prison wasn't that long …

Meanwhile, I kept busy. The prison ran educational classes and, since I'd never finished school, I guessed I might as well go for a High School Equivalency diploma. I attended regularly, did the homework and sat the tests. I came out with the highest mark ever scored in the prison system – or so they told me.

While I tried to steer my mind away from the transfer problem, Chris was hard at work. He was getting seriously pissed off that the government was ignoring him, and he was not a guy you would willingly antagonise. He knew a lot of different ways of screwing people around. On the phone one day he told me he'd taken enough shit from the government. He was going to sue them for contempt. I thought he was joking, but he did it.

If his aim was to make them take notice, he hit the frigging jackpot. They fired back via the IRS, coming at me for criminal tax evasion. When that failed – it was a part of my plea bargain that they would waive any such action – they hit me with an income tax demand on the money they'd found in my safety deposit boxes. The bill came to $350,000.

But if that stung me, their next broadside scared the living shit out of me. It turned out that the Grünwald brothers had finally come out from under the table and told their story to the Lichtenstein police. Interpol got to hear about it, the feds picked it up, did a little figuring, and soon matched my name and activities to the late William Hammond. Next thing I knew, Lichtenstein had filed an extradition warrant for my arrest on extortion, kidnapping and money laundering charges – and I dare say the US government guys went downtown and celebrated.

There I was, a year left to serve, and now I was going to be extradited to Lichtenstein. Worse, as far as the Department of Justice was concerned, the transfer treaty was off. Chris was fighting like hell to prevent my extradition, but it wasn't looking good. Glenn Altman, Chris's young protégé who had been second in command of my case, now took the driver's seat, as Chris had become involved in another major trial. Glenn and I got along from the get-go.

It was a stand-off. The US could not extradite me so long as they were legally bound to transfer me to Canada. Unless I agreed, that is. Chris and Glenn cooked up a deal whereby I would agree to the extradition if the Department of Justice would reduce my sentence in the US to time already served. They nearly bit Chris's hand off. They thought that if I went to Canada I'd be out in six months. Send me to Europe and I'd stay inside for five years, minimum. They knew that Lichtenstein didn't take kindly to guys who pulled guns on innocent bankers, so the deal suited them fine. On Chris's advice, I agreed. I had no choice really.

As I prepared to make the move, Murphy's Law kicked in again. The Lichtenstein authorities were unable to send their police officers to pick me up. The US marshals couldn't take me over there because once I was out of the prison and across the border I would no longer be a US prisoner. So it was agreed that the law firm Jackson & Schneider would be responsible, and Glenn was assigned to escort me back across the Atlantic. It seemed I was good to go.

But what's the point of a justice system if it doesn't screw you around from time to time? Flights to Vaduz were routed through Zurich, and I'd been banned from entering Switzerland for ten years from the day I shipped out. Glenn was back on the case, arranging a special dispensation from the Swiss government which allowed me to land in Zurich, then continue to Vaduz immediately.

Glenn and Chris had both assured me that there were no problems. Everything was set for the next day. I reminded them to make sure there was a change of clothes and some money. I tried hard to stop myself, but when I went to bed that night all I could think about was the moment when I would set foot on Canadian soil. Big mistake. At three in the morning the cell doors slid open, the guards burst in and shouted at me to get up. They slammed me against the wall, cuffed me and took me to the hole. I had no idea what was happening, and nobody was going to tell me. Several hours passed before they came back and asked what I had to say about my escape plans.

'Escape?' I said. 'Why would I want to do a dumb thing like that? I got a pass outta here, man.' I heard myself cackling, like I was demented. It wasn't deliberate; it wasn't about the absurdity of their accusation; it was sheer terror that they'd have me on Con Air again and ship me round the country buried in their garbage runs 'til they got bored. 'Look,' I said, 'I'm being extradited to Lichtenstein. My sentence here has been reduced to time served. It's over. I'm on my fucking way.'

Now it was their turn to laugh. They hadn't heard a damned thing about any of this, but they'd sure as hell had plenty of cons like me dreaming up last-minute reprieves and pardons. Now they knew for sure I was cracking up, so it was back in the hole.

The cavalry showed up the next day. Glenn arrived with all the paperwork. The prison staff still didn't believe the story and kept him stewing while they went to the Department of Justice to seek verification. There followed another two days of waiting and sweating as I fought off a suicidal despair. Time seemed to have stopped, and things looked as bleak as they possibly could.

Only later did I get the heads up. It was the weather. A blizzard had blown in off the Great Lakes and dumped 15 or 18in of snow. It was the biggest storm in a decade. The driver assigned to take me north had refused to leave 'til the roads were cleared. Glenn tried to get them to let me go and said he would take me to the border. No way: their orders were to take me up there themselves and hand me over. It was two more days before the van driver decided he could risk it, two days that I spent in the hole, convinced it was all over.

When they took me out to the transport it was still snowing heavily. Armed guards were everywhere. We formed a convoy of three trucks, with me in the middle one, US marshals in front and behind, while Glenn followed in his own car.

At the border we were the only people around. Snow was coming in horizontally on a biting north wind; it cut right through my canvas prison clothes. The marshals escorted me out of the United States and Glenn handed me my passport. I had a job holding it, my fingers were so cold. They took me the last few yards to the Canadian post. There was a pink-faced immigration guy in a heated booth. I felt a blast of hot air as soon as he opened the window. I stood there, hunched and shaking, my passport in my hand. He took it from me, flipped it open and asked, 'How long have you been in the States?'

'Thirteen months,' I said.

'And what have you been doing?'

I thought for a moment, then said, 'Thirteen months.'

He looked at me, then at the marshals, then at Glenn. He got the joke. He grinned, and nodded, 'Welcome back,' he said.

30

Extradited to Lichtenstein, December 1995

I stepped onto Canadian soil just ahead of Glenn. The truth is, I elbowed my way past him. I couldn't wait. As the guards returned to their vehicle, it was just me and him in the parking space, a few yards beyond the Canadian border checkpoint buildings. Turning back, I could see the US Customs and Immigration facilities at Port Champlain. We embraced on the highway and I congratulated him. 'So far so good,' was all he said at that moment, 'let's see what happens now.'

For the next stage of my journey, heading towards Montreal, I felt like a free man. There were no chains, no guards; I was strangely disorientated. My lawyers had negotiated an agreement whereby I could enter Switzerland for the sole purpose of proceeding to Vaduz. Glenn would accompany me all the way. Once there, I would surrender myself to the Lichtenstein authorities. As we drove north towards the city I was chewing over the possibility of a further sentence of five years, maybe more, still uncertain how we were going to play it.

We pulled off the highway next to a shopping mall. 'Come on,' Glenn said. 'We're going shopping.'

'What is this?' I said, stepping out of the car.

'Take a look at yourself.' I thought I looked pretty presentable in my neatly tailored prison clothes. Glenn was not impressed. 'We need to get you dressed properly,' he said. We bought a couple of pairs of smart trousers, a blazer, two shirts and a few other things suitable for a court appearance, plus a winter coat. We went for some food and I found a payphone to call Linda and put her in the picture. Before driving away, we dumped my prison clothes in a bin – all except my sneakers. I guessed I might want them in my new prison.

Once we got to the airport, it was like the old days – we flew business class. There were a lot of things I wanted to talk over with Glenn, but we kept the conversation light. The last thing I wanted was to be overheard discussing my misdemeanours when surrounded by all those respectable people in suits.

No such luck in Zurich. I got to the head of the queue for immigration and was beckoned to the desk. I handed over my passport and the letter of authority from the Swiss government allowing me entry, explaining that I was in direct transit to Vaduz in the care of my lawyer and had permission to pass through. The officer glanced at it, then, at the top of his voice, he called out to the people waiting in line behind me, '*Und wo ist dieser* … where is this – this criminal's attorney?'

Glenn walked forward and said quietly, 'Ah that would be me, sir.'

We had a hire car booked. We set off south and east along the lakeshore, discussing our strategy. Both Glenn and Chris had been in many hours of negotiation with the prosecuting judge and were hopeful of striking a deal. In Vaduz we checked into a hotel, had dinner and made it an early night. I felt I ought to sleep, but I was buzzing. I had something brewing up in my mind, and it was only after I'd spent some hours figuring it out that I nodded off.

I'd got into a way of doing things in prison and wasn't about to break the habit. I was awake soon after five, up and doing my workout routine. It helped me revise what I'd been thinking about three or four hours previously. Was it totally crazy? I didn't think so. Did it still make sense? Sure it did.

Two hours later, I was dressed and drinking coffee in the lounge. As soon as Glenn appeared I was ready to head out to catch the Lichtenstein attorney we had to have on board for procedural reasons. The only real reason he was there was that Glenn was not licensed to practise law in Vaduz. The fee? Ten grand. We discussed the strategy and headed to the courthouse to see what the fates had cooked up for me.

The Grünwald brothers were already in court with their own attorneys. When I saw them, I nodded. They shifted in their seats. One of them turned and whispered something to the other.

The judge walked in, everybody rose, and she told us we could sit down. She read out the charges. Despite the fact that I'd gone over them a dozen times with Chris on the phone, they sounded shocking when they were read out in court. Did I really do that? Me? Glenn rose to reply, but just as he was about to begin I tapped his arm and asked him to sit back down. 'What is it?' he whispered.

I didn't answer, just got to my feet and addressed the judge. 'Now that I've had time to think this over,' I said, 'I fully understand why the Grünwald brothers here concocted their story.' The brothers stared at me, then at their lawyers, who were already on their feet protesting. I waited 'til the judge had silenced them, and said, 'Please be patient and listen to what I have to say. I've thought this through, and it's all clear to me now. The reason you made up this story about me was your fear – and, believe me, I can understand that fear – that I might be an associate of Jack McBain. And that the money you were holding on my behalf was earned through trading in narcotics.'

I then addressed the judge. 'It seems perfectly reasonable to me, if that's what they thought, that they would panic. It makes absolute sense. They were afraid that I was in a position to implicate them in …' I paused, milking the moment, 'well, to put it bluntly, in laundering the proceeds of drug trafficking. If I also confirmed the source of Jack's money as being the drug trade – and could show that they were aware of it – they would be in serious trouble.'

The brothers suddenly looked a lot less comfortable. Beside me Glenn was whispering, 'Where the hell are you going with this?'

'Just trust me,' I said, and carried on, addressing the brothers directly. 'Now, let's get one thing straight here. I didn't come to Vaduz to testify against you for money laundering. I came here to testify that at no time did Jack tell you where his money came from.' I turned to the judge. 'You have to understand, my intention was never to suggest that the principality of Lichtenstein is a safe haven for drug money.' I paused to let that sink in, then continued. 'I came here to exonerate the Grünwald brothers and to tell them I forgive them for making up this story – the story about how I forced them to give me money. At gunpoint. Most importantly, I am not here to fight over the $4 million still in my accounts. All I want is the forgiveness of the court for whatever role I had in this, and to forgive the Grünwalds for what they only did out of fear.' Again, I addressed the judge directly. 'My motive in this is simple: all I want is to secure the earliest possible release date so that I can get back to my family in Scotland. Nothing more than that.'

I sat down. Glenn was shaking his head. 'Have you lost your fucking mind?' he whispered.

'No,' I said.

'Well, you'll lose every last cent you have in the world if you keep this up. Look, the whole idea of implicating the Grünwalds was to guarantee you a light sentence – absolutely guarantee it. And now you've thrown all that money down the drain. For nothing.'

I wanted to point out to him that I'd already signed off 40 million bucks' worth of property to get me this far. And besides, what was this 'light sentence'? There was no such thing for the sonofabitch who had to serve it – as he would find out, if he ever had to spend a single night in jail. Four million was small change in comparison. But I was now watching the Grünwalds, deep in conversation with their attorneys. Their professional futures were on the line here, and they knew it.

It didn't take them long. When their lawyer stood up to speak, he looked at me and said, 'The facts are as the accused states them. My clients admit that, under severe duress – and in fear of their safety – yes, they invented the story. They also wish to make it plain that the accused at no time threatened them; in fact, there never was a second man in the incident. It was a one-man operation.'

The judge raised her eyebrows and said to me, 'But you say on the one hand these are legitimate earnings, while on the other you will not fight for them?' I guess she was with Glenn on this one: she too thought I was nuts.

'Your Honour, I grew up in a violent and broken home. We never had any money. When I left I just wanted what I thought every kid deserved – all the things I'd missed out on – and I figured the way to get them was by making money. I told myself that one day I would have a family and I would make it right for them. When I look back, I can see I was doing that all for myself. It was my own dream I was following. What my wife wanted was honesty, and I gave her lies. She wanted a proper family, but in ten years of marriage I was never there. One of my children is 3, the other one is 4, and they hardly know who I am.' I shrugged. 'I want to be a father to them, a proper husband to my wife, and then see whether I can right some of the wrongs I've done to society.'

I paused for a moment. Everybody in the room was staring at me. I could hear Glenn breathing heavily, through pursed lips. I held up my hands. 'I'll serve my sentence,' I said. 'I accept that. I just don't want to serve any longer than I have to. If I can get out a day earlier by giving up the money, take it. Give it to someone who needs it.' As I sat down, I added, 'One thing I learned in jail: you can't put a price on time.'

The judge had been listening intently. Now she ordered a recess. Glenn watched her leave the room. Then he said, 'You realise you've left everything to her?' he said. 'It's now her decision entirely. We have no say. You do realise that, don't you?'

'Sure,' I said. 'I know it.'

We took a break and walked outside. It was milder than when we showed up, and the sun was shining. Across the road a woman was walking a toddler through a park. Another woman was putting a baby into a pram, tucking a blanket under its chin and speaking to it in a gentle voice.

We went and sat on a bench for a few minutes before going back inside. I asked Glenn if he had the faintest idea what this felt like, to sit in the park and watch the world go by. He nodded. He got it now.

It was two hours before the judge returned to the court-room. We all stood. She spoke first to the Grünwalds. 'Do you agree to drop all charges against Mister Stone?'

They looked at each other, nodded at their attorney and answered, one after the other, 'We do.'

She turned to me. 'And do you, Mr Stone, agree to forfeit the monies held in your various accounts?'

'Yes,' I said. 'I do.'

She sighed. She seemed kind of weary. Maybe she was simply relieved. Or baffled. Most likely both. 'In that case,' she said, 'you are free to go, Mr Stone. The charges against you are dismissed.' She picked up her papers from the desk, nodded to the Grünwalds, and left the courtroom.

31

Home, December 1995

Glenn and I decided to drive straight back to Zurich before anyone changed their mind. For a while he hardly spoke. Good job, really, because I wouldn't have been able to answer. When I managed to sling a couple of coherent thoughts together, I figured he was pissed off at what I'd done in court. But when he did open his mouth, it was to tell me that he flat out couldn't believe what I'd pulled off, that I was a free man.

At the airport, he was planning to fly straight home to DC, but I wasn't happy about that. I had a feeling that my re-entry into Britain might not be the smoothest. He agreed to come with me, at my expense. He could get a flight easily enough from Heathrow.

My fears were justified. As soon as I got to LHR Immigration and showed my passport, the officer at the desk studied it, referred to some kind of index he had there, and told me he needed to question me further. Allowing Glenn to accompany me, he led me to a sort of holding room where he explained that the British authorities didn't want to let me in the country. It was all about my criminal record. They brought in a Special Branch officer to question me. The fact that I had a British wife and children seemed irrelevant. The fact that I had a serious criminal record was what concerned them.

'But that's abroad,' I said. 'And I've served my time.'

'Yes,' the cop said, 'but you also have a criminal record over here.' I had no idea what he was talking about, and told him so. 'For vagrancy and begging?' he said. That's when it hit me: he was talking about one of the aliases I'd had through my man in Malaga, the guy who supplied UK passports. He knew damned well what had happened and was fishing to see whether I'd admit it.

A chief immigration officer arrived and introduced herself. After the other officer had briefed her, she asked, 'Are you telling me your wife actually wants you home?'

'Of course she does,' I said.

She was sure I was lying. 'Okay,' she said, 'let's call her and find out, shall we?'

I gave her Linda's number and crossed my fingers, hoping she'd be in. The woman made the call right there, from a phone at the desk where we were seated. I could hear Linda answer. 'Hello?'

'Is that Mrs Stone?'

'It is. Who's calling?'

The woman told her it was immigration at London Heathrow. 'We have your husband here.' There was a pause. I guessed she was wanting Linda to say, 'That scumbag!' Instead she got a whoop of joy.

'Oh, that's *wonderful!*'

'He's just arrived in the UK. He claims that you're expecting him to join you at your home.' She was about to say more but Linda cut right across her.

'You're telling me he's here? That's fantastic news!'

'Yes, but are you quite sure you want us to let him into the country?'

'Well, of course. Why wouldn't I?'

'You don't feel you're in any danger?'

Linda gave a knowing snort of a laugh. I knew damned well what was on her mind. 'No,' she said. 'No danger.'

'Do you know about his record?'

'Yes, and I know he's paid the price for his mistakes.'

'So you want him back? Because if you don't we can have him on the next plane out of here.'

'Oh no,' Linda said. I could hear every word. 'I want him back. And it's not just me. There's two bairns here needing their dad.' The last thing I heard before she hung up was Linda shouting to the kids, 'Guess who's coming home for Christmas? Your daddy!'

The immigration officer gave me a two-week permit. After that, I would have to fly to Canada and apply from there for permanent residency as the husband of a British citizen and the father of British-born children.

As the woman took my passport and bent it open at a clean page she looked at me and growled, 'And if you lay a finger on that woman, I will come and throw you out of Britain with my bare hands. Yes?'

'Sure,' I said, as I watched her whack the stamp in my passport, shaking the table and rattling the pens in the jar next to the phone. She got up and went to the door, called Glenn in and explained what she'd done.

After that I was free to go. I thanked Glenn for all that he'd done for me over the last year and a half. He said he would get to work on the residency application. He knew some good people in Ottawa who would handle it. I hugged the guy and told him I owed him and Chris my life. 'It's what you pay us for,' he replied.

Night had fallen by the time my plane took off for Aberdeen. Down below, scattered flares marked the positions of oil rigs scattered across the North Sea. I shuddered as I remembered the icy waters in which I'd dived to earn my living all those years ago. I wondered what might have happened if I'd stuck at that. Who knows how life would've turned out? I certainly wouldn't have had the yachts and private planes, or the millions of dollars. Of course, I didn't have them now, either, but would life have been the domestic bliss that Linda pictured? Maybe. And maybe I would have been killed, like a half dozen of my diving buddies were. Could it be that the life I'd lived had saved me from dying in the life I'd left behind? Only time can tell you which decisions are the mistakes and which are strokes of good fortune.

The stewardess was coming down the aisle with a drinks trolley. I took out my wallet and counted my money. I had £50 in sterling that Glenn had given me before we split. I put it back in my pocket. I didn't need a drink, I had my freedom. It occurred to me that what I was bringing home was pretty much the same amount I'd had in my jeans in Canadian dollars the day I ran away from home and hopped that flight to Florida. In the years since, I'd made several fortunes and lost them all, but on balance I hadn't done too badly. You could argue I'd broken even.

The plane landed and taxied up to the terminal. I was first out of the rear doors and down the stairs. A cold wind, straight down from the Arctic, cut through my clothes. A few stray flakes of sleet smacked into my face. I had no checked baggage to wait for and was able to walk right out through the sliding doors into the arrivals lounge.

There was Linda, dabbing at her eyes with a Kleenex, then running towards me, the kids on either side of her. As she reached out to embrace me, laughing and sobbing at the same time, I felt my little boy tugging at my trouser leg, and my daughter, looking up at me and saying, 'So you're my daddy.'

★★★

I'd been back a few years – something like that. It was mid-evening. The kids were asleep and Linda was out, visiting her dad. I was sitting by the open fire, eyes narrowed against the heat that blasted out from the logs. Not for the first time, I was thinking over the events of the previous several years. I got up, went to the bookcase and found my battered old copy of *Diving to Adventure*. Returning to my seat, I flipped through it. My own past now seemed as remote as the yellowing pages and the faded monochrome pictures of my hero, down on the ocean floor with his mask and his spear. I got about halfway through, and there, on the blank lower half of a page, were the co-ordinates I'd jotted down as we left Glacier Bay. I thought briefly about how much they might be worth to someone with sufficient balls, sufficient drive … and shook my head.

I closed the book and looked at the image on the cover of Hans diving down to spear a giant ray. I was just about to throw the book into the flames when I heard Linda's key turning in the front door. Coming into the room, she said, 'Oh, you've got that down. You know, I did finally read it when you were … when you were away. Helped me understand you, just as you said. I'm really glad you hung onto it.'

'Is that right?' I said. 'So I guess it's pretty important to both of us.' And as she slipped her coat off, I stood up and replaced it on the shelf.

Postscript

Throughout my time in jail, and the years that followed, I never could be sure who it was that had ratted on me. It gnawed away at me. For a long time I'd suspected Jack, then I convinced myself it wasn't him, then fresh doubts crept in. Later, I convinced myself it must be Doug. At the same time, I was aware that it could've been one of my crew on the Alaska trip – any of them.

I was doing some background reading in preparation for this memoir when I stumbled across an article in the *Washington Post*. It was about legal cases, involving state and federal agencies, which had been sealed and buried away in secret files, in many instances for the protection of informers. The clerk's office had begun disclosing hidden cases eighteen months previously, after an appeals court in Atlanta said the practice was unconstitutional. What caught my eye was the fact that the writer had come across a series of such cases in south Florida – 400 of them. Their existence had been acknowledged, but no details had been disclosed.

The article went on to say that details were finally coming to light. Of all the cases available, this reporter had, for some reason, chosen to quote from 'a marijuana conspiracy', and that naturally caught my eye. The case, I read, was referred to in the official records as 'USA v. Sealed Defendant', but records obtained by the *Post* revealed the case number and the defendant's name and age. And there it was, right in front of me. Not Jack, not Eric, not Darren, but 'former New Orleans resident and informant, Douglas Kane, 55'. I felt like I'd been kicked in the chest with both hind legs by a mule.

There's a satisfaction in solving mysteries, but sometimes with that satisfaction comes pain. Maybe I mean that there are some things you wish you hadn't found out. I hardly needed to read on, but of course I did. I read that my former partner, the man who had been like a brother to me, the man who coolly suggested we wipe Jack out, and the man who wanted me to sign over my company to him so he could look after my family, had been indicted right along with me in Denver in 1993. His case had been transferred to Miami. Then, the killer line that confirmed my very worst suspicions: 'In 2002 he pleaded guilty, was sentenced in secret, and walked free, without any custodial sentence.'

There was only one way Douglas Kane could have negotiated a deal like that. For four years, until December 2006, Kane's case did not appear to exist on the docket of the Southern District of Florida. Then, for a brief period of time, it did, and the reporters found it.

My lawyers, however, found a heavy veil has since been drawn over the case. Kane's name is a secret. The style of the case is 'USA v. Sealed Defendant' – and every document in the file is sealed. Now, the case simply does not exist.

Rob Stone
March 2015

Also from The History Press …

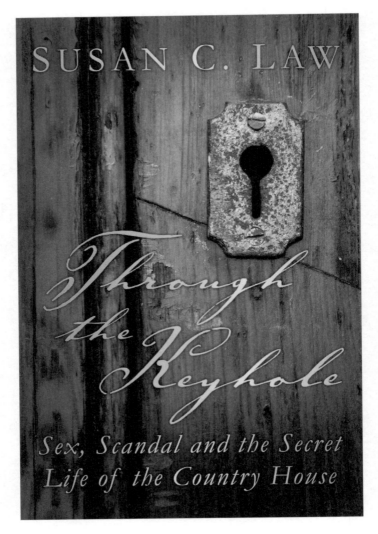

SUSAN C. LAW

Through the Keyhole

Sex, Scandal and the Secret Life of the Country House

9780750956697

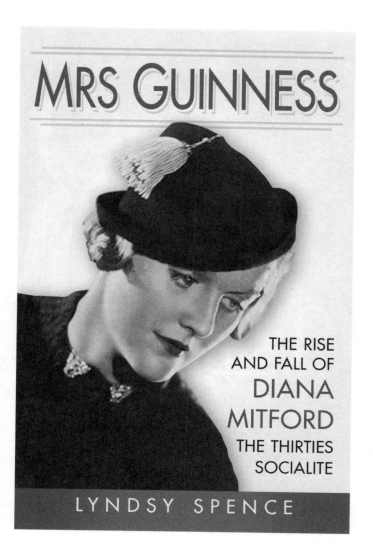

MRS GUINNESS

THE RISE
AND FALL OF
DIANA
MITFORD
THE THIRTIES
SOCIALITE

LYNDSY SPENCE

9780750959735

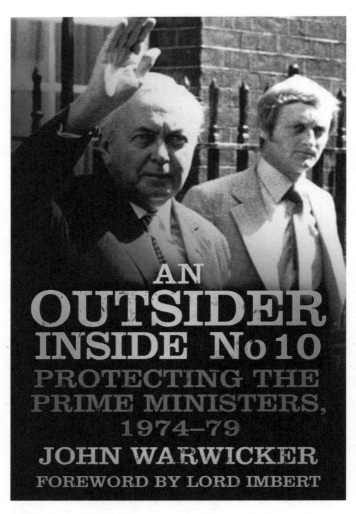

AN
OUTSIDER
INSIDE No 10
PROTECTING THE
PRIME MINISTERS,
1974–79
JOHN WARWICKER
FOREWORD BY LORD IMBERT

9780750956697